due for return on ... shown below.

Cheat
IN
Adobe Flash CC

The art of design and animation

Chris Georgenes

Focal Press
Taylor & Francis Group

NEW YORK AND LONDON

First published 2014
by Focal Press
70 Blanchard Road, Suite 402, Burlington, MA 01803

Simultaneously published in the UK
by Focal Press
2 Park Square, Milton Park, Abingdon, Oxon OX14 4RN

Focal Press is an imprint of the Taylor & Francis Group, an informa business

Library of Congress Cataloging-in-Publication Data application submitted.

ISBN: 978-0-240-52591-4 (pbk)
ISBN: 978-0-240-52595-2 (ebk)

Typeset in Rotis Semi Sans
by Apex CoVantage, LLC

MIX
Paper from
responsible sources
FSC
www.fsc.org   FSC® C014174

Printed and bound in the United States of America by Sheridan Books, Inc. (a Sheridan Group Company).

Contents

Contents

7 Animation examples...214

8 Working with sound .. 256

Contents

Foreword

Over ten years ago in a dimly lit basement, I started using the Flash authoring tool to create unpalatable, short, frame-by-frame animations - and discovered it was much easier than other tools I had been using to do the same thing. It's hard to believe what Flash has become over the years, and how many more people are out there using it to create content and share their work. One of the nice and inspiring things about Flash is that it attracts so many different users, from creative animators to hardcore programmers, and all sorts of people in-between.

I was assigned to work on testing a new type of motion tween for Flash a few years ago. Because the feature was already developed (but at the time untested), I needed to learn how everything worked from the ground up. Similar to other migrating Flash users, I have experienced and understand the learning curve between new and classic motion tweens! The new motion tweens are a different way of thinking about animation in Flash, however they do offer many advantages such as fewer "broken" tweens, attached motion paths, independent tweenable properties, tween presets, and preset eases. Some animations I've created in the past were faster or easier to accomplish after a bit of time spent with the new model. What about using "classic" motion tweens? Yes, there are some workflows where classic tweens are necessary and a couple cases where they're faster to use. However, the goal is to enhance and improve new motion tweens and the Motion Editor so using them is always possible and preferred.

You certainly don't need to learn everything there is to know about Flash and ActionScript to master the tool – you can choose to focus your talents on design or development, or challenge yourself from time to time by crossing over between graphics and code. But now that Flash is full of features and capable of so much, the tools can seem rather daunting to learn. But if you have helpful resources at your side, like this book, learning Flash doesn't need to be difficult. I believe the key to learning Flash is to keep it simple when you start out, take it slow, use the available resources (like books), and try to be patient. Also don't be afraid to go online and ask for help, we've all been there! Learning Flash takes some time, but it is a lot of fun and very rewarding.

Flash is an incredible tool for expressing your creativity, style, and unique ideas. Whether you're a new or existing Flash user, now is a great time to learn or use the software and get involved with the Flash community online. I hope that you use Flash with this book to get inspired, learn valuable new tricks and techniques, and create some wonderful animation. And of course, make sure to have fun with the software while you read and learn all about how to animate!

Jen deHaan
Sr. Software Quality Engineer, Flash Authoring
Adobe Systems Inc.

How to cheat, and why

The truth about cheating
The word "cheat", in most cases, has a negative connotation. To "cheat" implies deception and trickery associated with a fraudulent act. In some ways this book will show you how you can trick your audience, not unlike a magician's "sleight of hand" technique where you can control not only what is being seen, but how the viewer sees it. But this book will certainly not teach you how to be a fraud.
To "cheat" in Flash is to find shortcuts to help you work more efficiently and economically. Time translates to money and if you can deliver a great looking project on time, that means you stayed within budget and everybody wins.

My philosophy
At the end of the day, if I didn't have any fun, then it would be time to find another job. But I had to learn this lesson the hard way a few years ago while working with an animation company designing a network television series. I was designing the main characters for a show called *Science Court* (ABC), and there was a conflict between us and the network as to the choice of skin color for one of the characters. I liked green and the network preferred orange. I felt strongly that my color choice was the best and I admit I may have let myself become emotionally charged about the issue. One day I went to lunch with the animation director and we were casually talking about the color issue. It was something he said that changed my outlook on work from that day forward: "*We must have pretty cool jobs when the most stressful part of our day is whether or not a character looks too much like a frog.*"
I stopped dead in my tracks, instantly realizing how right he was and how silly I felt about the matter. After lunch we returned to the studio where I immediately changed the character to orange and never uttered another word about it. I even ended up liking the orange more than the green. Since then, my philosophy has always been to have fun no matter how stressful my workday gets. My job, in comparison to all other possible occupations, is the best job even on the worst of days.

Workthroughs and examples
Each workthrough in this book is designed as a double-page spread so you can prop the book up behind your keyboard or next to your monitor as a visual reference while working alongside it. Many of the workthroughs are real-world client projects I have been commissioned to design and animate. Using these projects as examples has allowed me to provide you with a downloadable zip file containing the source files for you to open and explore. Each chapter ends with an Interlude in which I talk about

everything from my own experiences as a designer and animator as well as some relevant and useful information based on the topic at hand.

Flash terminology

Not much has changed when it comes to terminology in Flash. **Symbols** have been around since the beginning and so has the behavior any symbol can have (Graphic, Movie Clip and Button). The **Timeline** has remained unchanged and **nesting** still pertains to assets and animations within symbols, one of the key strengths of Flash. If you already have a basic understanding of Flash then you will most likely be familiar with most of the terminology in this book.

Download Example Files

The download icon indicates the source file for that particular example is available for you to download from **www.howtocheatinflash.com/ downloads**. Download the ZIP file and unpackage it to your local hard drive. The unpackaged file contains all the example files found in this book and are for your learning pleasure.

Companion Website

Please visit the companion website for this book by navigating your browser to **www.howtocheatinflash.com** where you can keep up to date with the information regarding this book and download the example files.

Beyond the book

Be social. Visit **facebook.com/howtocheatinflash** to ask questions, get answers or post your own works of art and animation.

Follow me on Twitter@keyframer. I'm pretty consistent when it comes to tweeting about trends and technologies as well as cool new gadgets. You can also find out where and when my next speaking engagement will be.

Acknowledgments

This book is dedicated to James Williamson, who I'm proud to call my friend.

Special thanks to
David Bevans of Focal Press for his support and dealing with all of my missed deadlines.

David Crawford for Moo Cows and Apple Strudel. Spinkee!

Myra Ferguson and Erika Scopino for making my own words sound better than I ever could.

Fred Wessel and Dennis Nolan for giving me my greatest tool of all: the ability to draw.

Mom and Dad for encouraging me to choose my own path in life.

Jay Schuh for stepping up to help out with this book when deadlines got tight.

Tom McCaren for his sound design talents.

I am eternally indebted to
Becky, Bobby, Billy and Andrea for being the greatest family a guy could ever have.

Warm and fuzzy feelings to
Laith Bahrani, April Clark, Joe Corrao, Jarred Hope, Thibault Imbert, Kevin Kolde, Shine Lee, Stephen Levinson, Dave Logan, Eric Mueller, Ben Palczynski, Davendra Pateel, Adam Phillips, Benedetta Pontiroli, Todd Sanders, Tim Saguinson, Aaron Simpson, Evan and Gregg Spiridellis.

A tip of my hat to
Tom Barclay and the entire Adobe Flash team for continuing to evolve Flash, the coolest animation program on the planet.

Thanks to the following people and companies for their approval to use their projects as examples: *David Crawford, Tom McCaren, Katie Osowiecki-Zolnik, Ben Palczynski, Colter Avara, Laith Bahrani, GSN Games, Adobe Systems, Audacity, Cone Inc., Eltima, Erain, Fablevision, istockphoto, Jib Jab Media, M-Audio, PercyPea Ltd, Samson, Sony, Superbusy Records and Wacom.*

Some of the photographic images used in this book are from the following royalty-free image sources: Adobe Stock Images & www.istockphoto.com.

How to use this book

I am a digital animator – a *Digimator* if you will. I learned how to animate using a computer. Any animation program can have a mechanical feel to it since we work by selecting options from menus much of the time. The trick I have learned is how to make a software program like Flash feel more organic, as if it were a ball of clay, starting with a basic shape and pushing and pulling it into something unique. If this book teaches anything, I hope it teaches you to think differently as to how you approach Flash. Just because the Help docs, online resources or even other books tell you how something can or should be done, don't take that as carved in stone. Take it as carved in clay, meaning you can continue to expand upon the ways the tools are used, even beyond what you may have read elsewhere.

The first few chapters focus on some of the basics of using Flash in real-world situations. I do not explain the rudimentary features of Flash, such as how to convert objects to symbols and what the differences are between Movie Clips and Graphic symbols. That is what the Help docs are for and are simply a keystroke (F1) or a Google search away. You bought this book to learn what goes beyond the Help docs and what can only be learned through the span of several years of experience using Flash. For you, this is the true essence of "cheating" because this book condenses those years into 300+ pages.

Just in case you do get stuck on something that you simply can't find an explanation to, I'm a pretty easy guy to find if you want to send me your questions. You can send me a tweet **@keyframer** or message me on Facebook: **www.facebook.com/howtocheatinflash**

Fl

Adobe® Creative Cloud™
Flash Professional® CC

Building Workspace...

It's back to basics for Flash CC as the least used tools and features have been removed completely. Most of us weren't using them anyway, so chances are they won't be missed.

1
What's new in CC

ADOBE FLASH PROFESSIONAL CC MAY BE PROOF THAT less is more. The least popular and lesser-used features have been stripped from the Flash authoring tool. This lighter, more streamlined version of Flash is the version that finally fits into that polka dot bikini just in time for summer.

Let's take a look at what's new in Flash CC and what's been exiled to the land of misfit features.

Under the hood

W ITH EACH NEW UPDATE comes new expectations for Flash to be better, faster and packed with more features. Flash CC is an interesting release because in many ways it meets these expectations and even exceeds them. But in other ways Flash CC may come up short for some users due to features that have been removed completely. This chapter takes a look at how the latest version of Flash stacks up for the designer and animator.

Right off the bat, you will notice something different about Adobe Flash Professional CC. It happens so quickly, there's a chance you might miss it. Launching Flash CC takes merely seconds thanks to a complete rewrite of its code base to support the Cocoa framework on Mac OS X. My unofficial benchmark testing shows Flash CC takes about 3 seconds to fully launch. Previous versions of Flash, such as CS6, take upwards of 30 seconds or more to launch. The updated code base is not just to speed up start times but more importantly to improve the overall stability and performance of Flash to ensure longevity on OS X.

Based on my experience running Flash CC for several months throughout the prerelease and now the shipped version, this may be the most stable version of Flash I have ever used. Flash CC has yet to crash on my system (Mavericks, the newest Mac OS X) and I have it running nearly all day, every day. I even purposely leave it running while putting my MacBook Pro into sleep mode, just to try and get Flash to crash when waking up the operating system. So far, Flash has proven stable.

Flash Professional CC has been enhanced to support HiDPI displays including Retina Display available on the new MacBook Pro. HiDPI display facilitates a dramatic improvement in image fidelity and resolution. With Flash Professional CS6, which was not native to HiDPI display, the text was not as sharp and images did not have much detailing. The increased resolution of these displays required the Flash Professional user interface to be updated completely and ensure that the content is displayed with appropriate levels of fidelity. With Flash Professional CC, the icons, font, drawing on stage, general content rendering, and the whole IDE itself are displayed with superior clarity and crispness.

By default, Flash Professional CC enables HiDPI display on MAC. However, you could turn off retina display on MAC, and Flash Professional CC will accommodate this change.

Other performance improvements

• Publishing time improved significantly for FLA/XFL files, having a large number of AS linkages with Warnings mode enabled.

• Performance improvements for Import to Stage and Import to Library that ensure the file open dialog launches faster.

• Launch time for Flash Professional has been reduced significantly.

• Significantly reduced time for opening AS & FLA/XFL files.

• Smoother drawing experiences with the live color preview of objects.

• Unlimited pasteboard size.

Darker user interface

S INCE ITS INCEPTION, Flash has sported a very bright interface. From the white of the stage to the light gray menus, Flash has been a beacon of brightness in an otherwise contrasting suite of tools. When Flash became part of the Adobe Creative Suite, the contrast suddenly became more apparent as applications such as Photoshop and After Effects had already converted to a bold, dark interface design. Now with a complete overhaul to its core code base, we have the choice between the light or the dark side of Flash CC.

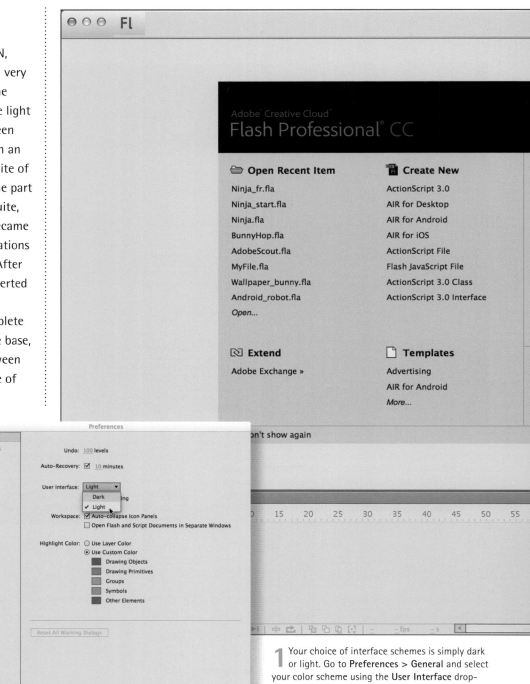

1 Your choice of interface schemes is simply dark or light. Go to **Preferences > General** and select your color scheme using the **User Interface** drop-down menu.

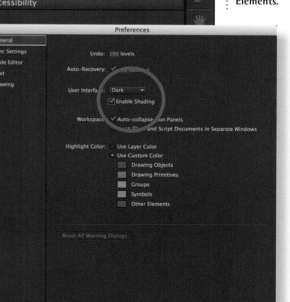

HOT TIP

You can customize the interface further in terms of how objects react when highlighted. In the same section of the Preferences panel you can select custom colors for Drawing Objects, Primitives, Groups, Symbols and Other Elements.

2 If you choose the dark interface, you have the option to turn off **Shading**. With Shading on, some of the menu headers and various other details will have a subtle amount of added depth. With Shading turned off, the effect is substituted for a flat shade of dark gray which provides a cleaner look and slightly faster redrawing of the panels when opened or moved across the screen.

Unlimited pasteboard size

LIFE IS FULL OF LIMITATIONS. Lots of them. Almost everything around us is restricted to some degree of certainty. From warranties to natural resources, a run on stamps, clothing, automobiles and television shows, limitations are a fact of life we're forced to accept. It's difficult to find anything that is truly unlimited. Until now.

For the first time ever, Flash CC has an unlimited pasteboard (the area beyond the stage). If you are new to Flash and CC is the first version you've ever used, this new feature may not seem like a big deal. But for those of us who have used previous versions of Flash, we were all too familiar with a pasteboard limitation of no greater than 2,880 pixels. We were forced to design and animate within the confines of a limited environment. Flash was The Truman Show of the software world. As of Flash CC the confines of the pasteboard have been lifted, and all is right in the world.

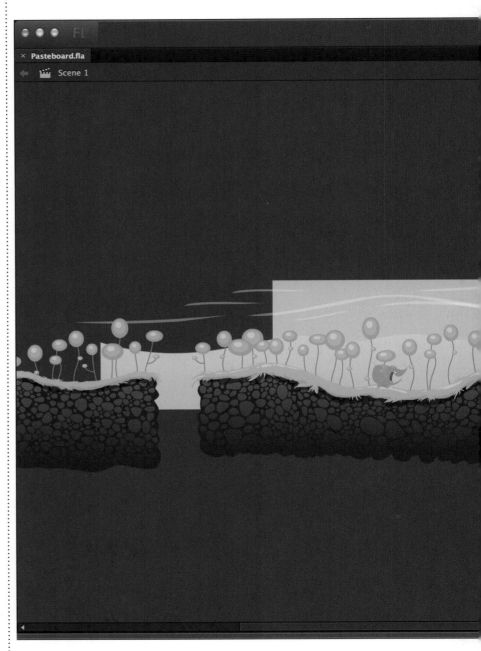

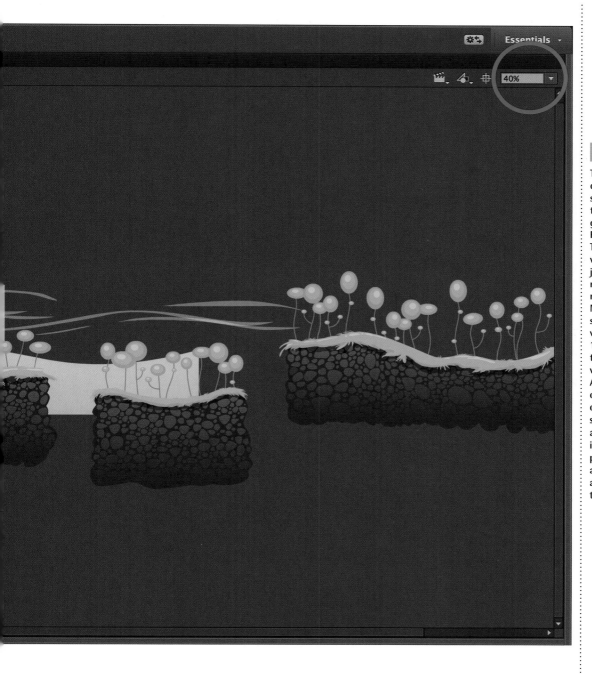

Distribute symbols & bitmaps to keyframes

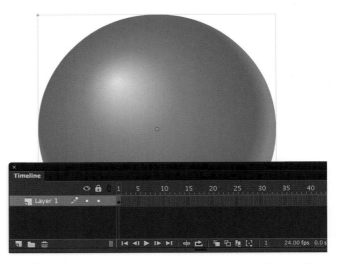

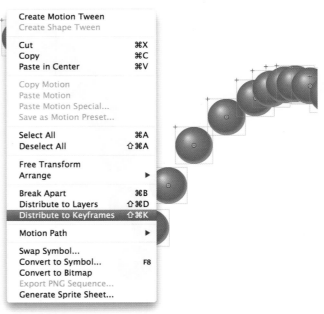

SOMETIMES CERTAIN FEATURES COME along that allow you to take advantage of them in ways they may not have been originally designed. It took some thinking on my part to come up with an example to showcase the new Distribute to Keyframes feature. Once the idea came to me, I quickly realized how much of a game changer this feature could be for anyone using Flash for frame-by-frame animation. Typically, frame-by-frame animation requires an image or a series of images to be drawn or positioned across individual subsequent keyframes, a technique that requires frequent testing to make sure the timing is right. With Distribute to Keyframes, you can create all of your "animation" on a single keyframe with the convenience of seeing the spatial relationship of the object throughout each pose or, in this example, each position.

1 In frame 1 of a new document I created a simple ball graphic using the Oval **O** tool and a radial gradient for depth. The plan is to animate this ball bouncing from left to right across the stage.

4 With the entire range of motion complete, the hard part is done. Select all **ctrl** **A**, then right-click over any of the selected objects on the stage and select **Distribute to Keyframes** from the context menu.

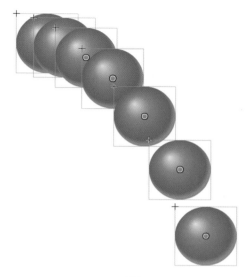

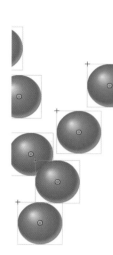

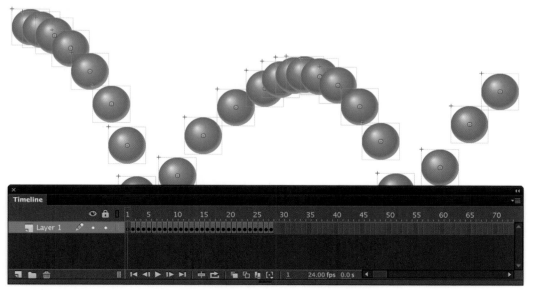

2 Hold down the Option ⌥ key and then click and drag the symbol to duplicate it. Position it using the Selection **V** tool. To simulate gravity the ball must increase speed as it descends, otherwise known as an *easing in* effect. The distance between each ball gradually increases as the ball arcs downward.

3 Here the duplicate ball symbols are positioned in an acsending arc with the space between each of them decreasing to simulate an *easing out* movement. The advantage to animating this way is seeing the entire range of motion of the object, which provides a overall sense of timing based on the intended action.

HOT TIP

Distribute to Keyframes will work with objects other than symbols. You can distribute grouped objects, Object Drawings and imported bitmaps. Distribute to Keyframes will even work with multiple objects of various formats. Select any combination of bitmaps, symbols, grouped objects and Object Drawings and you can still distribute them all to keyframes with a single command.

5 Flash CC will distribute each selected object to its own keyframe. Play the timeline to see the animation of the ball bouncing. The timing will be dictated by a combination of the document frame rate as well as the relative placement of each object. Creating animation using the Distribute to Keyframes method has become a part of my workflow whenever possible. In situations such as the ball bouncing example, it can be a real time saver to create your animation as a single image first, and then let Flash do the hard part by distributing everything to keyframes.

11

Swap multiple symbols and bitmaps

Oۤ FTEN IT IS THE SIMPLEST OF features that can make the biggest differences. Whenever we get the chance to automate repetitive tasks, our productivity increases and workflows get easier. Swapping symbols has been a Flash workflow feature for as long as Flash has been around. Up until Flash CC, however, we have only been able to swap one symbol at a time. If you've ever had to endure the process of manually swapping a large number of symbols, then I'm happy to tell you those days are now over.

1 There is nothing complicated about this example, but more often than not we find ourselves needing to perform repetitive, mundane tasks. Each balloon is a separate symbol, and the task at hand is to swap each one with a different symbol so that they are all *instances* of the same balloon symbol. Previous versions of Flash dictated that we repeat the swap for each individual symbol which is no longer the case in Flash CC.

4 In the **Swap Symbol** panel select the symbol to replace the selected symbols on the stage and then click **OK**.

2 Select all symbols you want to swap for a different symbol. Hold down the **Shift** key to select multiple symbols.

3 The replacement symbol already resides in the library represented by the purple balloon. In the Properties panel click the Swap button.

5 Each of the selected symbols on the stage have now been swapped to a the newly selected symbol. We have never been able to achieve swapping of multiple symbols in previous versions of Flash, as simple as it may be.

Toggle guides and masks

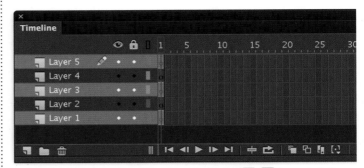

M ULTIPLE LAYER SELECTION: YOU can now select and assign/modify properties to multiple layers using the **Layer Properties** dialog. Convert layers to Guides or Masks with the Toggle Guides and Toggle Masks options. In addition to Guides and Masks, other layer properties include:

- **Lock Others**
- **Hide Others**
- **Expand Folders**
- **Collapse Folders**

From within the Layer Properties panel you can change the layer color and height across multiple selected layers.

1 Select multiple layers by holding down the Control ⌘ *ctrl* key and clicking on each layer in the Timeline panel. If you want to select all layers, hold down the Shift *Shift* key, select the first layer and then the last layer. All the layers in between will also be selected.

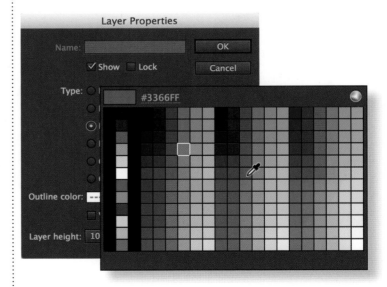

3 In addition to layer types, a new outline color can be applied by clicking on the color swatch and selecting a new color from the popup palette. The new color will be assigned to all selected layers.

Show All
Lock Others
Hide Others

Insert Layer
Delete Layers

Cut Layers
Copy Layers
Paste Layers
Duplicate Layers

Guide
Add Classic Motion Guide

Mask
Show Masking

Insert Folder
Delete Folders
Expand Folders
Collapse Folders

Expand All Folders
Collapse All Folders

Properties...

2 Right-click over any of the selected layers to bring up the context menu. The options available to you in Flash CC are **Lock** and **Hide Others, Insert** and **Delete** layers, **Cut, Copy, Duplicate layers** and convert all selected layers to **Guide** or **Mask layers.** You can also select **Properties** to access the **Layer Properties** panel. From here you can toggle layer visibility, lock or unlock and select the layer type.

Layer Properties

Name: 　　　　　　　　　　　OK

☑ Show ☐ Lock 　Cancel

Type: ○ Normal
○ Mask
⦿ Masked
○ Folder
○ Guide
○ Guided

Outline color: ▭

☐ View layer as outlines

Layer height: 100% ▾

HOT TIP

If you convert a layer property from Normal to Folder and then back to Normal again, you will need to insert at least 1 frame before drawing or placing objects on the stage. Press the F5 (Insert Frames) key to insert at least 1 frame in the converted layer to allow objects to be added to your scene as intended.

Layer Properties

Name: 　　　　　　　　　　OK

☑ Show ☑ Lock 　Cancel

Type: ○ Normal
○ Mask
○ Masked
⦿ Folder
○ Guide
○ Guided

Outline color: ▭

☐ View layer as outlines

Layer height: 300% ▾
　　　　100%
　　　　200%
　　✓ 300%

4 Click the **Layer Height** drop-down menu to select a new layer height. You can choose between **100%**, **200%** and **300%** layer heights. Click **OK,** and all selected layers will adopt your new settings.

Timeline

Layer 5
Layer 4
Layer 3
Layer 2
Layer 1

1 5 10 15 20 25 30 35 40 45 50 55

24.00 fps 0.0 s

Scale to Anchor point

CHANGING THE STAGE size in Flash has been limited to the right and bottom sides of the stage in previous versions. The composition of your design was ignored during this process as well. If you have ever wanted to scale the stage along with the contents of your Flash document, you would have to do so manually, which can get complicated if your document contains long animations. In Flash CC we can now scale the stage size and its content together based on any one of nine anchor points.

1 The Flash document has its stage size set to **1024 x 768** pixels. This example will show you how to scale the stage size along with the entire contents of the timeline. Even if your Flash document contains long timeline animations, everything will be scaled according to the stage size and anchor point. Scaling the stage is very useful if you have a project that you want to publish to various devices or mediums that have varying aspect ratios. Imagine being able to author content for output to video to be uploaded to **YouTube** or **Vimeo** but then scale that same content for an iPhone or Android smartphone or tablet.

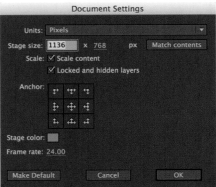

3 To enable the scaling of the document contents, click to select either the width or height text fields of the stage size. Type in a new value for both the width and height. In this example I have chosen a new stage size of **1136 x 640** to support the **iPhone 5** screen resolution. The Scale checkbox will become active, allowing you to select it, by clicking in the box to allow the content to scale. You can also choose to scale locked and hidden layers as an option. The **Anchor** feature allows you to select how the content is positioned. Click on any one of the 9 squares to determine the placement of your content. For this example I selected the middle square so that all my content is centered based on the new width and height. Click the OK button.

Document...	⌘J
Convert to Symbol...	F8
Convert to Bitmap	
Break Apart	⌘B
Bitmap	▶
Symbol	▶
Shape	▶
Combine Objects	▶
Timeline	▶
Transform	▶
Arrange	▶
Align	▶
Group	⌘G
Ungroup	⇧⌘G

Document Settings

Units: Pixels

Stage size: 1024 × 768 px Match contents

Scale: ☐ Scale content
☑ Locked and hidden layers

Anchor:

Stage color:

Frame rate: 24.00

Make Default   Cancel   OK

2 Open the **Document Settings** panel by going to **Modify > Document** or ⌘ J. You will find several options within the **Document Settings** panel that include stage size, scale, anchor, stage color and frame rate.

4 Flash will change the stage width and height as specified in the **Document Settings** panel and scale the entire content of the timeline based on the selected anchor point. Pictured to the right is the new size **1136 x 640** that publishes perfectly for the **iPhone 5** screen resolution.

17

DragonBones extension

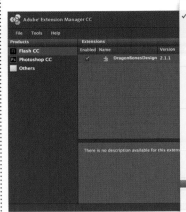

DRAGONBONES IS AN OPEN SOURCE 2D skeleton animation program that contains a Flash Professional design panel and an AS3-based library. The design panel converts Flash vector animation to a texture atlas (also known as a Sprite Sheet). DragonBones integrates well with the Starling Framework, which takes advantage of GPU accelerated animation. The DragonBones extension is both designer and developer friendly. Animations can be handled entirely by the designer who can then export the necessary data to be handed off to a developer for game integration. To learn more and download the DragonBones extension, visit
http://dragonbones.github.io.
For more information on the Starling Framework, visit
http://gamua.com/starling.

1 Download the **DragonBones** extension from **http://dragonbones.github.io**. Once downloaded, double-click the **XMP** extension file to launch the **Adobe Extension Manager CC** to install

DragonBones for Flash CC. If Flash CC is already running, you will need to restart the application. With Flash CC running, launch the DragonBones extension by going to **Window > Extensions > DragonBonesDesignPanel**.

4 Add a new layer to the Movie Clip timeline containing the character to be animated. Create Blank Keyframes (F7) on every other frame and add the following frame labels: **idle**, **walk**, **run**, **crouch** and **jump**. The DragonBones extension will reference these frame labels once the Movie Clip has been imported later in this example.

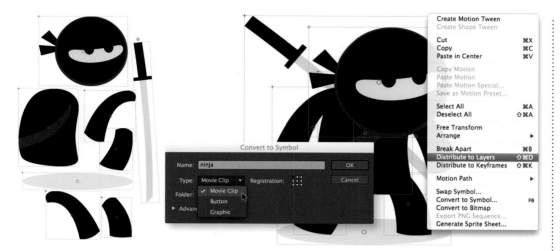

2 The DragonBones extension uses characters that are setup in traditional Flash fashion. Objects are converted to symbols and organized in cut-out animation style. The ninja pictured above is comprised of 8 different symbols, each in their own layer and within a Movie Clip symbol.

3 The entire character is converted to a Movie Clip symbol. Edit the Movie Clip symbol, select all the symbols of the character, right-click over them and select Distribute to Layers from the context menu.

HOT TIP

DragonBones will only work with the same set of symbols across the entire timeline. Keep your characters simple because you will not have the luxury of swapping symbols throughout the animations. If you do, the DragonBones workflow will break and cause errors.

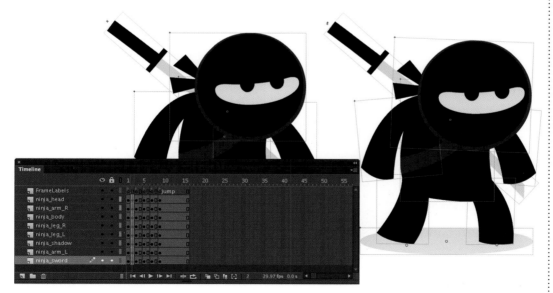

5 The animator needs only to create 2 poses per animation state as DragonBones will do all the interpolation. For the idle animation I just want to create the ninja standing still, yet with a subtle motion as if he's breathing a little heavy. Insert Keyframes (F6) in frame 2.

6 In frame 2 each symbol of the ninja character is in a slightly different position. It's hard to notice but the head has been moved down a few pixels, the arms rotated inward slightly, the body also repositioned as well as the sword and legs.

Continued…

19

1 Launch the DragonBones panel by going to Window > Extensions > DragonBonesDesignPanel. To begin working with DragonBones you must import the Movie Clip symbol containing the character poses and frame labels. Make sure the Library panel is open and

the Movie Clip is selected. In the DragonBones panel click the **Import** button. In the **Import** popup panel, select **Selected Items** from the Import drop-down menu.

4 Adjust the total length of the animation by using the slider, up or down arrows or selecting the numeric value and typing in the desired duration manually. The longer the duration, the slower the animation will be. Blending Times is the number of tween frames needed to switch from one motion to another. If you enter a blending time value of 5, then 5 tweened frames will be used to transition from one motion to the currently selected motion.

5 You can select each bone independently in the Bone Tree window and adjust their behaviors individually using the sliders to the right. The **Total Frames Scale** slider controls the number of frames of the selected bone relative to the total frames of motion. The **Play Delay** slider controls the delay of the current bone relative to the motion it belongs to. What the 2 sliders can do is provide a secondary motion to your animations which adds a level of realism.

2 DragonBones will import the selected Movie Clip and display its contents in the preview panel on the left, the frame label data in the **Behavior List** panel on the right and the Bone Tree hierarchy just below that. You will notice that DragonBones has applied motion to the poses in the selected frame label using a tweening engine.

3 You will likely want to adjust the timing of the animation as well as some easing. To access the behavior controls, click on the double arrow to expand the window. You will find Total and Blending time controls as well as Keyframe Easing and a Loop option.

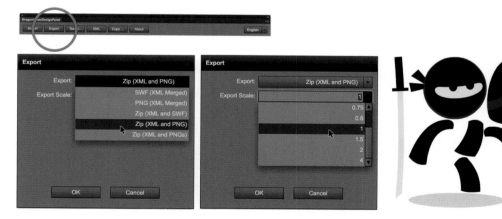

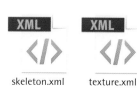

6 When you are finished adjusting each behavior, it is time to export the animations by clicking the Export button. In the Export drop-down menu, choose from several export options based on your needs. Here I have selected Zip (XML and PNG) format. In Export Scale dropdown box, you can set the scale of the exported texture atlas to export assets with different dimensions for devices with different resolutions. The PNG file is the atlas (or Sprite sheet) generated by DragonBones and contains all the character assets. The **texture.xml** file contains the atlas sheet data while the **skeletal.xml** file contains the animation data file. If you are purely a designer/animator, your work here is done. You can safely pass the exported XML and PNG files off to the developer who will incorporate them into the game engine.

skeleton.xml

texture.xml

Multi-device connectivity

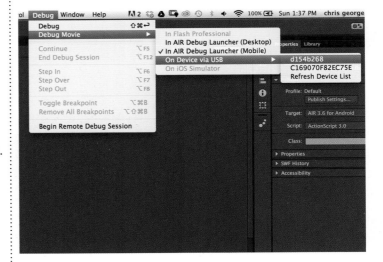

1 Create a new **AIR for Android** or **AIR for iOS** document by going to **File > New...** ⌘ N *ctrl* N. For this example I selected **AIR for Android**. I have 2 devices connected to my computer via USB: a Galaxy Tab and a Galaxy S4.

FLASH CC NOW SUPPORTS the testing of applications on multiple devices simultaneously via USB functionality. You can conveniently select from a list of devices of varying screen sizes, OS versions, and hardware configurations directly from your Flash CC application. The advantages here are being able to see how your application looks and performs across a range of platforms before submitting to an official store.

4 You can debug your application from within the Flash CC document by going to **Debug > Debug Movie > On Device via USB** and selecting the connected device from the list. If you don't see your device listed, select **Refresh Device List**.

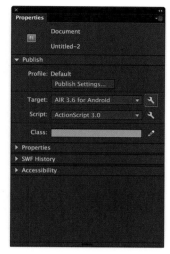

2 In the Properties panel click on the wrench icon to the right of the Target drop-down menu to open the AIR for Android settings.

3 In the AIR for Android settings panel you will see the connected devices in the After publishing section at the bottom. If you don't see a device listed, click on the Refresh button.

HOT TIP

If you are having problems with your device not being recognized, make sure USB debugging mode is turned on. You can access this option by going to the system settings for your device and locating the developer tools category. On my Android devices USB Debugging is found under Settings > Developer Options > USB Debugging.

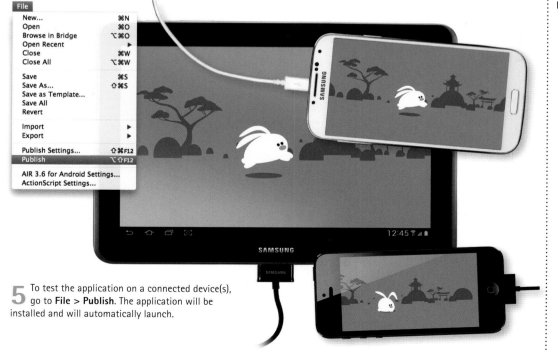

5 To test the application on a connected device(s), go to **File > Publish**. The application will be installed and will automatically launch.

Exporting Video

1 The Flash document above contains a timeline based animation using nested Graphic symbols. The entire timeline is about 15 seconds in duration. The stage size is 1920 x 1080 at 24 frames per second.

THIS IMPROVEMENT MAY BE THE most exciting for animators! We've needed a reliable way to export our content directly from Flash to video format. In the past, we've experienced dropped frames or unexpected quality issues when exporting our animations due to an error-prone process that demanded large amounts of memory. The enhancements to the video exporter are the direct result of integrating the Adobe Media Encoder in Flash CC. This integration simplifies the video export workflow while providing many more encoding options for output to a variety of mediums.

4 Once the video has been exported, the Adobe Media Encoder will launch automatically. The MOV file from Flash will be added to the Queue panel. Using the AME, you can select from a variety of presets in the Preset Browser on the right side. I want to upload my animation to **YouTube**, so I have selected the H.264 format, specifically the YouTube HD 1080p 29.97 preset in the Preset Browser. When you are ready to export, click the green arrow near the top of the AME to begin the encoding process.

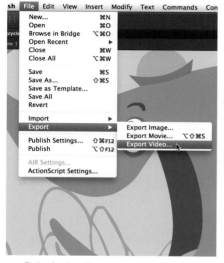

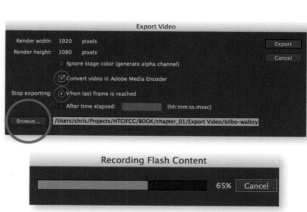

2 To begin the video export process go to File > Export Video...

3 In the Export Video settings panel, make sure **Convert video in Adobe Media Encoder** is checked. Since my document contains timeline animation, I have selected **When last frame is reached** as the stopping point of the export process. Click **Browse** to select the path where to save your video file and then click the Export button. The **Recording Flash Content** progress bar will display the export process.

5 With the encoding process complete, the video file can be opened and played in the Quicktime Player to verify the quality of the video is acceptable. In my experience with the new video exporter in Flash CC, each frame is flawless – even at 1920 x 1080 and with no dropped frames.

Find & Replace enhancements

IF ONLY LIFE HAD A FIND AND replace panel. I could imagine a world where if something needed to be fixed, it could be located and remedied with the help of a few input fields and a checkbox or 2. My to-do list would take minutes instead of hours or even days. Find and Replace is not new to Flash, but for the first time, Flash CC introduces a few subtle updates to the panel.

I've always considered the Find and Replace panel to be the unsung hero of Flash. Surprisingly, very few Flash users even know it exists, probably because it's relatively hidden under the Edit menu as opposed to under the Window menu where most of the other panels reside. Once you've been introduced to this wonderful time-saving gem, you will find countless ways to use it.

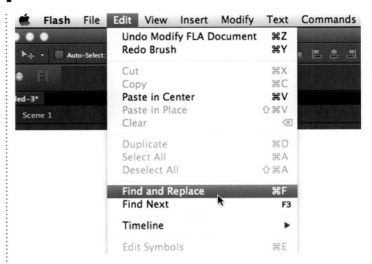

1 The Find and Replace panel can be found under the Edit menu or by pressing ⌘ F ctrl F on your keyboard.

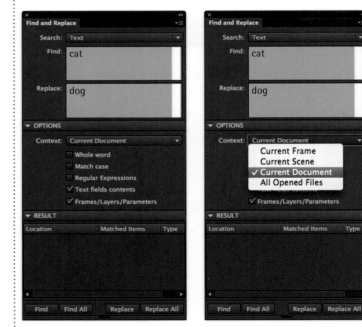

4 You can refine your search by entering specific text in the Find input field, and replace it with text entered in the Replace field.

5 In the Options category, select Current Document from the Context drop-down menu, then click Replace or Replace All if there's more than 1 instance that needs changing.

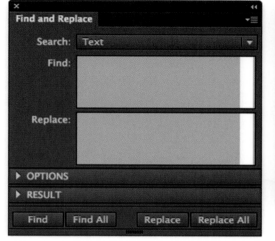

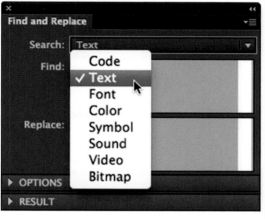

2 The main improvement of this panel is the organization of its features into categories. Each category can be expanded or collapsed based on the content you wish to edit.

3 Using the Search drop-down menu, select from Code, Text, Font, Color, Symbol, Sound, Video or Bitmap.

HOT TIP

If you need to replace assets across multiple documents, make sure they are all open, and then select All Opened Files from the Context drop-down menu in the Context category. The Find and Replace dialog is also integrated into the Actions panel.

6 Here I am changing the color of the character across several different symbols from orange to blue. I've chosen Color from the Search drop-down menu and selected the original color in the Find swatch. In the Replace swatch I have chosen the new color to replace the original color and then clicked the Replace All button.

Live preview for drawing tools

IF YOU USE THE SHAPE tools often in Flash, this enhancement will be significant for you. In Flash CS6, when drawing on the stage, you only saw the outlines of shapes. In Flash CC this is no longer the case. You can now preview a shape when using the Line, Rectangle and Oval tools instantaneously. The Live Preview feature displays the stroke and fill color for the shape along with the outline in real time as you are drawing.

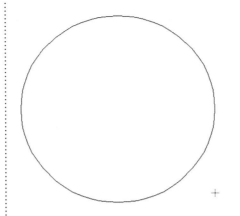

In Flash CS6, the circle shape displays the outline while actively being drawn with the Oval tool.

The circle is filled with color only after the cursor has been released.

In Flash CC, shapes are filled with color as they are being drawn in real time as shown above using the Rectangle tool.

The circle preview includes the selected fill color

Live Preview also includes strokes (if selected) for shapes as well as strokes made with the Line tool.

Other notable enhancements

Performance improvements

Publishing time improved significantly for FLA/XFL files having a large number of AS linkages with Warnings mode enabled.

Performance improvements for **Import to Stage** and **Import to Library** ensure that the file open dialog launches faster.

Unlimited pasteboard size means the area outside the Flash CC stage is endless.

Enhancements to the ActionScript Editor

The Code Commenting feature can now intelligently comment or uncomment based on your selection of single or multiple lines of code.

Scintilla, an open source code editing component, has now been integrated with Flash CC.

Enhancements to panels

Several panels have been redesigned in Flash CC to improve efficiency and to provide a better user experience:

A number of options have been reduced on the Preferences panel to provide a simplified experience.

Filters UI and Accessibility Properties have been included in the Properties panel.

Changes to the PSD and AI Importers

The experience of importing a PSD file in to Flash CC has been simplified significantly. The following is the list of changes made to the PSD file Import dialog:

The **Layer Panel View** has been excluded.

Hidden layers bundled in to a **Layer Comp** stay hidden and cannot be selected or edited when importing a **PSD** or an **AI** file.

HOT TIP

Many of the improvements to Flash CC are under the hood. Gone are the bells and whistles which have been removed in lieu of a solid core functionality this version has been on improving the very core of Flash: its foundation. Flash CC is much faster and more stable than previous versions which paves the way for a bright future.

Deprecated features

Help Improve Adobe's Products

Adobe strives to provide the best possible user experience to our customers. To facilitate the continued development of products, anonymous data will be collected and sent to Adobe periodically detailing how Adobe's products are used. No information is collected that could be used to either identify you or be used to contact you.

Learn More

See Participating Products

[Do Not Participate] [Participate]

THIS MAY STING A LITTLE. FOR THE first time in the history of Flash, or at least in my recollection, the number of removed features seemingly outweighs the number of added features. But before we freak out, let's take a moment to learn how and why Adobe made these decisions. When you install and launch Flash for the first time, a popup window asks if you want to participate in the Adobe Product Improvement Program. If you click Participate, you will be helping Adobe improve the very product you love. Don't worry, involvement in the program requires no effort on your part except using the application. The data collected by Adobe consists of your system information, browser type and version, Adobe product information and feature usage such as menu options and button selections. The information collected is used to develop new features and improve existing ones. In the case of Flash CC, Adobe removed the least used features based on the information collected from those who participated. You can choose to not participate or stop participating at any point.

In memoriam...

ActionScript 1 and 2

Some of you may have seen this coming but for those who didn't, ActionScript 1 and 2 are no longer supported in Adobe Flash CC. ActionScript 3 is the version of choice moving forward.

TLF Text

If your FLA, created with an older version of Flash Professional, contains TLF Text, then Flash CC will automatically convert it to Classic text upon opening the FLA.

Motion Editor

For some animators, the loss of the Motion Editor may be surprising. Flash CC no longer includes the Motion Editor, which supported the control of individual properties for the new Motion tween model. Motion paths, however, will remain. Not many animators used the Motion Editor but those who tried, including myself, found it somewhat clumsy to use. As a self-contained panel, the Motion Editor felt too disconnected from the main timeline and the object that was being animated on the stage. The Motion Editor demanded a large amount of screen real estate, arguably its own display. As powerful as it was to control each individual property within the same tween span, the implementation of the Motion Editor made the workflow cumbersome. For this reason the Flash team decided to remove it for now, step back and rethink the Motion Editor completely. I can assure you there are many internal discussions about how best to redesign and implement the Motion Editor in a future update.

Deco Tools

Adobe introduced the Deco tool in CS4 and subsequently Deco brushes in CS5. From Vine Fill to Symmetry Brush to Lightning Brush, we had automated animation in the form of brushes. As cool as they were, nobody really used them. I'll admit, I never did either. I was excited about them at first, but they never became my go-to tool of choice. It seems like this was a similar story for most Flash designers and animators.

Bone Tool

The Bone tool was one of the most promising new Flash features that simply never fulfilled our inverse kinematic needs. It could be said that I was one of the most vocal proponents for getting the Bone feature into Flash. I've been part of the Flash prerelease team for as long as I can remember and have always had a direct line of communication to the Flash engineering team. Back in 2004, when Macromedia still owned Flash, the annual Max event was held in New Orleans. I was there as a speaker showing the audience my typical animation workflow of editing the center point of symbols to simulate the hinging of character body parts. After my session was over, Eric Mueller, an engineer on the Flash team, approached me with his laptop and showed me a prototype plugin running inside Flash. That plugin eventually became the Bone tool and was introduced in Flash CS4. Now, 3 versions later, it has been removed. Based on user feedback and analytics, the Bone tool simply didn't live up to expectations.

Also removed from Flash CC

Project panel

Launch & Edit (L&E Photoshop works)

Printing

Strings panel

Behaviors panel

Object-level undo

Check Spelling panel

Movie Explorer

Bandwidth Profiler

FXG Import/Export

Actions toolbox

Kuler panel

Share My Screen

Code Hinting for JSFL

Video Cue Points

Closed Captioning

Video playback on stage

Device Central

Customize Tools panel

Drag-and-drop from Stage to Library or another application

Importing some bitmap formats (BMP, TIFF, AutoCad)

Importing some sound formats (AIFF, Sound Designer, Around AU, Adobe Sounds Document)

File info (XMP Metadata)

Projectors

Fireworks PNG Import

With all that has been deprecated in Flash CC, your initial reaction may range anywhere from anger to disappointment. It would be easy and a bit justified to react negatively to the decisions Adobe has made for Flash, but let's take a deep breath, step back and think about this for a minute. Not too long ago the word on the street was that Flash is dead. Marketing buzzwords such as HTML5 and Canvas have seemed to cast a shadow over the term Flash, more specifically the Flash Player. Even I began to consider adopting a completely different animation program.

Amidst all the "Flash is dead" rumors, Adobe was busy examining the data from Flash users participating in the Product Improvement Program and made some executive decisions – completely rebuild the core of Flash for a strong future. This direction is proof that Adobe is investing in Flash long term as a viable authoring tool and an important member of the Creative Cloud family. Think of it as a new beginning, a shedding of old skin, a Flash reimagined.

I taught 2 sessions at Adobe Max this past year and had the distinct pleasure of having members of the Flash engineering team, who came all the way from India, as my assistants. They got to see me use and teach the tool they help build. I then got to know them a little better over lunch; they were warm, receptive and open to ideas that promote a better Flash experience moving forward. Meeting the engineering team put faces behind the application and cemented in my heart and mind that Flash is not only here to stay but more importantly is built by caring people.

Adobe® Creative Cloud™

What is the Creative Cloud?

To explain this new direction in as simple as terms possible, I would describe the Adobe Creative Cloud as a subscription-based file storage service. But what separates this from other storage services such as Google Drive, Dropbox and Apple iCloud is that Adobe not only allows you to store and share your files on the Creative Cloud but also download, install and update all your Adobe applications as part of the same service. Installation is performed after you've subscribed to the service and downloaded the Adobe Application Manager.

How much does it cost?

The Adobe Creative Cloud offers a multi-tier subscription service based on your needs and history using Adobe products.

Individual plan: $49.99 US per month or about $600 US annually.

Individual CS customer plan: If you've been an Adobe customer since CS3, the Creative Cloud membership costs $29.99 monthly ($360 annually). If you are already using CS6 then the Creative Cloud membership will be $19.99 monthly ($240 annually).

Single app plan: Just need a single application? $19.99 per month, and it's yours along with 20GB of cloud storage.

Team plan: **$69.99** per month or **$840** annually. If your team is a CS3 or later customer, the price drops to **$39.99** monthly.

The idea behind the Creative Cloud subscription service is the more apps you use, the more bang for your buck. Adobe no longer supports perpetual software versions. You will not see another boxed version of any Adobe application nor will you have to wait for 18 months or longer for an updated version.

What does this mean for you?

Not only will you have a cloud service to save and share project files with collaborators and clients, you will also have the option to download any application from Adobe's collection. Don't need every Adobe app? Fine, just download and use what you need and only when you need it. Adobe Creative Cloud is like your own personal à la carte app store that allows you to pick and choose only the apps you need. Of course, you may be the type that needs all applications all the time. Indulge yourself. Adobe won't judge you.

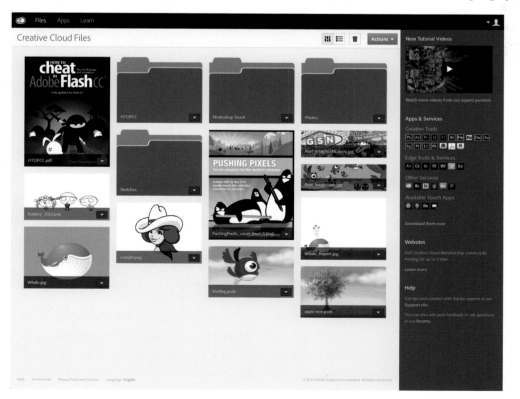

Do I own the applications I download?

No. But you never did anyway. When we purchase software we never truly "own" it but rather license it from the developer. There's a big difference between owning and licensing that isn't worth getting into here because of all the legalities involved. The biggest advantage of the Creative Cloud apps is that you'll always have access to the latest updates which will come more frequently than the now deprecated perpetual versions.

Multiple installations

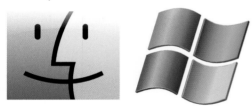

You can install Creative Cloud apps on up to 2 computers regardless of platform. Let's say you have a Mac at home and use Windows at work. You can install Adobe applications on both, a huge advantage over previous versions of the Creative Suite. In the past, if you needed to install on Mac and Windows, then you needed to purchase 2 different licenses.

Does Adobe own my files?

No. Adobe owning your work would be kind of crazy and not what the Creative Cloud was designed for. Your files belong to you and always will. After all, you created them.

Do I have to save files to the Creative Cloud?

No again. The Adobe Creative Cloud is for the sharing of your files if you decide that's what you want to do. The Cloud is also great for accessing your files across multiple computers. Alternatively you can save files to your local hard drive the same way you've been doing it for years; File > Save as.

Membership cancellation

In the event you want to cancel your Adobe Creative Cloud membership, you will have a 90-day grace period to download your files from your Creative Cloud account.

Behance community

Included with your Creative Cloud subscription is access to an amazing creative community called Behance. If you are looking for inspiration from fellow creatives or looking to get your own creations noticed, Behance will not disappoint. I personally love perusing the Behance site for inspirational work, and your Creative Cloud paid membership gets you the Behance Pro features such as ProSite – a customizable professional portfolio with your own unique URL.

Edge tools and other Creative Cloud perks

But wait, there's more! As part of your Creative Cloud subscription you also get access to the Edge suite of tools such as Animate, Code, Inspect, Reflow and Web Fonts. Typekit and PhoneGap Build are also included. Other available services include Business Catalyst, Story Plus, Digital Publishing Suite and more.

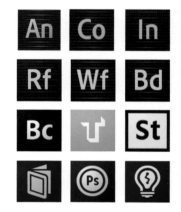

Need more information? Visit the Creative Cloud at http://www.adobe.com/products/creativecloud/faq.html

■No two snowflakes are exactly alike and the same can be said for artists and designers. A good drawing program will allow this individuality to be expressed without limitation.

Design styles

THE FLASH DRAWING ENGINE IS AS COMPLICATED OR
as simple as you make it. Drawing in Flash is like
building with Legos. Each individual tool is simple
to use but capable of creating complicated designs
when necessary. Even with so many drawing programs
at my disposal, Flash is almost always my go-to tool
because of its ease of use. This chapter will show you
the fundamentals of designing in Flash with a few cool
drawing techniques along the way.

Drawing with basic shapes

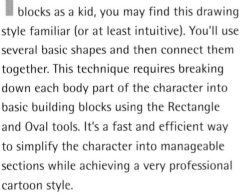

I F YOU PLAYED WITH LEGO BUILDING blocks as a kid, you may find this drawing style familiar (or at least intuitive). You'll use several basic shapes and then connect them together. This technique requires breaking down each body part of the character into basic building blocks using the Rectangle and Oval tools. It's a fast and efficient way to simplify the character into manageable sections while achieving a very professional cartoon style.

Here, we will use shapes to cut into other shapes. This technique is very useful for cutting holes out of objects as well as altering the edges of shapes. Of course these techniques can be applied to background elements as well.

The key here is using simple shapes to build complex images suitable for Flash style animation, which we will get to in later chapters.

1 Here is my original pencil sketch that I have scanned and saved as a JPG file. I prefer to start with pencil on paper because I simply like the feel of this medium and the results are always a little more, shall we say, artistic.

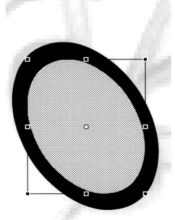

6 To achieve the black outline, select the shape, copy it using ⌘ C ctrl C and paste it in place using ⌘ Shift V ctrl Shift V. While it's still selected, select a different color from the Mixer panel and scale it about 80% smaller.

2 After importing the scanned image, insert a blank keyframe on frame 2 and turn on the Onionskin tool. Onionskinning allows you to trace the image in a new frame while using the original image as a reference.

7 The original shape is still present underneath your new shape. The trick is to position the new shape off-center from the original to achieve an outline with a varied weight.

3 Using the Oval **O** and Rectangle **R** tools allows you to quickly achieve the basic forms of the character. The Selection tool is great for pushing and pulling these basic fills into custom shapes based on the sketch.

4 Turn on the Snap option (magnet icon), and drag corners to each other so they snap together. This process is not unlike those Lego building blocks you played with when you were a kid.

5 Next, click and drag the sides of your shapes to push and pull them into curves. This process is fun as your character really starts to take shape.

8 The parachute uses a slightly different technique I like to call "cutting in". Let's start with the Oval tool for the parachute's basic shape.

9 You can cut into this shape using different colored shapes such as this blue oval. Position it over the area you want to cut into, deselect it, then select it and hit the Delete key *Delete*.

10 Once your shape is the way you want it, you can use the Ink Bottle tool **S** to quickly add an outline to it.

2

Design styles

Geometric and organic shapes

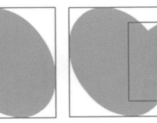

DESIGNING WITH BASIC SHAPES is not limited to characters. For most Flash projects, I start with primitive shapes for all objects, including props and backgrounds. At their most basic level, my designs start with simple ovals or rectangles, and from there I build upon these shapes to create relatively complex images. What I love about working with vectors is the ability to push and pull them into anything I want as if they were made of clay.

1 To suggest a fully mature tree with a plumage of leaves, you don't actually have to draw each individual leaf. Since the design style is targeted at young children, it's valid to keep the level of detail to a minimum. Select the Oval **O** tool and your desired fill color and create an oval shape. Next rotate it or skew to position it at an angle. Copy and paste it and scale it to add more "leaves". Rotate and position the new oval as shown above. There's no wrong decision at this stage as it is entirely up to you as to how much variation you want your tree to have.

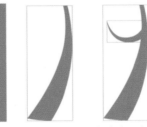

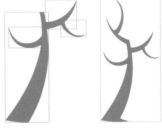

3 The trunk of the tree is designed in a similar fashion. Create a basic rectangle using the Rectangle **R** tool and use the Selection tool **V** to push and pull the sides and corners to give the trunk a slight curve and taper. Each branch is a duplicate of the tree trunk shape. Hold down **alt** and then click and drag the trunk to create as many duplicates of it as you want. Scale, skew, rotate and position each duplicate shape so that they resemble tree branches.

5 With Snap to Objects on, drag a corner point to another corner point until they snap together. Snapping to an object makes it easy to merge different shapes together accurately. To complete the front side of the birdhouse, create another square and drag the top 2 corner points to the bottom 2 corner points of the triangle with the Selection **V** tool until they snap together. Skew the shape with the Distort tool (subselection of the Free Transform **Q** tool) to suggest perspective.

2 Repeat the previous step by copying and pasting the same oval to suggest a larger plumage of leaves. Scale, skew and rotate the shape and position it off-center from the original oval. The objective here is to to create a non-symmetrical organic shape to suggest the imperfections that are found in nature. Remember, nothing in nature is perfectly horizontal, vertical, round or square, which is why there's no

wrong way to position these. As you can see I used a total of 4 ovals to complete my plumage of leaves. I could have used more or less, but I felt this was just the right amount. Feel free to experiment with the number of shapes and variations for your tree. At this stage I couldn't help but add a little bit of texture to suggest some volume using the Brush **B** tool and a subtle yellow color.

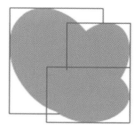

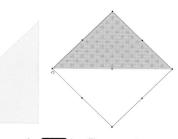

4 The birdhouse is also built using simple shapes. The key here is to turn on the Snap to Objects feature represented by the magnet icon in the toolbar when you select the Rectangle **R** tool. Create a perfect square by dragging with the Rectangle tool while holding down the **Shift** key. Using the Subselection **A** tool, select one of the

corner points and press the **Delete** key. The square is now a triangle. Rotate the triangle using the Free Transform **Q** tool. Hold down the **Shift** key to constrain the rotation to 45 degree increments. Rotate the triangle until the bottom side is flat and the top side is pointed.

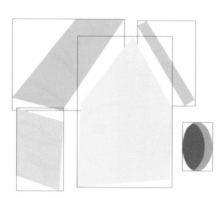

6 The remaining additional shapes for the birdhouse are also (you guessed it) simple rectangles and ovals. Keeping the Snap option turned on, drag corner points to each other to join shapes and as Object Drawings you can also overlap shapes to complete the image.

HOT TIP

As you can see each shape has a bounding box around it because Object Drawing mode **J** was turned on at the time the objects were drawn. Object Drawing Mode allows you to overlap objects without merging them together.

41

The Brush tool

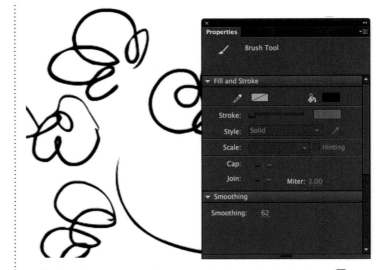

THE BRUSH TOOL IS PROBABLY the most versatile of all the drawing tools, especially when combined with a pressure-sensitive tablet. Drawing with the Brush tool is essentially drawing with shapes. It's the tool that feels the most natural due to the support of pressure sensitivity and tilt features.

Wacom makes a series of popular tablets that work great with Flash. They can work in conjunction with your existing mouse or replace your mouse completely. Many digital designers use a tablet with any number of graphics editors including Adobe Photoshop and Adobe Illustrator.

Deciding to use the Brush tool is really a matter of style and preference. For this character, I wanted to achieve a loose, hand-drawn feel, so the Brush was a perfect choice.

1 The first adjustment you will want to make when using the Brush tool **B** will be the amount of smoothing you want applied. This option appears as a hot text slider in the Properties panel when the Brush tool is selected. The right amount of smoothing to use depends on personal preference. The higher the number, the smoother the line (and vice versa). For this character, we'll choose a low amount of smoothing to maintain an organic quality to the line work.

3 To remain consistent with the loose drawing style, you may want to add a fill color that bleeds outside of the outlines a little. There are several ways to achieve this effect by painting on a new layer below the outline art or setting the brush to "Paint Behind" and painting on the same layer.

2 Always design your characters with the intended purpose in mind: animation. Form follows function, and the animation style can often dictate how a character is designed. If you're a perfectionist like me, you'll want the hair to look as much like individual curls as possible. To do this, avoid designing the hair as one large flat object. Instead, draw individual sections of curls to keep them as separate objects, so they can be moved independently of each other. Turn on Object Drawing mode **J** (subselection of the Brush tool). Object Drawing mode allows you to draw shapes as separate objects. These objects can be drawn over each other without them being merged together. You can select each Object Drawing with the Selection tool **V** and then convert each one to a symbol.

HOT TIP

Experiment with different stage magnifications when drawing. I prefer to draw on a larger scale and with the stage magnified about 400%. The result is typically a smoother line quality.

4 The final result represents the loose hand-drawn style we were after. The line quality feels natural and reflects the imperfections the human hand is capable of. We are not trying to achieve a slick design style here but rather to convey a looser line quality representative of hand-drawn artwork. This style lends itself well to a child character as the integrity of the line is similar to how a real child would draw.

1 The character sketch was created using ProCreate, a powerful drawing app for the Apple iPad. I used a drawing stylus instead of my finger because of its accuracy .

2 After importing the scanned image, I inserted a blank keyframe on frame 2 and turned on the Onionskin tool. I began tracing the image in a new frame while using the original image as a reference.

I N ITS DEFAULT MODE, THE BRUSH TOOL along with a graphics tablet that supports pressure sensitivity – is great for drawing shapes with a varied width. The success of the Brush tool may be due to its simplicity, but that doesn't mean you can't achieve sophisticated results when using it. The Brush tool provides several options that affect how the paint is applied, and with a little ingenuity you can dictate how the Brush works based on your needs and workflow. This example shows my use of the Paint Selection setting for the Brush, allowing it to paint within the confines of a selected fill color only.

6 Paint anywhere inside the selected fill color without destroying any other part of the drawing. The shapes made with this Brush tool setting will be limited to the selected area only.

7 The Paint Selection setting is perfect for adding lines to suggest strands of hair. I also used this same technique for adding the shadows around the character's eyes.

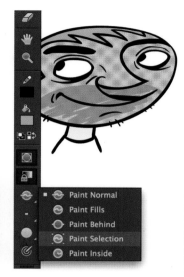

3 I traced the character using the Brush **B** tool. Typically I have the Brush tool smoothness setting at a value between 60 and 75, which is a setting found in the Properties panel.

4 With the character outline complete, it's time to mix a color for his skin tone and fill the head using the Paint Bucket **K** tool.

5 Select the fill color using the Selection **V** tool. To add some shading to the character, mix a darker value of the skin tone and then select the Paint Selection option from the Brush tool subselection menu.

HOT TIP

You can apply smoothing after a shape has been drawn with the Brush tool. Select the shape with the Selection tool and click the Smooth tool in the Tools panel. Alternately you can click the Straighten tool to straighten the edges of the selected shape.

8 The Smoothing value was set to 72 for this drawing, meaning Flash smoothed the shapes created with the Brush tool just enough to remove most of my natural imperfections of drawing by hand. For a more natural-looking drawing, adjust the Smoothness to a lower numerical value.

9 Here's a version of the same character drawn with a Smoothing value of 0. The difference in line quality is subtle, but if you look closely it's quite noticeable how imperfect the overall image is. With no smoothing applied, the drawing can take on a completely different look and feel.

Mixing colors

A S OF FLASH CS6, the Color panel got a slight facelift. Instead of choosing between HSB or RGB, we now have both displayed simultaneously and all color values are accurately controlled using hot text sliders.

Mixing colors in Flash since then has never been easier or more accurate. The creative folks over at Big Pink asked me to create an animation for children between 2 and 5 years of age. Because of the target audience, I wanted the animation to have a soft yet inviting color palette.

1 My typical workflow when mixing colors is to click and drag within the gradient window in order to select the approximate color I'm after. Once I have this color selected I like to use the hot text sliders to fine-tune my color selection. Hue and saturation can play an important role in the design process, and for this particular background image I wanted to keep the colors muted to avoid overpowering the characters that were added later on. As you can see here, the main color of the house has a very low level of saturation but enough brightness to maintain a good level of clarity.

3 Once I had the overall pink color selected, mixing the darker shade of pink required a simple brightness adjustment. The large color swatch at the bottom of the Color panel will split to reveal the current color being mixed on top of the original color. This split provides a visual reference for how the new color will contrast against the original color.

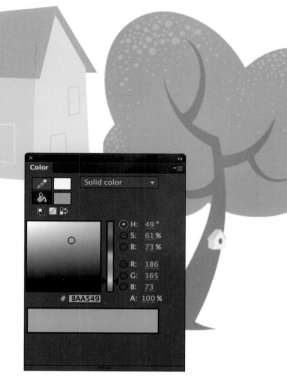

2 Once again the colors of this house are easily muted by lowering the saturation and keeping their brightness relatively high. The green for the tree is slightly more saturated compared to the other colors but overall still muted.

HOT TIP

You can use the Flash Color panel to pick any color from anywhere on your screen – even outside of Flash! Just click on the fill color swatch to activate the color picker and then click on the area of your screen that contains the color you desire.

47

Advanced color effect

THE ADVANCED COLOR EFFECT
separately adjusts the alpha, red, green
and blue values of the instance of a symbol.
It can be used in a variety of ways to suggest
the tone of your graphic design or the mood
of an entire animated scene. Let's take a
look at how to adjust the color values of a
symbol using the RGB hot text sliders. In the
Color Effect section of the Properties panel,
change the style mode to Advanced.

1 Select the symbol containing your
artwork. Using the hot text sliders,
change the value for red to 100% and
both green and blue values to 0%. An
overall hue of red will be applied to
the symbol. Increasing the amount of

green while decreasing red and blue
will result in an overall greenish hue.
Increasing the amount of blue while
decreasing red and green will follow
suit with an overall bluish hue.

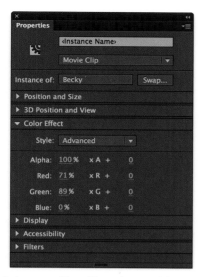

2 Red, green or blue will not always satisfy your color needs. By varying the amount of red, green and blue you can come up with almost unlimited variations of color tones. Here I have an almost equal mix of red and green but no blue at all.

3 If the red, green and blue percentages aren't enough, you can produce more values by adjusting the values in the right column. These values will get added to the percentage values in the left column. For example, if the current red value is 100, setting the left slider to 50% and the right slider to 100% produces a new red value of 150 ([100 x .5] + 100 = 150).

HOT TIP

The advanced color values can also be animated over time using Classic and Motion tweens. Check out the animated example on page 50.

Animated color effect

1 As animators we occasionally need to find ways to visually suggest the passing of time. One of the easiest ways to do this is to change the overall hue of an entire scene or background. As we know, this process naturally takes several hours, but through animation we can speed up time to convey the effect. In its initial shot, this quaint suburban home is designed to represent daytime, probably early afternoon given the angle of the shadow across the front door. The entire background has been converted to a symbol and a Motion tween has been created by right clicking over the symbol and selecting Create Motion Tween. Insert frames in the tween span by pressing on a frame further down the Timeline and pressing the F5 key. With the tween span extended, the hue of the entire scene can now be changed via the Color Effect section of the Properties panel.

2 Make sure the frame indicator is at or near the end of the tween span. With the Properties panel open and Color Effect section expanded, select the symbol containing the background image. Using the hot text sliders, adjust the hue of the symbol instance. Here I have removed the red and green values by entering a numerical value of "0" for both and increased the amount of blue to suggest a cooler range of colors across the entire image. These settings imply a lack of sunlight and create a convincing night time mood. Position the frame indicator back at frame 1 and press the **Enter** key to playback the animation. The Motion Tween span will interpolate the difference in color values between the keyframes, resulting in a dramatic time lapse animation similar to the transition from day into night. You are not limited to just day and night as this technique can be used to imply a change of mood for dramatic effect.

Using gradients

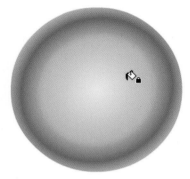

1 A simple radial gradient is used to fill most of the shapes that make up the monkey. The trick here is providing the illusion of a 3D object in a 2D environment. Four colors are used for this gradient. The critical color for this illusion is the fourth color (far right). It represents a light source coming from behind the sphere, suggesting the sphere is truly round.

GRADIENTS CAN BE VERY effective when you want to break away from the flatness of solid color fills. They can be used to add a sense of depth and dimensionality to your characters, backgrounds and graphics in general.

Gradients can also work against you due to their ease of use, resulting in generic and often lackluster images. When in the right hands, however, both linear and radial gradients can contribute to a very effective and sometimes realistic design.

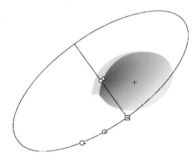

4 To make the ear look concave, mix another radial gradient going from darkest in the center to a lighter value on the outer edge. Fill the shape with this gradient and position it off-center so that only half of the gradient is shown. Since darker colors will recede and lighter colors will appear closer to us, this otherwise flat shape now gives us the impression it is concave.

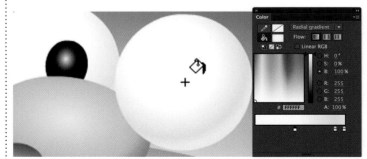

7 For those classic cartoon "ping-pong" eyeballs, mix a radial gradient the same way using white and gray colors. Color theory teaches us that to show light, you must show dark. Apply this technique to the eyes by placing them in front of a darker shape. The contrast will help make the eyeballs *pop*, thereby adding depth.

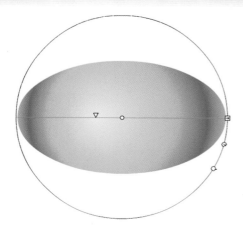

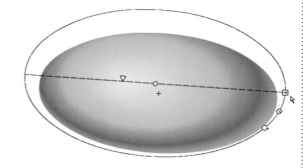

2 Edit the gradient to conform to the shape using the Gradient Transform tool **F**. Use the handles to rotate, scale and skew the gradient, so it is slightly larger than the shape. Select the center control point, drag the entire gradient and position it slightly off-center from the shape.

3 Click and drag the focal point tool so that the highlight is positioned between the center of the shape and its edge. This position suggests that the light source is at more of an angle. Notice the fourth color of our gradient is showing along the bottom and right edge which implies light wrapping around the sphere from behind.

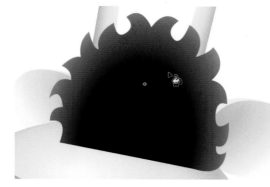

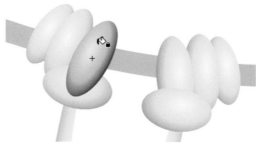

5 The hair is a shape filled with another radial gradient. Most of this shape will be hidden behind other graphics, so you only need to concern yourself with how the outer edge looks when the character is fully assembled.

6 The hands are really just a few strategically positioned spheres with the same radial gradient as the face and body and are used to suggest hands.

8 The nose is a combination of spheres filled with radial and linear gradients. To create the nostrils, use a linear gradient and edit it so that the darker color is above the lighter color. By themselves, the spheres are just shapes. But placed against the radial sphere, they become holes.

9 Good designs are consistent in technique. When each element is comprised of the same graphical style, the overall result is typically consistent and fluid. Don't deviate from your plan; choose a technique and stick with it.

HOT TIP

Gradients, in my opinion, look more realistic when the change in color values is subtle. Gradients that have strong contrasting colors have a tendency to look unrealistic.

53

Adding texture

1 The first task is to design your textures. A digital camera is a very handy device for this purpose. Take a walk around your neighborhood and you'll quickly find an unlimited supply of interesting textures that can be used for your designs. Use Photoshop to adjust the color, add filters and crop your images. Remember to keep the image small enough for web output.

BITMAPS DON'T ALWAYS HAVE TO BE imported as static elements in your projects. Instead, they can be an effective source of adding texture to your designs. Since any image could be a potential texture, the possibilities are endless. For this frog character, I wanted a slightly more sophisticated look while still maintaining a cartoon feel. Instead of using solid color fills and some spot color shading, the use of imported bitmap textures added that extra sense of depth and richness.

3 You can use the Bucket tool to fill your shapes with the different bitmaps you imported, broke apart and picked with the eyedropper.

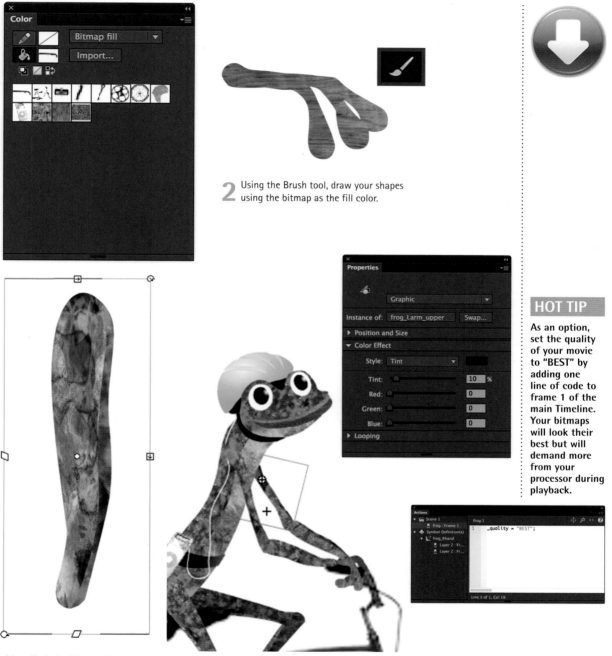

2 Using the Brush tool, draw your shapes using the bitmap as the fill color.

4 Most likely the bitmap fill will need to be scaled, rotated or re-positioned. Select the Gradient Transform tool **F**, and edit your fill using the various handles around the bounding box.

5 The final step is to convert all parts to symbols and add a slight amount of dark tint to the instances behind the character. This helps separate similar bitmap textures from each other and adds a touch of depth.

55

BITMAPS DON'T ALWAYS have to look flat. Introducing "Grotto," a character made almost entirely of bitmap fills and some carefully placed Flash gradients, which provide the illusion of form, volume and, most of all, texture.

Here we'll look at how to give otherwise flat bitmap textures a bit more depth using some basic gradients and alpha.

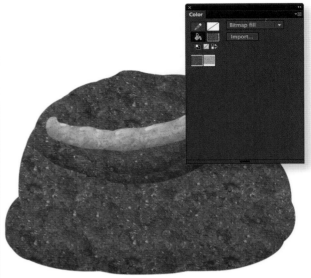

1 The first step is to create your texture in Adobe Photoshop, import it into Flash, break it apart and then select it with the Eyedropper tool *I*. I created the shape for Grotto's body with the paint brush and the bitmap swatch as my fill "color". Select the body shape and convert it to a Graphic symbol.

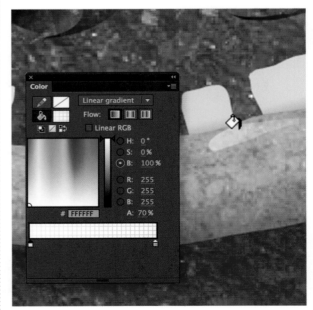

4 Sometimes the devil is in the detail, which is evident here with the additon of some subtle highlights to the lip. On a new layer use the Brush tool to paint some shapes and then fill them with a linear gradient containing 30% white to 0% white. Use the Fill Transform tool *F* to edit the gradient as necessary.

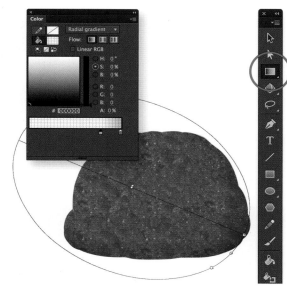

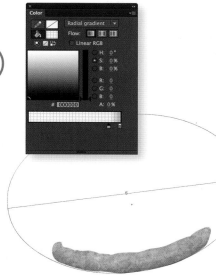

2 Edit the symbol by adding another layer above the shape layer. Copy ⌘C ctrl C and paste in place ⌘ Shift V ctrl Shift V the body shape into this new layer. Fill it with a radial gradient with two colors; black with about 30% alpha and black with 0% alpha.

3 The mouth/lip symbol was made the same way by layering a radial gradient over the bitmap fill shape. Use the Fill Transform tool to position the gradient so it forms a shadow along the bottom half of the shape.

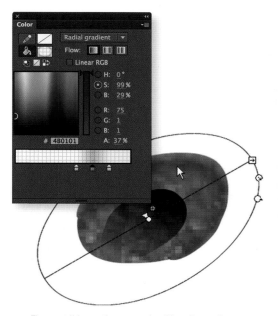

5 The nostril is another example of layering various gradients over the original shape containing the bitmap fill. Here I used a linear gradient for the inner nostril shape and a radial gradient to provide some shading for a more realistic effect.

6 When all these subtle details are combined, they can add up to a very sophisticated image. The shapes that make up Grotto are simple yet convincing, simply by layering some basic gradients over our textures.

HOT TIP

You may also want to adjust the properties of the imported bitmap (double-click the bitmap icon in the document library and select "Apply Smoothing.") This will apply anti-aliasing to your image and make it appear smoother.

The Pen tool

S O FAR IN THIS CHAPTER WE have looked at several ways of achieving different styles of drawing, from the basics of snapping simple shapes together forming bigger, more complex shapes to using bitmaps as textural fills. Most of the time the design process demands a combination of tools and techniques to get the job done. For this character design I went from a rough pencil sketch to a fully rendered vector drawing using the Pen tool and basic shapes. The Pen tool, in combination with the Selection tool, offers infinite flexibility when it comes to manipulating strokes and shapes.

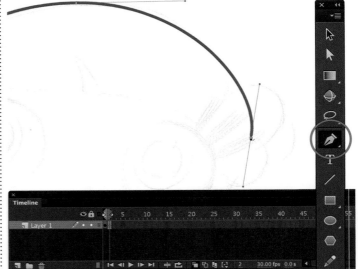

1 Start with a scanned sketch or draw directly into Flash. Create a blank keyframe on frame 2 and turn on the Onionskin feature. Using the sketch as reference, trace the hair using the Pen tool by clicking and dragging each point as you go. This technique will automatically create curves with Bezier handles, allowing you to manipulate the stroke each time a point is made.

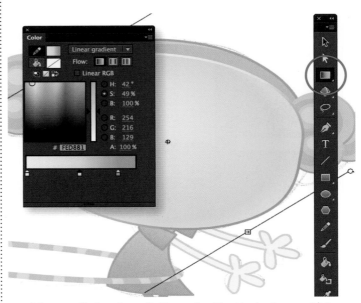

5 A linear gradient can be applied to a path without having to convert it to a shape like in older versions. For this gradient I chose to mix 3 colors: a light, mid and dark tone. With this gradient selected in the stroke color swatch in the Color panel, click on the path using the Ink Bottle **S** tool to apply it. Edit the gradient using the Gradient Transform tool **F**.

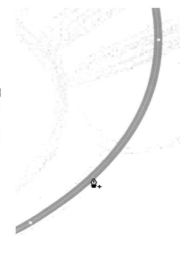

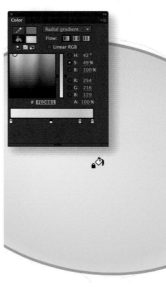

2 Using the Subselection tool **A**, modify the contours of the hair by clicking an anchor point and adjusting its Bezier handles. Once this shape is complete, temporarily cut and paste it to a new layer and lock it to avoid editing it unintentionally.

3 To add an anchor point, hover the Pen **P** tool over the path until you see the "+" symbol appear and click. Remove an anchor point by hovering over and clicking it.

4 Once you have closed the path, fill it with a color. Here I have mixed a radial gradient to provide a sense of volume to the shape.

6 The Pen tool is clearly a useful tool for drawing paths, but in some situations the Oval and Rectangle tools are a better and faster alternative. The Selection tool **V** can be used for basic editing of paths made with the shape tools.

7 The final result is a combination of shapes and paths created with the Pen, Oval and Rectangle tools. Editing of these paths and shapes was the result of using the Selection, Subselection and Pen tools.

Trace Bitmap

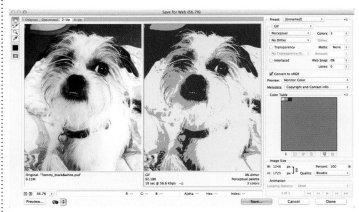

1 Start with a good quality image that has enough color contrast. Open it in Adobe Photoshop and save it as a PSD file. Now may be a good time to adjust the contrast, saturation, colors or whatever else you prefer to edit. Save for Web using ⌘ Shift ⌥ S ctrl Shift alt S and select GIF as the file format. Select Grayscale from the Color Reduction drop-down menu and limit the number of colors to two or three depending on the image and amount of colors your prefer to keep. Click Save and name your new GIF image.

PHOTOGRAPHIC IMAGES CAN BE used to add a measure of realism to any Flash project. They can be imported and used in their original state, or they can be simpified for a unique, stylized look. The obvious approach to vectorizing photographs is to import the image into Flash and use the drawing tools to trace it by hand. But that can be very time-consuming depending on the complexity of the image. The trick here is to average down the amount of colors your image contains, and Adobe Photoshop makes this an almost effortless task.

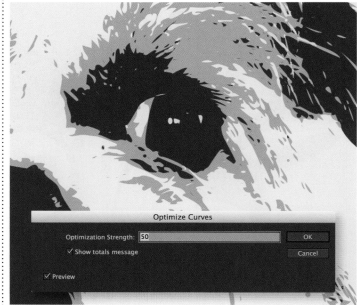

4 Select the entire image and go to Modify > Shape > Optimize to open the Optimize Curves panel. With Preview selected use the slider to adjust the amount of smoothing desired and click OK.

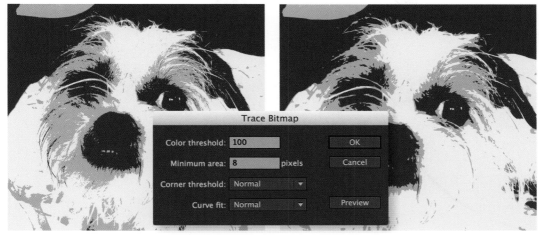

2 Import the optimized GIF into Flash ⌘ R ctrl R. Make sure it is selected and go to Modify > Bitmap > Trace Bitmap. In the Trace Bitmap dialog panel, you can adjust individual settings that will ultimately dictate the level of complexity your image will have when converted to vectors. The proper setting will vary depending on your image and personal preference.

3 Once the trace is complete, your image will be all vector and fully scalable. The resulting image of this dog is now only 88k, but we can get it even smaller by using Flash's built-in Optimize engine.

5 Flash CC offers Advanced Smooth and Straighten panels that provide more control over how your vector image is optimized. Both of these panels can be found by going to the Modify > Shape menu.

6 The end result is an image that is very lightweight for the Web, weighing in at only six kilobytes. It is also easy to change its color scheme using the Paint Bucket tool **K** and the Color Mixer.

Image Trace (Illustrator) Ai

1 The original sketch was drawn by Hussam in Adobe Photoshop using subtle variations in color and shading. It will be interesting to see how well the Trace Image engine converts these subtle nuances in color from pixels to vectors. Place the bitmap into an Illustrator document by choosing File > Place...

ADOBE ILLUSTRATOR AND ADOBE Flash are 2 of the best vector drawing applications available. In terms of drawing tools, Illustrator has a much more sophisticated toolset than Flash, and for this reason it's worth taking a look at a feature introduced in Illustrator CS6: Image Trace.

Image Trace was the replacement for the Live Trace tool and for good reason: Image Trace is much more powerful and does a much better job at tracing your bitmap images.

The dinosaur character I'm using for this example was created by my friend Hussam Nassour of Dubai, India. Hussam is a wonderfully talented character designer and CG artist. The dinosaur sketch is a perfect example for vectorizing using the Image Trace feature. Visit sketchwings.com to see more of Hussam's work.

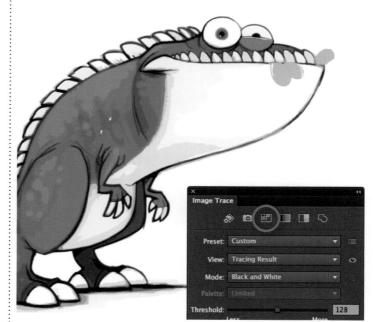

4 Low Color will trace the image with fewer colors than the High Color option. Low Color is useful if you want fewer colors and a more stylized look to your image.

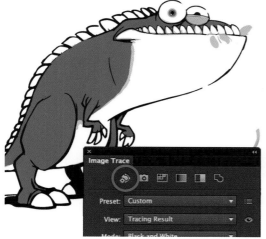

2 Open the Image Trace panel by choosing Window > Image Trace. Select the bitmap and click the Auto Color icon to begin the Trace Image conversion. The Auto Color preset will convert the image to vectors while averaging the colors to a limited number of values.

3 The High Color option does a remarkable job of converting the image to vector paths while maintaining the same integrity of the original. The converted paths look almost identical to the original bitmap.

5 Grayscale converts the image to vectors while converting the colors to gray tones.

6 Black and White converts the image to black and white vector fill colors only. To edit the paths in Illustrator CS6+, click the Expand button located in the main tool bar.

Shading 1: line trick

1 Start with a basic shape that contains a fill and outline. This technique will work just as well with shapes that have no outlines.

2 Select the Line tool **N** and make sure the Snap to Objects tool is also selected in the toolbox.

CEL SHADING IS COMMONLY referred to as "toon shading." This style of shading is popular with comic book style artwork and classic Disney films. I have discovered four different ways to achieve cel-style shading in Flash for you to consider. This particular example demonstrates a stroke drawn across an existing fill color. The stroke can be edited without disrupting the shape below it. Once the stroke has been defined and a shadow color added, the stroke can easily be removed, leaving behind the shadow and original fill color.

6 An alternative way to mix colors in Flash is to click the color wheel button in the upper right corner. This button will open the color palette mixer that is native to your operating system. Mix your new color and click "OK".

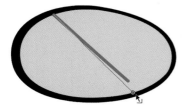

3 Draw a diagonal line inside the fill of your shape. Use the Selection tool **V** to drag each end point of the line so they snap to the edge of the fill.

4 Use the Selection tool to bend the line so that its arc reflects the shape of the oval.

5 With the fill color selected, mix a slightly darker color using the Color panel mixer.

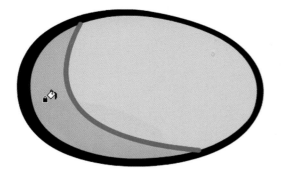

7 Use the Bucket tool **K** to fill the shape you created with the Line tool.

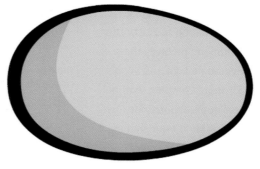

8 Select the line and delete it. Easy right? If it still isn't perfect, you can continue to use the Selection tool to edit the edge of the new fill you created.

HOT TIP

Cel-style shading can be difficult to achieve. You have to imagine that your two-dimensional shapes have a third dimension and they are affected by light and shadow. Choose a light source and keep it consistent throughout your design when adding shading.

Shading 2: shape it

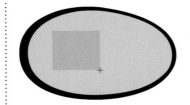

1 Using the Rectangle tool **R**, draw a box inside your shape that contains a darker fill color (no outline).

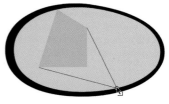

2 Use the Selection tool **V** to pull the corners until they snap to the edges of the shape (make sure the Snap feature is turned on).

HERE'S ANOTHER variation on cel-style shading in Flash. This technique involves the Rectangle tool and allows for more complex shading. This approach may be preferable if your shapes require more complex shadows.

5 Let's take this technique one step further by adding more shading for a more realistic effect. Repeat the above procedure using an even darker color inside the shaded area.

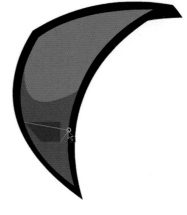

6 Use the Selection tool to pull the corners until they snap to the edges of the shaded shape.

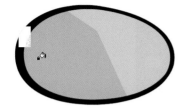

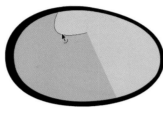

3 Fill the gap area created after snapping the corners to the edge of the shape.

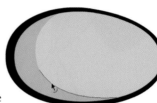

4 Use the Selection tool to bend the edge of the darker fill color so that its arc reflects the shape of the oval. Having used the Rectangle tool, you have an extra corner to play around with. The extra control can be useful for creating more complex shading such as with the ear shape.

7 Fill the gap area created after snapping the corners to the edge of the shape.

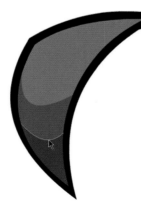

8 Use the Selection tool to bend the edge of the darker fill color so that its arc reflects the contour of the shape.

9 You can repeat this procedure as many times as you like. The more color values you add, the more realistic the image will be.

HOT TIP

If you would like a cool and easy way to create various hues based on your original color, give Adobe's Kuler tool a try (kuler.adobe. com). You can mix shades of color very easily and then save and download them as ASE (Adobe Swatch Exchange file). Open the downloaded ASE file(s) in Illustrator and then save your new swatch panel as an AI file and import it into Flash. An easier way would be to manually copy the HEX value from the Kuler site and paste into the Flash Color Mixer panel.

Shading 3: paint selected

1 Start with a shape.

2 Select the Brush tool **B** and then from the brush mode subselection menu, select Paint Selection. This subselection will restrict any paint to selected fills only.

W E'RE ALL DIFFERENT AND we tend to find different ways of using the same tools. Certain techniques become familiar to our workflow, and we become comfortable in our individual habits. Here is yet another technique for creating cel-style shading that you may prefer over the previous versions. It lends itself well to the designer who likes a more hand-drawn feel to their work.

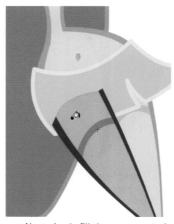

6 Next, simply fill the space created with the new fill you just painted.

7 Voila! Now you've got a convincing cel-style shading for the leg.

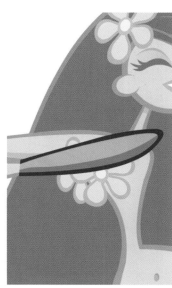

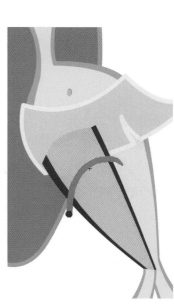

3 Use the Selection tool **V** to select the fill color you'll be adding the shade color to. Now use the Brush tool and adjust the amount of smoothing desired for the shape you'll paint. Next, paint inside the selected fill.

4 Don't worry about being sloppy. Once you release the brush, the painted fill will exist only inside the selected area you intended.

5 Sometimes the area may be too large to paint entirely by hand. In this situation, just draw the contour of the edge for the shaded area.

8 The face shading can be drawn the same way. Remember the direction your light source is coming and paint a crescent fill.

9 Fill the space created by the new fill and you are done.

10 Cel shading can add that extra dimension to your designs, giving them depth and realism.

Shading 4: outlines

THIS VARIATION ON CEL-STYLE shading works well for both simple and very complex shapes. If you have line work that is very loose in a hand-drawn style, this technique may be the one for you. You'll use the Ink Bottle to create a line around your fill. Then you can reposition this line off-center and fill the space created with a darker shade of color.

1 Start with the Ink Bottle tool 🖊 and a stroke color that doesn't exist anywhere in your design. Set the stroke height to around 3 or 4 point. Click anywhere within the fill to outline it with a stroke in the color you chose. Don't worry about how it looks because you will eventually delete this line entirely after you are done.

4 For this character's outfit, I applied a stroke outline to the overalls as well.

5 The stroke is selected and repositioned based on the same light source as in the previous example.

2 Select the line by double-clicking on it with the Selection tool **V**. Next, use the arrow keys to nudge it away from the original shape in the direction of your light source. Fill this area created between the stroke and the original edge of your shape with your shade color.

3 Delete the entire stroke by pressing the *Delete* key. If your stroke has been deselected, select it by double-clicking on it with the Selection tool. Double-clicking the stroke will select the entire stroke while single-clicking on it will select a segment of it if it contains multiple points.

HOT TIP

Set your stroke height large enough to make working with the stroke easier. A larger value will allow you to select it more easily. Choosing a bright color that is high in contrast from your original design will make it easier for you visually.

6 A darker shade of color is mixed and filled to create the illusion of form and realism.

7 With the stroke still selected, delete it. In some cases, the resulting shape created may need some tweaking.

8 Use the Selection **V** tool to further refine your shading based on your needs and design sense.

Realism with gradients

1 The first step is to outline the basic shape of the flower's petal with a stroke color that is high in contrast to the original image. Be as precise as you want, but I recommend using the original image as a guide, simplifying where needed along the way.

2 The Pen tool **P** is perfect for this task simply because it is quick and easy to manually trace the contour of the petal by clicking and dragging along the contour of the image.

6 The initial gradient will provide the overall hue and tonal range of the flower petal. Flash lets you apply up to 15 color transitions to a gradient.

7 Fill your shape with your radial gradient and then use the Gradient Transform tool **F** to edit its size, position and rotation. You can delete the stroke at this stage as it is no longer needed.

LASH IS MUCH MORE THAN A tool for designing cartoon characters. Its full array of vector drawing tools is suitable for many styles of illustration. Here we'll go step by step creating a realistic flower illustration. Flowers are always appealing to draw and at the same time challenging due to the subtle variations of color they often contain.

The main tools used in this example are the Pen tool and Gradients. Flash has adopted the core functionality of Illustrator's Pen tool including identical shortcut keys and hot key modifiers – not to mention identical pen cursors as well. Integration is bliss.

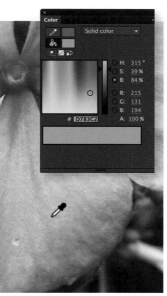

3 To close the path, position the Pen tool over the first anchor point. A small circle appears next to the Pen tool pointer when positioned correctly. Click or drag to close the path.

4 Use the Subselection tool *A* to refine your path if you desire. To adjust the shape of the curve on either side of an anchor point, drag the anchor point, or drag the tangent handle. You can also move an anchor point by dragging it with the Subselection tool.

5 Next we need to mix some radial gradients. Flash's color picker can grab colors from anywhere on your screen if you click on any of the color swatches found in the Color Mixer, Properties panel or the toolbox and drag to the area containing your desired color.

HOT TIP

To constrain the curve to multiples of 45°, hold down the Shift key while dragging. To drag tangent handles individually, Alt-drag (Windows) or Option-drag (Macintosh).

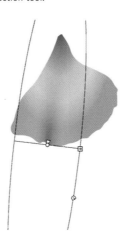

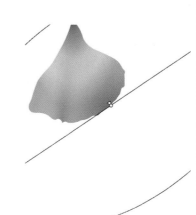

8 Copy ⌘ *C* *ctrl* *C* and Paste in Place ⌘ *Shift* *V* *ctrl* *Shift* *V* this shape to a new layer as you will be layering several gradients on top of each other to create a realistic effect. The following gradients contain varied amounts of alpha to create subtle transitions in color.

9 Fill the duplicated shape with your new gradient and use the Gradient Transform tool *F* to create the suggestion of subtle undulations within the shape. Repeat the process of copying and pasting in place this shape to new layers for each new gradient.

10 You can manipulate each new gradient using the Gradient Transform tool *F* to create soft shadows and highlights. In almost all cases you will only use partial gradients to create subtle transitions of light and shadow.

73

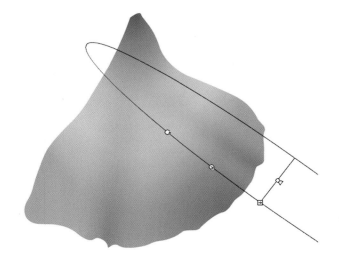

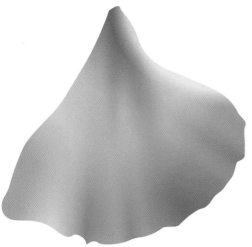

11 It's always convincing to position soft shadows where the edge of the shape contains an imperfection. The combination of gradient colors and irregular contours makes for a very convincing imperfection.

12 This end result is achieved by using several variations of layered radial gradients, producing beautiful and convincing variations of color.

15 To achieve the effect of depth in the center of the stigma, drag the little white arrow in the radial gradient's center to move the focal point towards the edge.

16 Here's what the flower image looks like once all the petals and stigma have been illustrated. But you don't have to stop here. Let's have some fun with Flash's filters. Convert the entire flower to a Movie Clip symbol.

13 Repeat the same procedure for each petal of the flower image. To keep your main timeline layers to a minimum, convert each layer to a group or an object drawing and convert each petal to a symbol.

14 The center of the flower, technically named the stigma, was created with a doughnut-shaped fill containing a radial gradient.

HOT TIP

The technique of mixing gradients with transparency and layering them so that they overlap each other can produce effects that go beyond radial and linear gradients. You can actually use this technique to create gradients with abstract shapes and curves that go beyond what the default gradients were designed to look like. It takes a measure of trial and error to achieve the look you want, but in the end the final results may be worth the extra effort.

17 From the Filters panel, add a Drop Shadow. Set the blur, alpha and distance to your desired amount. You may want to also add a Blur filter to soften the overall image of the flower.

18 Duplicate the instance of the flower movie clip. Scale and rotate them to create an appealing floral arrangement. It's almost hard to imagine this style of illustration can be made entirely in Flash, right?

Design styles
UI Design

YOU MIGHT BE WONDERING why I'm featuring a Flash design that looks like it was created with Adobe Photoshop or Fireworks or perhaps Illustrator. I chose this graphic because the *download available* icon used throughout this book was created entirely with Flash. I love using Flash to create graphics and buttons for user interfaces because it forces me to be simple. I also like how the Flash drawing engine allows me to quickly and easily manipulate vector shapes.

1 The first step is to create a circle using the Oval tool ⬭ with a fill color only. The stroke color swatch is puposely empty to avoid having a stroke added to the shape. The fill color is a linear gradient using a variation of 3 green colors. The mid-tone is the darkest color while the color swatch on the left is of a slightly lighter value and the swatch on the far right is the brightest. This shading simulates a light source coming from above. Select the shape and convert it to a Movie Clip symbol by pressing the F8 key.

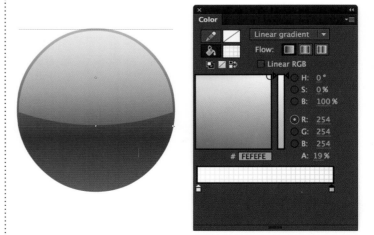

5 Since black doesn't necessarily convey a highlight very well, we need to mix a new color. In fact, another linear gradient will work well here. Using only 2 color swatches, use white for both but adjust the Alpha transparency of the left swatch to around 69% and the right swatch to 19%. Fill the shape with this gradient and adjust it by using the Gradient Transform tool. The end result should have the more opaque color at the top and the less opaque color at the bottom.

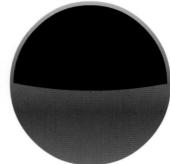

2 Copy and Paste in Place the original circle to a new layer. For illustration purposes I have filled it with a solid black color. Scale it so that it's slightly smaller than the original. I recommend locking the original layer.

3 Using the Selection tool **V**, start outside the shape and click and drag across the bottom half of the circle in order to select only the bottom half of the circle. Press the *Delete* key to remove it.

4 With the top half of the circle remaining, deselect it by clicking anywhere outside of it using the Selection tool. Now click and drag the lower edge down to create a slight curve.

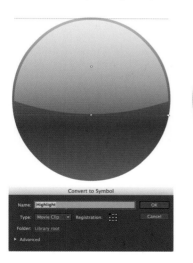

6 Select the highlight shape and press F8 to convert it to a symbol. Make sure the symbol type is Movie Clip. If it isn't, select Movie Clip from the drop-down menu. The Movie Clip type is important because it allows us to add a Blend Mode to it.

7 Select the Movie Clip and from the Blending drop-down menu in the Display section of the Properties panel select Overlay. Overlay combines Multiply and Screen blend modes resulting in light colors becoming lighter and dark colors becoming darker.

8 If the highlight is too bright, adjust its opacity using the Alpha slider in the Color Effect section of the Properties panel.

Continued...

9 A convincing shiny effect relies on the illusion of reflection. Adding a highlight along the top edge of the icon begins with using a copy of the larger highlight we just finished creating. Copy and Paste in Place the same shape to a new layer and break it apart. I have filled it with black for this example.

10 Select this shape, copy it and then Paste in Place again. With the shape still selected, choose a different color from the color panel (here I chose blue) and then nudge it few pixels downward using the arrow keys. The original black shape will be revealed underneath still intact. Click anywhere on the stage outside of the blue shape to deselect it.

11 With the Selection tool still selected, click the blue shape and press the Delete key. Deleting it will remove the blue shape as well as the original black section that was underneath it leaving behind the sliver of black as seen above. The remaining shape will be our edge highlight.

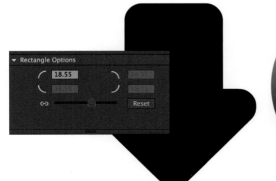

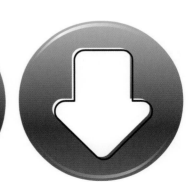

15 With both Rectangle Primitives selected, adjust the roundness of each corner using the Rectangle Options slider in the Properties panel. Break apart both rectangles and edit them to create the shape of an arrow.

16 I changed the fill color of the arrow to white and using the Ink Bottle tool ⑦ I selected black as the outline color and clicked inside the fill color to apply the outline.

17 Double-click the stroke outline using the Selection tool ⓥ to select it. Using the arrow keys nudge the outline down and to the right about 10 pixels.

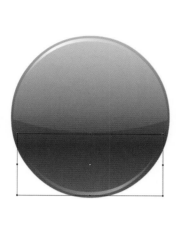

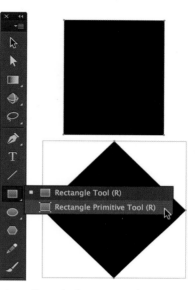

12 Mix a Linear gradient with 3 color swatches with white as the color for each. Select the swatch on the far right and adjust the color opacity to 0%. Repeat the same procedure for the far left color swatch. Select the middle swatch and lower its opacity to around 87%.

13 Copy and paste this highlight and then rotate it or flip it vertically. Position it at the bottom of the circle to create the illusion of light reflecting from below.

14 To create the arrow use the Rectangle Primitive Tool **R** and draw 2 rectangles. Rotate one of them 45 degrees by holding down the **Shift** key to rotate it in 45 degree increments.

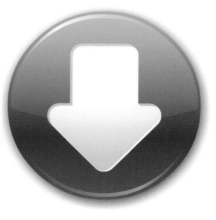

18 Using the Bucket Fill tool **K** and gray as the fill color, click in the area of the arrow in between the stroke and the edge of the shape as shown above. With the stroke still selected press the **Delete** key to remove it.

19 Select the Movie Clip symbol that was created in step 1. Apply a Drop Shadow filter from the Filters category of the Properties panel. Adjust the amount of blur, distance and strength.

20 The advantages of using Flash for creating graphics are that they are resolution independent and can be animated.

Character design

1 The first step is to sketch the character using your tool of choice. Here I have chosen to remain entirely in Flash by using the Brush tool. My sketch is kept loose as I only need to get the basic form drawn.

2 Select the Pencil tool and turn on Object Drawing mode. Create a new layer in the timeline and choose a bright stroke color that is high in contrast from the original sketch color.

DESIGN IS ONE THING, TECHNIQUE IS another. Everyone has their own way of working in Flash, and there are many ways to go about designing in Flash. For this character I chose a technique that a friend and talented illustrator showed me. It involves using the Pencil tool with Object Drawing mode and the Union feature to combine multiple Object Drawings into a single object. I love her technique so much I've started to incorporate it more into my daily workflow. Thanks to Katie Osowiecki-Zolnik for this cool Flash drawing technique. Check out her work at http://katieo.kuiki.net.

6 The mouth and teeth were drawn with the same technique of tracing in Object Drawing mode, combining each object using Union, and then editing the object as a whole.

7 Here I've added fill colors to the mouth, tongue and teeth. Once the shape and fill are finished I double-click the strokes to select them all and then press the Delete key to remove them.

Modify

Document...	⌘J
Convert to Symbol...	F8
Convert to Bitmap	
Break Apart	⌘B
Bitmap	▶
Symbol	▶
Shape	▶
Combine Objects	▶
Timeline	▶
Transform	▶
Arrange	▶
Align	▶
Group	⌘G
Ungroup	⇧⌘G

Delete Envelope	
Union	⌥⌘U
Intersect	
Punch	
Crop	

3 Using the sketch as my guide, I traced the image using the Pencil tool. It's ok to use as many different strokes as needed. In the next step we will combine the individual Object Drawing strokes into a single object.

4 Select all Object Drawings and then go to Modify > Combine Objects > Union to combine them into a single Object Drawing.

5 With drawing contained within a single Object Drawing, it's easy to edit the strokes to clean up the image. Select and delete any unneeded segments and use the Selection tool *V* to edit the curves if need be. Here I've also applied a fill color.

HOT TIP

The Union feature does not have a keyboard shortcut assigned to it by default. If you find yourself needing to combine Object Drawings often, then I recommend assigning a shortcut to the Union feature by editing your keyboard shortcuts. Once a shortcut has been assigned, you can take it a step further and assign the shortcut to an Express Key if you are using a Wacom drawing tablet.

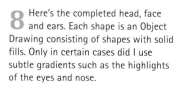

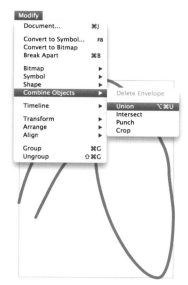

8 Here's the completed head, face and ears. Each shape is an Object Drawing consisting of shapes with solid fills. Only in certain cases did I use subtle gradients such as the highlights of the eyes and nose.

9 With the character designed in a neutral pose, I duplicated it a few times and edited the objects to create additional poses. In some cases new body parts were drawn to reflect the nature of the pose or gesture.

Object Drawing

I N THE PREVIOUS EXAMPLE, I SHOWED YOU a technique learned from fellow illustrator and animator Katie Osowiecki-Zolnik. Katie is not only extremely talented but probably the fastest illustrator I know. She chooses Flash exclusively due to the simplicity of its drawing tools. Impressed with her style, I asked Katie if she would show us her technique of drawing in Object Drawing mode and using the Union feature to combine objects. This example deconstructs a small detail of her mermaid image and shows how Katie uses Flash to quickly sketch, trace and polish her illustrations. Check out more of her work at http://katieo.kuiki.net.

1 The sketch is loosely drawn using the Brush **B** tool. Nothing fancy going on here. Just a quick and dirty drawing to get things started.

2 On a new layer, use the Pencil **Y** tool to trace over the original sketch. Make sure **Object Drawing** mode is turned on.

6 Draw a new stroke that dissects the leaf down the middle and bend it slightly. Use the Union feature to combine both objects.

7 Mix a darker value of the fill color and fill one of the halves of the shape defined by the new stroke. *Delete* the stroke.

11 Send the duplicated object to the back by holding down *ctrl* + the down arrow.

12 Scale and skew the object to create some variation.

3 Complete the drawing of a single leaf. Select all the Object Drawings and then go to Modify > Combine Objects > Union to combine them into a single Object Drawing.

4 Fill the object with your color of choice using the Color panel.

5 Delete the stroke by selecting it and pressing the *Delete* key.

8 repeat steps 2–7 except this time mix different color values to separate this leaf from the first one.

9 Duplicate the object by using *alt* or *⌥* + drag.

10 Flip the duplicated leaf horizontally by going to Modify > Transform > Flip Horizontal.

13 Continue to duplicate, flip, scale and skew existing objects to create additional leaves.

14 Arrange the individual leaf objects using *ctrl* + the up and down arrows.

15 Hide or remove the layer containing the original sketch when you are done.

HOT TIP

Keep a look out for holes that may get left behind by errant strokes. Often it is easy to spot small gaps in fill colors by zooming in to your image. If you spot a gap, select the color and fill it using the Bucket tool.

The most basic of objects, the cube, can be brought to life using just the Free Transform tool. With a little rotating and distorting, you can easily create an animation that gives an otherwise boring subject some life and personality. The same techniques can be applied to almost any object, including characters.

3

Transformation and distortion

SQUASH, STRETCH, BULGE – WHAT DO ALL THESE
transformations have in common? Hint: it's not how
you felt after eating that second baked bean burrito.
Answer: it's the Free Transform tool, the single most
efficient and versatile tool Flash offers, and it will prove
to be one of the most used tools in your daily animation
workflow. This chapter examines various ways of using
the transform tools to edit drawings and animate them.

Distorting bitmaps

A S A DESIGNER AND animator, I frequently use the Free Transform tool in Flash. It is the most multifaceted tool in the toolbox and is critical to the transformation and distortion of objects.

Free Transform is perfect for scaling, rotating, shearing and distorting your images. Free Transform is also used to edit the center point of instances of symbols. You can also use it to transform imported bitmaps or graphics created with the Flash drawing tools.

There are a variety of modifier keys used with the Free Transform tool that allow you to transform objects in different ways, as we will discuss here.

1 Enter Free Transform mode by selecting the Free Transform tool in the toolbox or by pressing the keyboard shortcut **Q**. Let's start by transforming an imported bitmap image.

2 Break apart your imported image **⌘ B** **ctrl B** before transforming it. If you want, you can convert it to a Drawing Object (Modify > Combine Objects > Union).

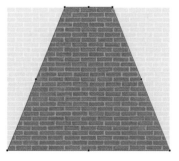

6 Position the cursor outside the bounding box between the handles and drag to shear the object. Hold down **⌥ alt** to shear based on the center of the object.

7 Hold down **⌘ ⌥ Shift** **ctrl alt Shift** and drag a corner handle to distort the object's perspective equally on both sides. Unfortunately, Flash does not distort the image but crops it instead.

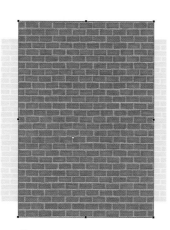

3 When you drag any of the four corner handles, you will scale the object. The corner you drag will move while the opposite corner will remain stationary. Hold down the **Shift** key to scale based on the object's center.

4 If you grab any of the four center side handles, you will scale the object horizontally or vertically which is great for squashing and stretching the object.

5 Grab one of the corner handles to rotate the object. Hold down **Shift** to constrain the rotation to 45 degree increments. Hold down **⌥** **alt** to hinge the object at the opposite corner.

HOT TIP

Some of the Free Transform tool features cannot modify instances of symbols, sounds, video objects or text. If you want to warp or distort text, make sure to break apart the text field into raw shapes first.

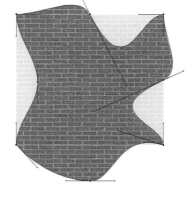

8 Hold down **⌘** **ctrl** to distort the object in a freeform manner. But unfortunately again, Flash doesn't truly distort a bitmap image but rather, crops it.

9 Select the Envelope tool (sub-selection of the Free Transform tool). The Envelope modifier lets you warp and distort objects.

10 Drag the points and tangent handles to modify the envelope. Changes made to the envelope will affect the shape but not the bitmap image itself.

The Envelope tool

WHEN USING THE FREE TRANSFORM tool with raw vector objects, the Distort and Envelope subselection tools become available. Using these tools is where you can really have some fun warping and deforming shapes as if they were clay. Think of how your reflection looks in a fun house mirror, and you'll start to get an idea as to what these tools are useful for. If you need to be precise with how your images are scaled, rotated or skewed, use the Transform panel to type in your values for the respective transformation.

1 Enter Free Transform mode by selecting the Free Transform tool in the toolbox or by pressing the keyboard shortcut **Q**. Select the Distort subselection tool at the bottom of the toolbox. Click and drag any of the corner handles to distort your shape.

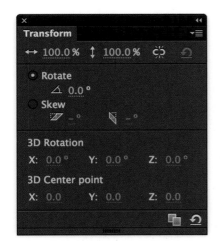

4 The Envelope modifier is great for warping and distorting shapes. When you select the Envelope subselection tool, you will notice multiple handles attached to the bounding box. Manipulating these handles will affect the shape contained within. Click and drag a corner handle to start warping your shape.

2 The Distort tool is useful for manipulating the perspective of a shape by clicking and dragging the corner handles.

3 Hold down the **Shift** key while dragging a corner handle to constrain the adjoining corner an equal distance and in the opposite direction from each other. Think of it as tapering your shape.

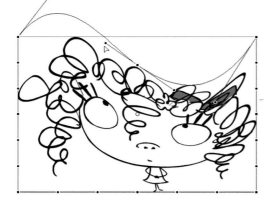

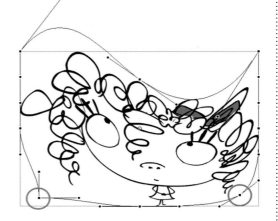

5 Drag any of the eight tangent handles to warp your shape in almost any direction. These tangent handles are located at each corner and along both horizontal and vertical sides as well.

6 You can move any of the points to a new location to further warp your shape. But be careful, once you click outside of the selected shape, the transformation will end. You can select it again and continue to warp and distort it, but the previous point and tangent positions will be lost.

Warping

THE ENVELOPE TOOL CAN help shave some time off your production schedule. In this case, the Envelope tool was used to deform the head of the Evil Mime character to represent the effect of being hit by a self-imposed upper-cut. Sure, the entire head could have been drawn, but not often do we have the luxury of time when a deadline is looming. It was much easier to start with the head already drawn and warp it to suit our needs.

1 Duplicate the artwork of the head by creating a new keyframe in the head symbol. Select the entire head and the Free Transform tool **Q**, then select the Envelope subselection tool.

2 Using the Envelope tool, you can move the handles to deform the relative area of the head.

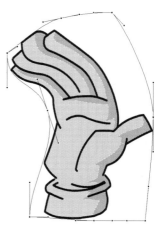

6 Here's the hand drawn in Flash using the Line tool. You may find the need for a variation of this same illustration and need to make it quickly.

7 Using the Envelope tool allows you to quickly distort the drawing into a different shape.

3 Continue to push and pull the Envelope's anchor points and control handles to deform the shape to your liking.

4 You can restart the envelope process by deselecting the artwork and selecting the Envelope tool again. When you reselect the Envelope tool it will reset anchors and handles which will allow you to distort your image further.

5 Don't be afraid to manually go back into the artwork and adjust your linework using the Selection tool. Often it's your own eye that is the best tool for the job.

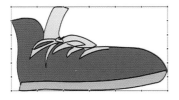

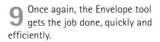

8 Here's the foot in its default state. Depending on your animation, you may need several feet in different shapes.

9 Once again, the Envelope tool gets the job done, quickly and efficiently.

10 Don't rely completely on the transform tools. In most cases, they only go so far. You may want to further refine the details of your image manually by using the drawing tools.

Card flip

A POPULAR ANIMATION REQUEST on the Flash public forums is how to animate a flat card rotating or flipping 360 degrees. What makes this animation often difficult to understand is the initial approach to actually creating it. It is easy to assume, since Flash is a two-dimensional program, adding a third dimension simply is not possible unless the object is redrawn manually one frame at a time. But with Flash, it's all in the approach, and it doesn't have to be taken literally. Two dimensions are plenty to work within for this animated effect.

1 Start with a simple rectangle with no stroke around it. Add a second keyframe on frame 10. Select the Free Transform tool **Q** and then the Distort subselection tool.

5 In Flash CC you have the ability to apply a Shape tween from the context menu in the timeline. So go ahead and apply one.

10 Let's add some shape hints to correct the problem. Select the first frame in the faulty tween and then go to Modify > Shape > Add Shape Hint **⌘** *Shift* **H** *ctrl* *Shift* **H**.

2 Hold down the *Shift* key and pull a top corner point away from the shape. With the *Shift* key still pressed, pull a bottom corner in the opposite direction.

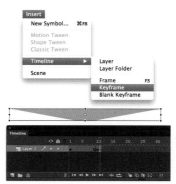

6 Now that you have the first half of the animation, you need to create the second half. Select frame 11 and insert a keyframe.

11 Drag the red "a" hint to one of the corners of your shape until it snaps.

3 Click outside the shape to end the transformation. Select it again, hold down the *Shift* key and drag the bottom middle handle upward. The *Shift* key will constrain the shape vertically.

4 Turn on the Onionskin tool, so you can see the previous frame. Position the newly transformed shape so that it is centered over the original shape seen through the onionskin.

While writing this topic, I experienced a common weakness with Shape tweens in Flash. Due to the nature of vectors and how Flash tries to calculate what it thinks you want to achieve, sometimes the tween implodes or twists in ways we never anticipated. Shape hints exist for this very reason and they are easy to learn about in the Flash Help docs. An alternative solution for this example would be to convert frames 1–10 to keyframes, copy and paste them in frames 11–20 and then reverse them.

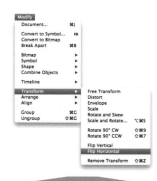

7 Modify the shape in frame 11 by flipping it vertically.

8 Select the keyframe in frame 1 and copy the frame *⌘ ⌥ C* *ctrl alt C*. Next, select frame 20 and paste the frame *⌘ ⌥ V* *ctrl alt V*.

9 Apply a Shape tween to the latter half of your frames. You may experience a misbehaving tween like I did when writing this topic. Let's fix it.

12 Go to the last keyframe in your tween and drag the green "a" hint to the same respective corner. Repeat this procedure again for the opposite corner.

13 The final visual effect is to mix a slightly darker version of the color of the card, and then use it to fill the shapes in frames 10 and 11.

14 The card will not only tween its shape but also its color from light to dark. This color change makes for a convincing three-dimensional effect.

3D Rotation

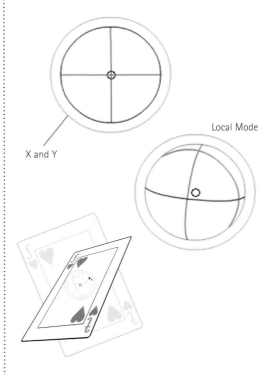

X and Y

Local Mode

THE PREVIOUS CARD FLIP example demonstrates how to transform a vector shape with the Free Transform tool and "Classic Tweens." Adobe Flash CC provides tools to simplify the same process. The 3D Rotation tool lets you transform objects not only along the X and Y axes but the Z axis as well.

1 The 3D Rotation tool **W** rotates Movie Clip instances in 3D space. A 3D rotation control appears on top of selected objects on the Stage. The X control is red, the Y control is green and the Z control is blue. Use the orange free rotate control to rotate around the X and Y axes at the same time.

The default mode of the 3D Rotation tool is global. Rotating an object in global 3D space is the same as moving it relative to the Stage. Rotating an object in local 3D space is the same as moving it relative to its parent Movie Clip if it has one. To toggle the 3D Rotation tool between global and local modes, click the Global toggle button in the Options section of the Tools panel while the 3D Rotation tool is selected. You can temporarily toggle the mode from global to local by pressing the **D** key while dragging with the 3D Rotation tool.

2 The first thing to do is to right-click over the Movie Clip and select Create Motion Tween. Flash CC will automatically insert frames based on the document frame rate to achieve a full second in the Timeline. This document is set to 24fps, therefore the duration of my motion tween is 24 frames.

3 Position the frame marker on frame 12. Select the 3D Rotation tool **W**. Click on the instance of the card and notice the 3D rotation controller that appears on top of the symbol. Click inside the 3D control and drag along the **Y** axis to rotate the card in 3D space. Notice that Flash has inserted a keyframe automatically for you.

4 Position the frame marker on the last frame and continue to rotate the Movie Clip along its Y axis in 3D space until it is 180 degrees from its original orientation. Repeat these steps as often as needed depending on the number of rotations you want to animate.

HOT TIP

Press the **D** key to toggle between global and local mode.

5 If you want to extend the Motion tween in the layer without affecting the existing keyframes, simply hold down the **Shift** key while dragging the right edge of the tween. Another way to do the same thing is to click on a frame further down the Timeline and press the F5 key to insert frames up to the selected frame.

Butterfly

I**N OLDER**
versions of Flash
the butterfly's wings were
animated using the Distort tool
(subselection of the Free Transform tool).
With the 3D tools in Flash CC, however, it is
much more efficient to use the 3D Rotation
tool for the flapping wing animation.
Here I have converted the original wing
graphic to a Movie Clip symbol and applied a
motion tween using the new Motion Model.
The advantages of using the 3D Rotation
tool for this animation are faster results and
a smaller file size. The smaller file size is on
account of using motion tweens and several
instances of the same symbol. Previous
methods required each frame to be re-drawn,
resulting in a frame-by-frame animation using
raw vector art for each keyframe which
created larger file sizes since each frame
contained all new data that needed
to be loaded sequentially when
viewing online.

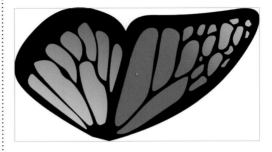

1 Convert the wing into a Movie Clip symbol twice so that
you end up with a movie clip inside a movie clip. You will
want to animate the wing inside a symbol, so a 2nd instance
can be used for the other wing later.
Select the 3D Rotation tool **W**. Click on the instance of the
wing and notice the 3D rotation controller that appears on
top of the symbol. Reposition the controller by dragging it to
a new location. The controller's position determines its center
point. Right click over the symbol and select Create Motion
Tween. Flash will automatically insert frames based on the
document frame rate to achieve a full second in the Timeline.
This document is set to play back at 30fps, therefore the
duration of my motion tween is 30 frames. The speed of the
animation can be easily changed by dragging the right edge
of the motion tween left or right.

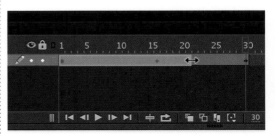

4 To adjust the speed of the wing animation, click and
drag the leading edge of the motion span. Here I've
decreased the length of the Motion span which increases the
speed of the animation.

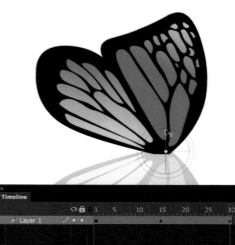

2 Position the frame marker about mid-way between frames 1 and 30 (frame 15 will work). Click inside the 3D control and drag along the **X** axis until the wing is 180 degrees from its original position. Notice that Flash has inserted a keyframe automatically for you.

3 Position the frame marker on the last frame in the tween. Drag along the **X** axis inside the 3D control until the wing is back in its original position. Play back your timeline by pressing the *Enter* key to see the wing flapping along the **X** axis.

HOT TIP

Double-click the center point of the 3D control to move it back to the center of the selected Movie Clip.

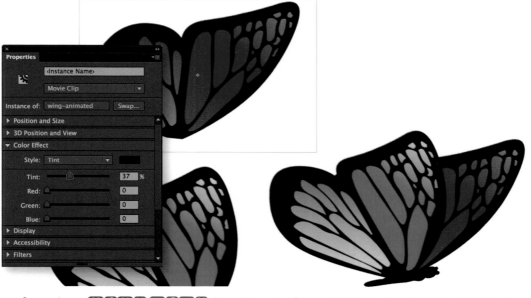

5 Copy and paste ⌘ C ⌘ V ctrl C ctrl V the movie clip containing the wing animation to use as the 2nd wing on a new layer below all existing layers. Select it and using the Tint color effect in the Properties panel, darken it slightly to provide a sense of depth.

6 Create a body shape, align the wings and publish your movie to see the butterfly take flight. To add some depth to the butterfly, move the back wing to the right a few pixels and skew it slightly. You can also move the front wing to the left and skew that a little also.

contributing the character above (joecorrao.com).

■ The hula hoop appears to be around the hulagirl's waist, or is it? In the original image, above, the hula hoop is clearly in a layer above the hulagirl. By creating a mask for the hula hoop, we can hide the portion of it that overlaps the girl's waist, making it appear to be around her.

4

Masking

MASKS ARE POWERFUL. THEY CAN BE USED IN MYRIAD ways to achieve limitless results. Masks can make your daily workflow easier, less time-consuming and, in most cases, become your most indispensable tool.

Having the ability to control the way two or more layers interact with each other through the use of masks is vital to your abilities as a designer and animator. The coolest thing about using masks in Flash is that not only do they help you to create stunning images, they can also be animated; a very powerful concept that can be mastered quite easily.

Rotating globe

1 First step is to create the continents. A quick online image search will yield plenty of examples. Import the image into Flash and leave it as a bitmap, use the Trace Bitmap feature or manually trace it using Flash's drawing tools. Convert it to a symbol.

WHENEVER I WORK WITH MASKS, I FEEL like a magician. Masks provide the ability for you to create illusions, much like a magician's "sleight of hand" technique. It's all about what the viewer doesn't see and you, as the designer, have the ability to control that.

One of the more popular animation requests from Flash users is how to make a rotating globe. The first thought is that a globe is a sphere and to animate anything rotating around a sphere requires either a 3D program or painstaking frame-by-frame animation. Not so if you can use a mask. Remember, it's not what you see, but rather, what you don't see.

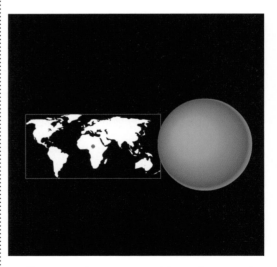

4 The next step is to create a mask layer using yet another copy of the circle in the bottom layer. Create a new layer above your continents, paste in place the circle and then convert this layer to a mask layer. This layer mask will prevent the continents from being visible outside this circle. All you need to do now is motion tween the continent symbol across this circle.

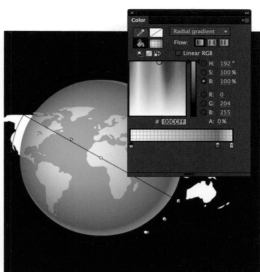

2 Create a new layer and move it below your continents. Draw a perfect circle using the Oval tool **O** while holding down the **Shift** key. Select this circle and copy it, then paste it in place on a new layer above your continents.

3 Mix a radial gradient similar to the one shown and fill the circle in the layer above your continents. Make sure to mix enough alpha into each color, so the continents will show through. Using the Gradient Transform tool **F**, edit your gradient so that the highlight edge is off-center to one side.

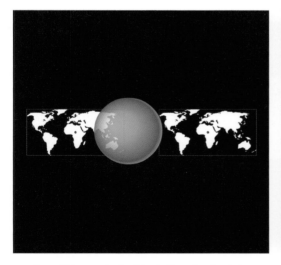

5 To avoid too much of a delay in the animation between the first and last frames, you can add a new masked layer with a new instance of your continent symbol. The best way to make this looping animation as seamless as possible is to copy the first frame of the continents and paste it in place into the last frame of your Timeline. Then work backwards in the Timeline and position the continents outside of the circle to the right.

6 Since the first frame is exactly the same as the last frame, and each frame in between represents a slightly different position for the continents, select the symbol in the last frame and use the arrow keys to nudge it over a few pixels. This will avoid the two-frame "hesitation" in the movement of the continents every time the playhead returns from the last frame to frame 1.

HOT TIP

You can always move your entire animation into a Movie Clip symbol so that it can be easier to position, add multiple globes and/ or target with ActionScript. To make it a Movie Clip, drag across all frames and layers to highlight them in black. Right-click or Command-click over them and select "Copy Frames" from the context menu. Open your Library and create a new Movie Clip symbol. Right-click or Command-click over frame 1 of this new symbol and select "Paste Frames".

Flag waving

1 You will begin by making a nice long repeating ribbon shape. Start with a simple rectangle with any color fill and no outlines. Make it a little wider than it is taller.

4 Repeat step three by pasting your new shape and flipping it vertically. Then attach it to the side of the shape again. See the ribbon pattern taking shape? But your ribbon is a solid color and lacking some depth, so let's continue by adding some shading.

7 Create a mask layer above the ribbon layer. Using the Rectangle tool, make a shape big enough to cover a section of the ribbon as shown. It helps to use a high contrast color.

THE WAVING FLAG IS A POPULAR "how do I...?" request in the Flash community. To be honest, it plagued me for quite some time as to how best to achieve this animation. My initial reaction was to use shape tweens and frame-by-frame animation, but that proved time-consuming and had unconvincing results. Then one day, out of the blue, it hit me; if I slide the right shape across a masked area, I could create the illusion of a flag waving without having to kill myself animating it in a traditional way. It suddenly became so easy anyone can do it.

10 Test your movie using `⌥` `ctrl` `Enter` to see the effect of the flag waving as it passes through the mask. But let us not stop there. Let's animate the mask using shape tweens to further emphasize the left and right edges of the flag waving. Use the Selection tool to bend the left and right edges. Create a keyframe further down the mask layer.

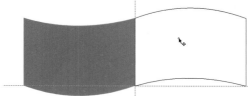

2 Use the Selection tool **V** to bend the top and bottom edges slightly, so they have a nice arc to them. You will want to repeat this shape to create a pattern, so select it and copy it.

3 Paste your shape and then flip it vertically. Use the Selection tool to drag it so that it connects to the original shape. Once these shapes are joined together, select it and copy it.

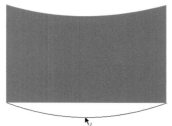

5 Mix two colors and add them to the Swatch panel. Mix a linear gradient with several color pointers alternating between these two color values. Fill your ribbon shape with this gradient and edit it so that the darker tones are in the concave sections of the ribbon shape.

6 Once you have the ribbon the way you want it, select it using ⌥**A** *ctrl* **A**, copy it using ⌥**C** *ctrl* **C** and then paste it using ⌥**V** *ctrl* **V**. Align it edge to edge with the original shape to essentially double its length. Convert it to a symbol.

HOT TIP

This example is a looping animation. For best results, make sure the first and last frames are identical by using copy frames and paste frames or by copying the object in the first frame and pasting it in place in the last frame

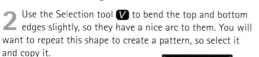

8 Next, create a keyframe somewhere down the timeline and reposition the ribbon to the left of the mask shape. Apply a motion tween.

9 To create a seamless loop of the ribbon, copy and paste in place a new instance to a second masked layer (using the same mask). Motion tween it so that it follows the original ribbon shape without creating any gaps.

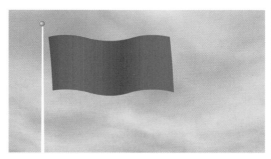

11 In this new keyframe, bend the left and right sides of the mask shape in the opposite direction. Apply a Shape tween. Repeat this procedure until the last frame is reached. The animated mask adds an extra animated touch to the overall flag waving effect. Presto! You are done.

12 Don't forget to add a flag pole and sky background for an even more convincing illusion. Try placing this animation in a Movie Clip symbol and drag a few instances of it to the stage. Scale them and arrange them in perspective for the ultimate flag waving effect.

Iris transition

THERE ARE USUALLY SEVERAL WAYS TO go about creating the same animations and effects in Flash. Whether it be animated on the Timeline or dynamically generated using ActionScript, it allows us as users to work within our own comfort zones. A simple iris transition is an example of an effect that could be done several different ways. I personally wouldn't know where to begin coding this kind of animation, but give me a Timeline and some keyframes and I am in my element. Using a mask for this example provides us with even more options; we can easily control the direction and focus of the iris itself, where it starts and where it ends. Animating the iris can be a nice touch to your storytelling if you want to focus the viewer's attention to a very specific area of the screen.

1 First step is to create a simple circle using the Oval tool **O**. The fill color is insignificant. Hold down *Shift* while dragging to constrain its proportions. Do not convert this shape to a symbol but, rather, convert the layer to a Mask layer.

4 Add a new layer and drag it over the mask layer, so it becomes linked to it as a "masked" layer. This layer is where your content will reside. If your content requires multiple layers, then make sure they are all masked or move all content into a new symbol and drag an instance of the symbol to the masked layer.

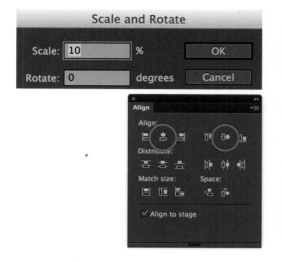

2 In frame 1, scale this circle as small as possible. Open the Scale and Rotate panel using `alt S` `ctrl alt S`, type in a percentage and click OK. Use the Align panel using `K` `ctrl K` to center the circle to the stage.

3 Create a keyframe a few frames down your Timeline in the same mask layer. Scale the circle so that it covers the stage completely. Convert the shape to outlines, so you can see the stage underneath it. Apply a Shape tween so that the circle grows from small to large, filling the stage completely.

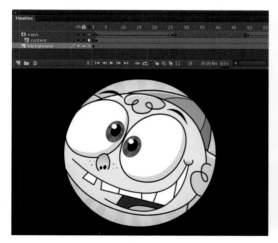

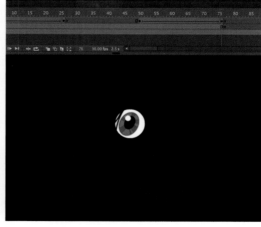

5 Create a new layer (not masked) below all the other layers and create a black rectangle the size and shape of the stage. The color can be anything you choose, but black typically works well for this type of effect. At this stage you can reverse the animated mask by copying keyframes in reverse order and applying another Shape tween.

6 Since you are creating the iris effect with an animated mask, you can easily control the iris' focus on a particular area of the stage. In the last keyframe, position the circle in the last frame over the character's eye. When the animation plays, the iris will animate and close in on the eye, a typical technique used in several cartoons.

Handwriting

THIS ANIMATED EFFECT is one of my favorites because I am asked frequently how it can be achieved, yet it is quite simple in technique. Every time I demonstrate how to make text "write" itself, the reaction is almost always the same: "Oh wow! That's all there is to it?"

The example here uses an animated mask which yields a very small file size, ideal for large blocks of text.

How to cheat in Flash

1 The first step is to type some text on the stage. It doesn't matter what it says; just choose a font and start typing. By default, text fields in Flash are set to Dynamic. In some situations this setting may be fine, but when an effect is added to the text field, the text may not render correctly in the Flash player. Such effects include masking, alpha, rotation and scaling. If you need to use Dynamic text, embed the font outlines.

|How to cl

3 Add a new layer above your text layer and convert it to a mask layer. The text layer will automatically be linked to it as a "masked" layer. In frame one, draw a rectangle just to the left of your text, making sure it is as tall as the text itself.

How to cheat in Fla

5 Now apply a Shape tween in between the 2 keyframes. Lock both layers and play the timeline to see the effect of the text appearing to write itself. If you want the animation to play faster or slower, insert more frames or remove frames respectively.

2 If you choose to change the behavior of your text field to Static, the font will be embedded in the compiled SWF, and the Flash player will render it correctly even with an effect added to it. Another option is to break apart the text until it becomes raw shapes. Breaking it apart will ensure the text renders correctly but also creates a larger file size, and it will be harder to edit the text if need be in the future.

4 In this same layer, create a keyframe further down the Timeline and select the Free Transform **Q** tool. Hold down the **alt** key while using the Free Transform tool to anchor the left edge of the shape in place. Grab the middle transform handle on the right side of the selected shape and drag it to the right until is spans the width of the text.

6 If you need to use Dynamic text, you must include the font outlines so that the text renders correctly in the Flash player. To embed the font, select the Dynamic text field and then click the "Embed..." button in the Properties panel. The Font Embedding panel will appear, allowing you to choose the range of characters used in your animation. Try to select the minimum number of characters because embedding all characters can increase file size significantly. There's a section in the Options panel that allows you to type in just the characters that you are using on the stage. These are the only characters that will be embedded, and as a result keep the file size as small as possible.

HOT TIP

If you want a more realistic technique to make text look like it is writing itself, check out the frame-by-frame method in Chapter 7.

Spotlight

ANIMATED MASKS, AS WE'VE SEEN, CAN provide an interesting dimension to your animation. It really doesn't take much effort to create various visual effects using an animated mask, such as this spotlight effect for a client's logo.

1 The first thing you need is some text or other image where you can shine a spotlight. Convert it to a symbol. The background should be dark if not completely black. In order to show light, we first need to create darkness. This technique wouldn't have the same effect if the background was very light.

2 Create a new layer above your image layer and convert it to a mask layer. The image layer will automatically be linked to it as a "masked" layer. Draw a shape using the Oval tool **O** while holding down the *Shift* key to constrain its proportions. Convert it to a symbol.

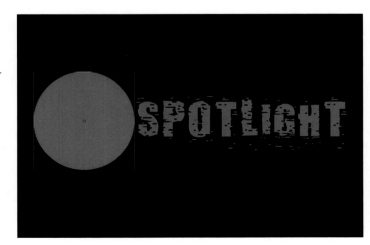

3 Add a keyframe further down the timeline and position the mask shape to the opposite side of the image. Apply a Motion tween so that the mask shape passes across the image.

4 The key to making this technique convincing is to copy and paste in place the image to a new layer below the original layer. Make sure it is a normal layer (not masked). Select the symbol and tint it to a dark color. This layer will not be affected by the mask .

5 Test your movie to see your animated mask pass over the original image layer while the darker instance remains unmasked and visible throughout the animation.

Focus

ONE OF THE MOST EXCITING features in Flash is the PSD and AI importer. Since CS3, we finally have wonderful integration between Photoshop and Illustrator alike. For this example we will edit an image in Photoshop, save it as a PSD file and import it into Flash via the PSD Importer wizard.

We will also add a slight touch of ActionScript for some added interactivity. If you suffer from ActionScript-phobia, don't panic; adding only a couple of lines of code will be painless. If I can do it, you can as well. The code will simply hide the cursor in the Flash player and allow us to drag a Movie Clip around the stage. The trick here is the mask itself, allowing us to see the sharper image through the mask shape only. Open wide and say "Ahhhh". This won't hurt a bit.

1 First you need to start with an image, of course. This might be a good time to browse your hard drive or grab your digital camera. It doesn't have to be a raster-based image or even a photograph. It can be vector art drawn in Flash or imported from a different program. Whatever image you choose, you will need two versions: the original and a blurred version of the original.

4 Once the import process is complete, your Flash document should contain both images on different layers. Make sure the blurred image is below the sharper image.

5 Create a new layer above the sharper image, draw a shape on that layer and convert it to a Movie Clip symbol. Convert that layer to a mask to automatically link it to the layer below. Both layers will be locked to show the effect of the mask.

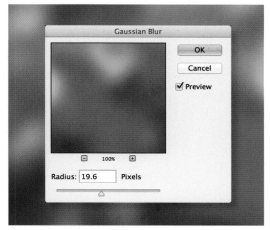

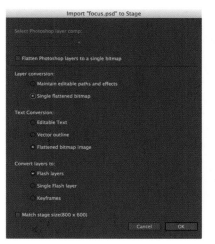

HOT TIP

The shape of your mask doesn't have to be a circle. It can be as simple or as complex as you wish to make it. Experiment in Photoshop with image effects beyond blurring. There's enough to choose from to keep you busy for a while. I particularly like the Glass filter (Filter > Distort > Glass...).

2 Open your image in Photoshop and duplicate its layer, so you have two copies of the same image. Apply a Gaussian Blur to one of your images. Save the file as a PSD file.

3 In Flash, import the PSD file you just created. The PSD import wizard will appear and prompt you with a variety of options. The left panel will display all the layers of the PSD file. Click on them to display options for each. You will also want to convert layers to Flash layers, place layers at original position and set your Flash stage to the same size as your Photoshop image.

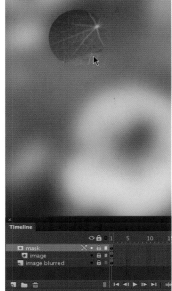

6 You are almost done! Lock all layers to see the effect. It works, but it is pretty boring as the mask just sits there. Time to add some functionality.

7 Use the Selection tool **V** to select the Movie Clip symbol containing the mask shape. In the Properties panel, type in an instance name. I chose "focus" for this example. With the Movie Clip still selected, open the

Actions panel and type the following ActionScript exactly:

ActionScript 3.0:
Mouse.hide();
focus.startDrag(true);

117

Feathered mask (ActionScript)

S INCE FLASH 8 AND THE INTRODUCTION OF A feature called "runtime bitmap caching", we have had the ability to create masks with that desired feathered edge. I know that oftentimes when the designer world overlaps the developer world, things can get a little blurry. To be honest, even the most code-phobic designer can use ActionScript to integrate dynamic masks into their designs. All that is required is a few lines of very simple code.

1 The first step is to create a radial gradient with two colors. The middle color should be solid and the outer color should be mixed with 0% alpha. The alpha transition from 100% to 0% will create the feathered edge that will later be used for the mask. Using this gradient as your fill color, select the Oval **O** tool and draw a circle on the stage. To constrain the circle so that it is perfectly round, hold down the **Shift** key while dragging. Convert this shape containing your radial gradient to a Movie Clip symbol. With this Movie Clip symbol selected, give it the instance name "maskMC" in the Properties panel.

3 You will need two different images to make the transition. Here I have chosen images from my trip to Amsterdam as a speaker at FITC (Flash in the Can). Place both images on different layers, one directly over the other. For clarity, I will refer to these as "Image A" and "Image B". Image A will simply reside on the bottom-most layer. Image B will be the one we reveal with the feathered mask using ActionScript.

4 Since the mask itself will be controlled with ActionScript, we will need to use actionScript to composite it to the image that will be revealed during the transition. Convert Image B to a Movie Clip symbol and give it the instance name "mask_image". The only thing left to do is apply the code that tells the radial gradient to act as a mask and apply itself to Image B.

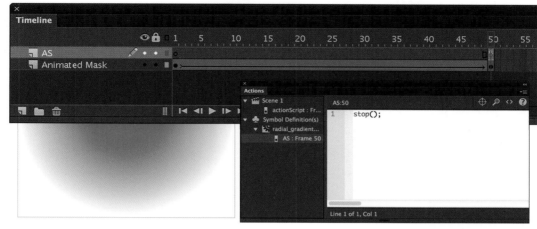

2 Double-click the Movie Clip to enter Edit mode. Select the radial gradient again and convert it to another symbol. Now we can create a nice transition effect by animating it. Using a tween, scale the symbol from very small to very large, large enough so that it covers the stage completely. Place a *stop();* action at the end of this timeline.

5 In the Actions panel (F9) type in the following code:
mask_image.cacheAsBitmap = true;
This code caches the image so that it can be masked at runtime in the Flash Player.
maskMC.cacheAsBitmap = true;
The code on Line 2 will assign the Movie Clip "maskMC" to act as a mask at runtime.

mask_image.mask = maskMC;
This last line of code will assign the mask and the image to be composited together.
That's all there is to it. Make sure you open the source file "feathered_mask_actionScript.fla" that you downloaded from **www.howtocheatinflash.com** to see this effect in action.

Medical pack

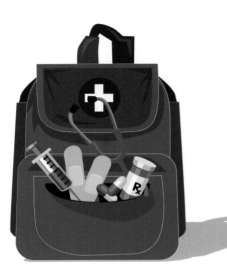

1 The medical pack is drawn as vectors inside Flash. The front pocket and zipper are the only objects to be animated, specifically the zipper, the shadow and the white "stitching". Each of these objects are placed on different layers.

2 The zipper requires just a horizontal motion tween across the pouch opening. The black shape represents the opening of the pocket. I created a Mask layer above the pouch opening and drew a thin green rectangle shape inside it.

AS WE'VE SEEN THROUGHOUT this chapter, masks can be used to help create compelling animations. But often the best animated effects are a combination of different techniques that come together to perform a single effect. In this medical pack animation, I needed to animate the front pocket unzipping and then opening to reveal the items inside. I used a combination of Shape tweens, Motion tweens and an animated masks. Each of these techniques alone aren't as compelling as when used together harmoniously.

6 Using Motion tweens, animate each object vertically over the "opening" of the pocket area. As long as each object is inside the mask shape, they will be visible. If by chance one or more objects needs to animate beyond the shape of the mask, you can edit the mask shape to accommodate the space needed. Make sure each object layer is assigned to the Mask layer.

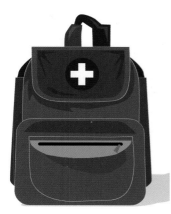

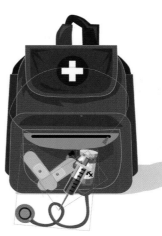

3 Using a Shape tween, animate the green shape in the Mask layer to span the black pocket opening below it. Make sure the pocket layer is assigned to the Mask layer. Lock both layers and play back the timeline to see the mask reveal the black pocket, providing the illusion of it opening.

4 Create a second mask shape that generously occupies the area above the pocket. The mask is drawn in the same shape as the opening from step 3, as well as a larger area to accommodate the space the objects will eventually occupy.

5 With the mask layer converted to outlines, we can position the objects "inside" the pocket just below the shape of the mask. The objects will not be seen because they are outside the area of the mask. Each object is a symbol on its own layer.

HOT TIP

The shadow of the pocket along with the white line that represents the stitching are animated using Shape tweens independent of the masks and masked layers. It's just the extra steps I like to take to provide a sense of added realism to the animation.

7 Add some **Easing out** to the Motion tweens and some rotation to each symbol. Lock both the mask and all masked layers to watch the objects appear to rise up from inside the pocket of the medical pack.

8 Here's the final frame of the animated effect. The use of masks helped solve the issue of literally creating a pocket for the medical pack.

121

Learning to be simple

ONE OF THE MOST DIFFICULT CHALLENGES FOR ME AS AN ARTIST WAS TO learn how to simplify my drawing style. Early in my career my work consisted of large scale lithographs depicting weeks of painstakingly complicated imagery. Spending days and often weeks on each print wasn't uncommon for me. But if you asked me to whip up a simple cartoon character, I wouldn't even know where to start.

Fact is, simplifying my drawing style didn't come easily. I was thrown into the world of cartoon animation when asked to join an animation team at a

local production company. They already had an established series on a popular cable network channel (*Dr. Katz,* Comedy Central), and my job was to design and animate a pilot for Dreamworks. It was a nice way to get thrown into the world of animation, resulting in a very diverse artistic direction for me. I embraced the challenge.

The next several years provided me the experience of designing and animating several successful television series and animated content for the Internet. We used Flash for everything, including storyboards, animatics, character and background design and, of course, animation. We were a paperless studio and Flash was our Swiss army knife of software tools. As Flash matured with each version, my skill level using it was maturing also.

Strict deadlines and cut-throat delivery dates meant working fast. Working fast meant keeping the drawing style simple, which I became very good at through practice. Not unlike a classical musician ending up performing children's pop music, I had my fine art training to help pave the road to cartoon animation.

Ironically today, I am considered a cartoonist and character animator as opposed to a fine artist. The ability to draw with simple shapes and lines did not come easy to me. Admittedly, I continue to find it a challenge creating graphics that are iconic in style. To break down an image into a few simple shapes and have it still be appealing and even the least bit amusing is a daunting task. Sometimes I can nail it in a few minutes of sketching; other times it can take a few hours of pushing and pulling shapes until I think they work together. All too often my efforts get tossed aside and spend the rest of their lives stored on a cold and dark back-up hard drive. Being asked to author this book has granted me the opportunity to choose some of the more successful designs as feature topics for the sole reason that they help make the book more visually appealing. What you don't see are the hundreds of failed attempts and design blunders I have created to reach this level in my career. There does exist an island of misfit characters where the majority of habitants are the result of my own handiwork.

Michelangelo was once quoted as saying "I saw the angel in the marble and carved until I set him free." As modest as he may have been, his perspective on design is timeless. Apply this thinking to your own approach when designing anything from a character, logo, background or even a website. All the best details are there in front of you; it's everything else that needs to be removed.

■ Animating movement often requires tricking the viewer's eye into thinking the motion is there when it is merely implied. The rocket isn't actually moving forward but your eye thinks it is because the background is animated in the opposite direction the rocket is pointing.

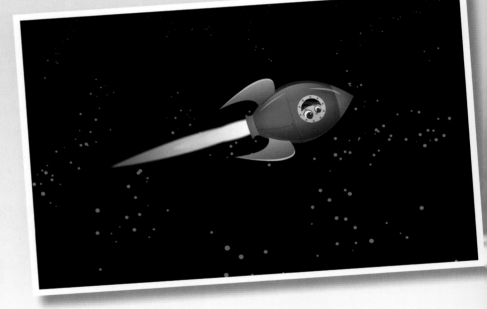

Motion techniques

LET'S FACE IT, FLASH IS ABOUT MOTION. IN SOME CASES, the more motion, the better. Motion can emphasize the intensity of an action sequence and can add a measure of realism to your animations. Whether it's making text fly around a website or animating a character in an action sequence, providing convincing motion effects can be critical to their visual success.

In this chapter, we'll examine the differences between the Motion tween and the Classic tween methods as well as look at a few of what I consider the most valuable motion effects that you can use in your everyday life as a Flash designer and animator.

Motion and Classic tweens

SO MUCH HAS CHANGED with Flash over the years, yet so much has remained the same. One of the fundamental features of Flash animation is the Motion Tween and as of Flash CS4 we have 2 different tween models. What are the differences between these 2 tween models? What tween model should you use and when?

If you remember one thing about the two tween methods in Flash CC, the Classic tween is frame-based while the new Motion tween is object-based. There are advantages and disadvantages to using either, and the difference depends on what kind of object you are animating and what that object needs to do. This example compares both tweening methods to show how they can both be used depending on your animation needs.

Motion tweens have more than 1 type of keyframe. The black circular dot in the first frame of the span indicates the assigned target object. If this dot is hollow (white), it means the object has been removed and a new object can be assigned.

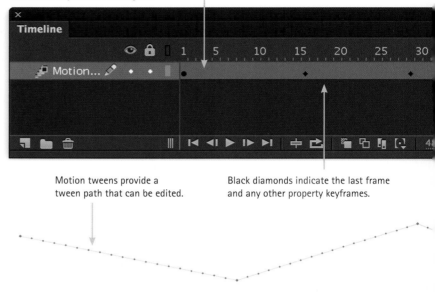

Motion tweens provide a tween path that can be edited.

Black diamonds indicate the last frame and any other property keyframes.

A black dot at the beginning keyframe with a black arrow and blue background indicates a Classic tween.

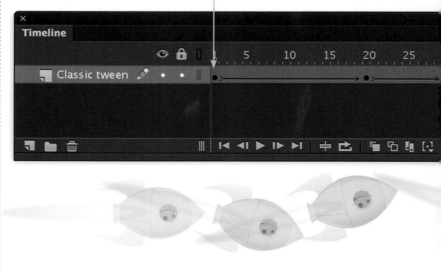

Use Classic tweens to animate between two different color properties, such as tint and alpha transparency. Motion tweens are limited to 1 color effect per tween.

Motion tweens are indicated by a solid light blue colored layer span. Unlike the Classic tween span, there are no horizontal dashed or solid lines or arrows indicating a broken or completed tween.

Classic tweens cannot be saved as Motion Presets. You can only save Motion tweens as preset animations in Flash CS4 or later.

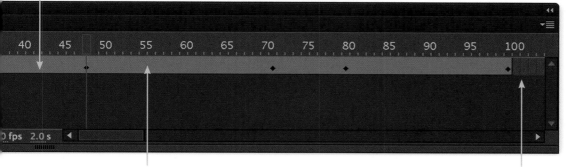

A *tweened frame* is any frame between keyframes within a tween span.

You can animate a 3D object using a Motion tween but 3D is not supported with Classic tweens.

Motion tween spans can be stretched and resized in the Timeline and are treated as a single object.

With Motion tweens, you cannot swap symbols or set the frame number of a graphic symbol to display in a property keyframe. Animations that include these techniques require Classic tweens.

Classic tweens use keyframes. Keyframes are frames in which a new instance of an object appears.

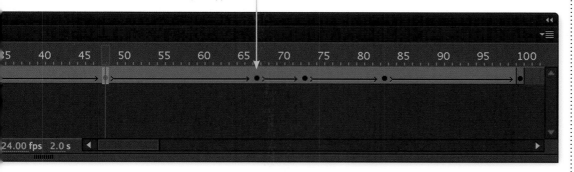

Classic tweens cannot be stretched and resized in the Timeline like Motion tween spans can. Classic tweens are comprised of frames that have to be selected individually and inserted or removed in order to stretch or shorten the animation.

Creating Motion tweens

THINK OF THE MOTION tween as a Classic tween on steroids, allowing you to animate each property individually across an entire motion span which was difficult if not impossible with previous versions of Flash and Classic tweens. One of the most popular timeline-related enhancement requests is now a reality: the ability to lengthen and shorten the Motion tween and have all keyframes interpolated automatically. With Classic tweens this can only be done manually and the more layers, frames and keyframes, the more of a nightmare this process can be. Let's take a look at more differences between these two tweening methods.

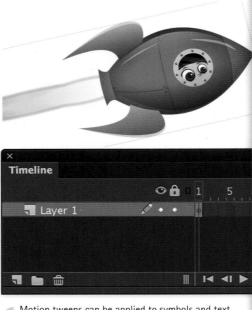

1 Motion tweens can be applied to symbols and text fields. A tween span in a layer can contain only one object or one text field. However, you can have multiple objects nested inside a single object being Motion tweened. To apply a Motion tween, right click over the object on the stage and select Create Motion Tween from the context menu.

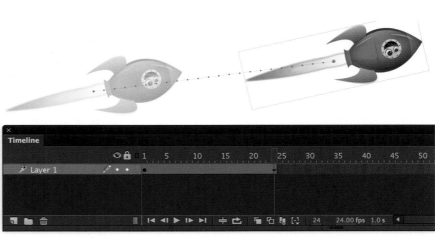

3 The quickest way to create an animation is to simply move the object to a new position on the stage. Flash will automatically create a motion path that can be edited using the Selection **V** and Subselection **A** tools.

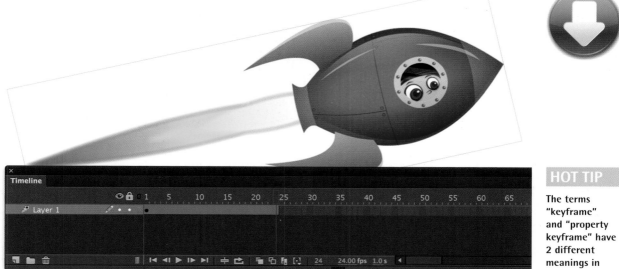

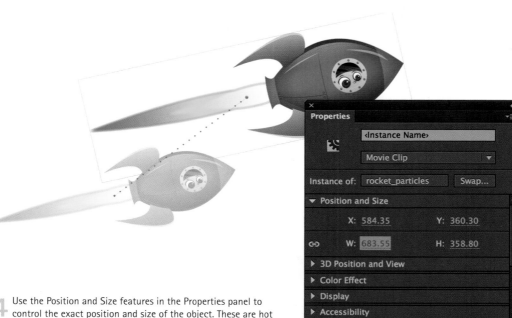

2 Flash automatically lengthens the tween span to accommodate a full second's worth of frames based on the document's frame rate. If your frame rate is set to 24 frames per second, then your span becomes 24 frames long. The playhead marker is automatically positioned at the end of the tween span.

4 Use the Position and Size features in the Properties panel to control the exact position and size of the object. These are hot text sliders that allow you to drag across them to change their values as well as select and type in the value manually.

HOT TIP

The terms "keyframe" and "property keyframe" have 2 different meanings in Flash CC. The term keyframe refers to a frame in the Timeline in which a symbol instance appears on the Stage for the first time. The separate term property keyframe refers to a value defined for a property at a specific time or frame in a Motion tween.

129

Working with Motion spans

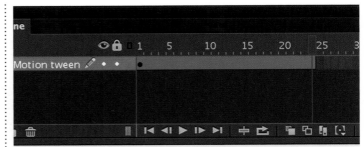

S O HOW DOES THIS NEW MOTION tween model work anyway? Not only has Adobe changed how tweens are created and applied but how we work with frames, keyframes and the tween span itself. The new Motion tween is very different from its predecessor visually, sans any dashed or solid horizontal arrows, or vertical lines indicating the "sync" feature being turned off. The Motion tween span is simple and straightforward, uncluttered and unadulterated, yet provides the ability to create sophisticated animations that go beyond the capabilities of the Classic tween method.

1 It's ironic that the Motion tween span since Flash CS5 looks so plain and simple, yet offers so much power and flexibility. You will not find horizontal lines with arrow heads between keyframes. You will not see dashed lines signifying broken tweens or vertical lines representing non-synced keyframes. This is a brave new world for Flash tweeners and to steal a line from Flash animation legend Laith Bahrani, "All of your tweens have finally come true."

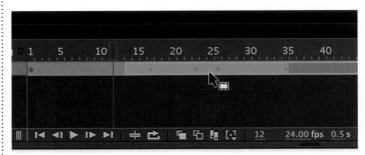

4 To move a span in the Timeline, select it by double-clicking on it and then click and drag it to a new location in the layer.

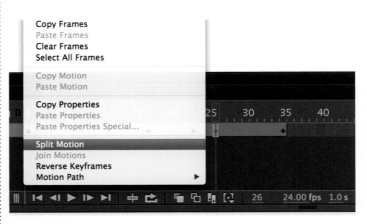

7 To split a tween span into two separate spans, *ctrl*-click or ⌘-click a single frame in the span and then choose Split Motion from the span context menu.

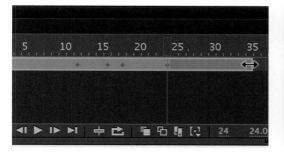

2 To lengthen the duration of your animation, drag either the left or right edge of the span to the desired frame. Flash will automatically interpolate all the keyframes in the span according to its new length. To add frames to a span without interpolating the existing keyframes, hold down *Shift* while dragging the edge of the span.

3 You can select a range of frames in a Motion span by dragging across the desired frames.

When working with Motion spans, keep in mind that controlling nested animations inside a Graphic symbol (see "Lip Syncing, nesting method"), is very limited. Any settings for Graphic symbols (Loop, Play Once and single frame) are applied once to the entire span. They cannot be applied to individual property keyframes in the span. Therefore your ability to control nested animations is lost, which is the main reason why Adobe retained the Classic tween method.

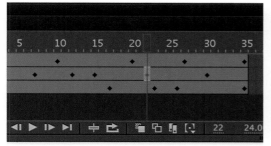

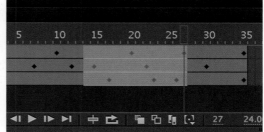

5 To select a single frame or keyframe in a Motion span, click the frame or keyframe. Once it's selected you can drag the keyframe to a new frame, or *alt* click to duplicate it while dragging it to a new frame.

6 To select a range of frames in a Motion span, drag across the range of frames and layers you want to select.

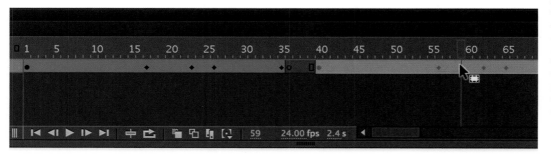

8 You can duplicate a Motion span by selecting it and then holding down the *alt* key while dragging it to a new location. This is super easy way to duplicate an animation across layers and other Motion spans.

If you drag a Motion span and overlap it with an existing span, the frames shared by both spans will be "consumed" by the span being moved into this position.

Editing Motion paths

IF YOU'RE ALREADY FAMILIAR with Flash and the Classic tween method, then you may have, at one time or another, experienced some frustrations trying to work with a frame-based tween model. Throw in the need to animate your object along a path and your workload just increased even more. Previously, if we needed to animate an object along a path, a guide layer was first created, then linked to the object layer, and then the object was manually *snapped* to both ends of the path with the aid of the Snap tool. The Motion tween method eliminates the need for all of these extra steps.

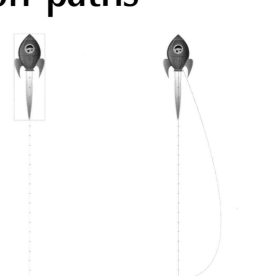

1 Right-click over the object and select Create Motion Tween. Flash automatically creates a Motion span in the Timeline. With the playhead over the last frame of the span, drag the object to a new location to expose the Motion path on the stage.

2 Use the Selection **V** tool and click anywhere on the stage away from the Motion path to ensure it is deselected. Reshape the path by simply dragging it anywhere along the segment.

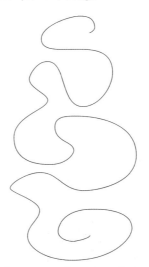

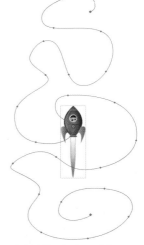

6 Use the Free Transform **Q** tool to scale, rotate and skew the Motion path as you would an object.

7 In some cases it may be easier to create a complex path by drawing it on a new layer with the Pencil **Y** or Pen **P** tool.

8 Select the stroke and then copy it **⌘ C** **ctrl C**. Select the Motion span in the Timeline or the object on the stage and paste your stroke **⌘ V** **ctrl V**.

3 With the Subselection tool, you can expose the control points and Bezier handles on the path that correspond to each position property keyframe. You can use these handles to reshape the path around the property keyframe points.

4 Position the play head on a frame where the object resides midpoint along the path. Drag the object to reshape the path automatically.

5 You can reposition the entire Motion path and the animation by selecting it with the Selection *V* tool and then dragging it to a new location.

Remove Motion
3D Tween
Convert to Frame-by-Frame Animation
Save as Motion Preset...

Insert Frame
Remove Frames

Insert Keyframe ▸
Insert Blank Keyframe
Clear Keyframe ▸
View Keyframes ▸

Cut Frames
Copy Frames
Paste Frames
Clear Frames
Select All Frames

Copy Motion
Paste Motion

Copy Properties
Paste Properties
Paste Properties Special...

Split Motion
Join Motions   Switch keyframes to roving
Reverse Keyframes   Switch keyframes to non-roving
Motion Path ▸   Reverse Path

9 If you dig a little deeper into Flash CC's context menu, you may discover yet another new feature called "switch keyframes to roving." The dictionary defines *roving* as: "*not assigned or restricted to any particular location, area, topic, etc.*" In keeping with that definition, Flash describes a *roving keyframe* as: "...keyframe that is not linked to a specific frame in the Timeline." What a roving keyframe means in Flash

terms: say you create an animation like the one pictured above, where an object is following a path with several unequal segments. Each segment spans a different number of frames causing the object to travel at different speeds along each segment. If you want the object's movement to be fixed, then right click over the span and go to Motion Path and select *Switch keyframes to roving*.

133

Motion Presets

MOTION PRESETS ARE pre-built Motion tweens that can be applied to an object on the stage. With the object already selected, choose the desired preset from the default list in the Motion Presets panel and click the Apply button. The preset animation has been applied to your new object. The default presets provide a great starting point, but you'll likely want to make your own. Flash CC provides the ability to save your custom animations as presets that can be reused over and over. You can build up libraries of animations that are not only easily applied to any object on the stage but can also be shared across the entire Flash design community.

1 Go to **Window > Motion Presets** to open the **Motion Presets** panel. This panel looks a lot like the Library panel with its preview window on top and list of folders and preset objects below. Select a preset to preview it and then select a Movie Clip symbol on the stage. Click the **Apply** button to assign the motion to the object.

3 The Motion path can be edited using the Selection **V** and Subselection **A** tools. Here the Selection tool is used to edit the curve of the path by dragging between its end points. Make sure you click on the stage away from the path to make sure the path is deselected first. Use the Subselection **A** tool to edit the control points using the Bezier handles that appear when selecting an end point or a property keyframe along the path. You can use these handles to reshape the path around the property keyframe points.

2 Once the preset is added, Flash applies a Motion tween to the
selected object. You can leave the animation as is or use it as a
starting point by editing the Motion span in the timeline as well as the
spline path that the object now follows.

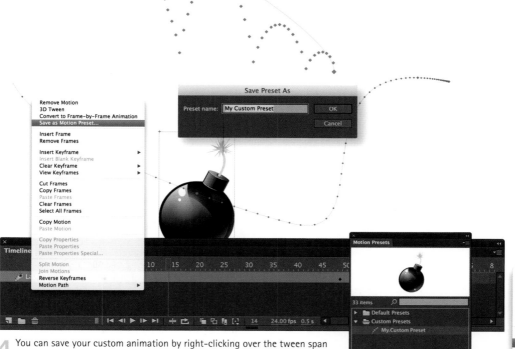

4 You can save your custom animation by right-clicking over the tween span
in the timeline or over the object on the stage and selecting **Save as Motion
Preset** from the popup menu. Provide a descriptive name and click **OK** to add it to
the **Custom Preset** folder in the **Motion Preset** panel. Your new custom preset can
now be applied to other objects the same way we just applied a default preset.

HOT TIP

To apply the
preset so that
its motion ends
at the current
position of the
object on the
stage, select
"End at current
location" from
the Motion
Preset's drop–
down menu
located in its
upper right
corner.

135

Motion tweens and 3D

FLASH HAS ALWAYS BEEN A 2-dimensional design and animation program. Making a 2-dimensional object appear to spin in a 3-dimensional space has been a popular effect but very difficult due to the lack of that 3rd dimension. Since CS4, Flash offers 3D capabilities in the form of 3D Rotation and Transformation tools.

1 Let's start with the image we want to spin. It can be anything you want, but I have chosen a coin because it seems this is the exact object many people want to use to animate spinning anyway. I'm using a bitmap of a 1 cent US penny, but you can use a coin of any currency either as an imported bitmap or drawn with Flash's drawing tools. Either way, make sure to convert the artwork to a Movie Clip symbol and then right click over it and select Create Motion Tween.

4 Next, position the playhead marker on the last frame and rotate the object the rest of the way so that it is facing us as it was in frame 1. Playback your animation to see the coin spin in 3D space.

5 But wait! Something's not right. Flash spins the coin to the right during the first half of the animation but then reverses direction during the second half. This reversal is easily corrected by placing the play head on the frame just after the second keyframe and rotating the object slightly more.

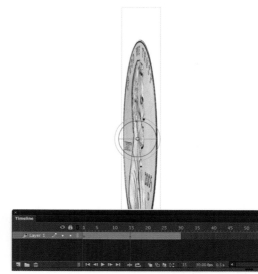

2 Select the 3D Rotation tool **W** and with the playhead on a frame other than frame 1, drag the object along its Y axis (horizontally).

3 Do not try to rotate the coin 360 degrees and expect Flash to know what you want it to do. You will need to divide the animation in half by stopping the coin rotation just short of the half way point.

HOT TIP

Experiment further by adjusting the Perspective angle and Vanishing point in the "3D Position and View" section of the Properties panel. You can get some very interesting 3D perspectives by applying more depth to your object.

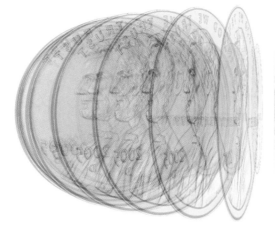

6 With the 3D rotation complete, try experimenting by editing the object's position relative to its center point. Edit the instance of the object by double-clicking on it. Move the object away from the center point (represented by the "+" cross hairs). The further you move the object from its center point, the more dramatic the effect of the 3D rotation. Here I turned on the Onionskin feature so you can see each frame of the effect when the symbol has been moved horizontally from its own center point.

3D Position and View

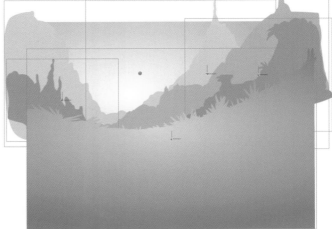

ONE OF THE MOST REQUESTED features from animators over the years has been the addition of a camera in Flash. Having the ability to build scenes involving a background, midground and foreground has always been a part of the production process. With a camera comes the ability to zoom and pan easily through a scene, requiring the movement of only 1 single object (the camera) instead of simulating a camera by moving all the contents around the stage.

Cameras only work in 3D environments and Flash, up until now, has never supported 3D except for ActionScript-generated 3D engines. But if you are like me, that level of ActionScript prowess is beyond reach.

Flash CC still doesn't support an actual camera, but we do have the next best thing: 3D Position and View, specifically a Z axis that we can now utilize to simulate a virtual 3D stage more effectively than with previous versions of Flash.

1 Setting up your stage is the most time consuming part of the process. The more elements in your scene, the more convincing the 3D effect will be. Here I have built a landscape consisting of background and midground elements, all converted to Movie Clip symbols and each residing on its own layer.

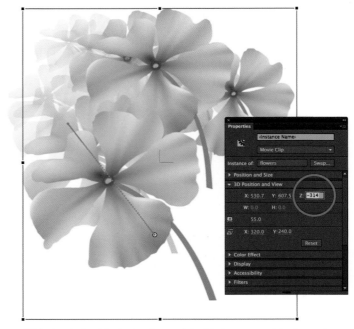

4 With the playhead in the last frame of the Motion span and the Properties panel open, select each Movie Clip individually and use the Z axis hot text slider to scale and position each object outside the stage. You will likely need to edit the X and Y axes to position the object precisely where you want it.

2 To suggest an even more convincing sense of depth I have included several foreground objects by adding several instances of a Movie Clip containing the flower graphic from Chapter 2.

3 Determine what frame you want the "camera" zoom to begin and insert keyframes for all of the layers containing the objects that will eventually be moved along the Z axis. Apply Motion tweens to each of the Movie Clips.

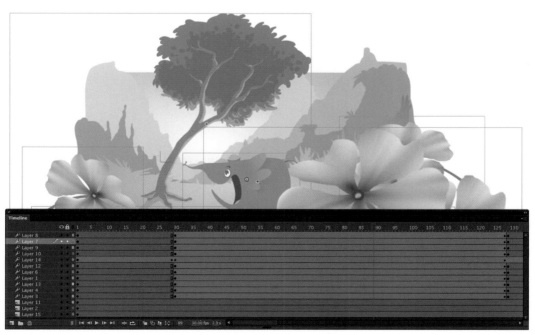

5 For this shot we are simulating a camera zoom, meaning the shot will move us into the scene. Since Flash doesn't have a true Camera, we simulate a zoom by scaling each object from its original size to a larger size. The direction of the zoom is dictated by the final position of each Movie Clip. The key to the success of this effect is how much the objects move in relation to each other. Foreground objects move faster and scale larger than the objects furthest away from us in the background. The sky and largest mountain range do not move at all while the flowers closest to us move and scale the most. These differences in movement give the viewer a sense of true depth in the scene.

HOT TIP

Locate this source file that was part of the downloadable package from the official website of this book. Scrub the timeline with various layers turned on and off to see just how each object is animated relative to other objects on other layers. The parallax motion is a sophisticated effect viewable when all objects are seen together in motion.

Basic shadow

SHADOWS CAN ADD depth to your project. This example is the most basic technique for adding a simple shadow to an animated character. Its simplicity does have its limitations, however. In this chapter you will learn more advanced shadow techniques with greater flexibility, but some may not be supported in older versions of the Flash player. Depending on your target audience and your client's technical requirements, you may need a technique that will allow you to publish to older player versions. This effect demonstrates one such technique.

1 For the best result, place your character animation inside a symbol which is commonly referred to as "nesting". The next step is to simply copy the symbol of your character using ⌘ C ctrl C. Create a new layer and move it below the character layer. Paste the copy of the symbol using ⌘ V ctrl V into this new layer.

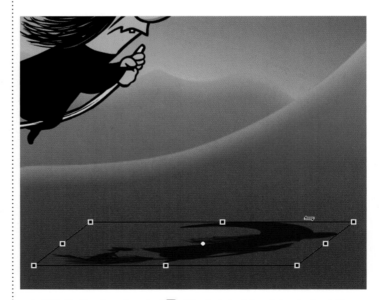

4 With the Free Transform tool Q still selected, click and drag horizontally outside the bounding box in between the handles to skew the shadow.

2 Next, apply a tint to the symbol instance you just pasted. The tint needs to have a strength of 100% to completely hide the character's details. The color of the tint should also be a darker color value than the background.

3 Position the shadow instance and with the Free Transform tool **Q**, scale it vertically to suggest some perspective of it being cast against the ground.

HOT TIP

This technique works great when your entire character animation resides in a symbol. Using a duplicate of this symbol for the shadow serves a dual purpose: since you are reusing a symbol, your movie will be efficient in terms of file size. Another advantage to using a duplicate symbol is evident when you revise or add more animation to the original symbol. Since both instances reference the same symbol in the Library, the shadow instance will be updated as well.

5 You may want to scale your shadow slightly smaller to suggest more depth. Play around with its position relative to the original character for the best results. Because the shadow symbol is a duplicate of the original animated character symbol, it will also animate in sync with the character. This synchronization will result in a convincing shadow effect. Since you have not used any special filters, this shadow effect is supported by all versions of the Flash Player.

Drop shadow

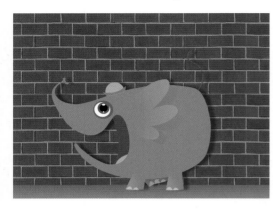

 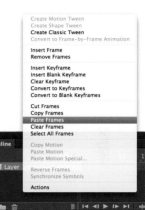

S EPARATION BETWEEN character and background can be critical to the overall impact of your animations. There are several ways to approach adding shadows for characters, but with animation the approach can seem a bit daunting at first. Flash CC makes adding shadows as easy as possible with the use of Filters.

For this example we'll take a look at the Drop Shadow filter in its purest form. The perspective shadow technique that follows this one will provide a cool way to use the same filter that adds more depth and perspective.

1 Filters can only be applied to Movie Clips. If your animation is not in a Movie Clip, you'll need to remedy this by selecting the entire range of frames and layers and then Copy Frames from the right-click context menu.

2 Create a new Movie Clip symbol from the Library panel. Select the first frame of this symbol, and from the right-click context menu, select Paste Frames.

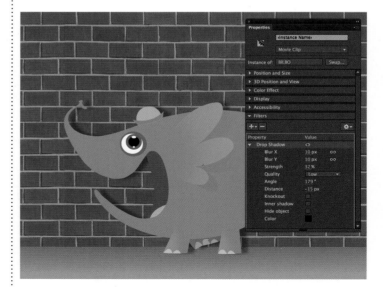

5 If you have a complex background, set the opacity to around 30–40%. This will allow the background values to show through the shadow itself for a realistic effect. I usually spend most of my time adjusting the angle and distance of the shadow relative to my light source. Test your movie to see the Movie Clip and shadow animation.

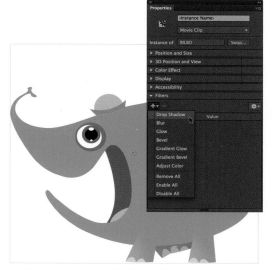

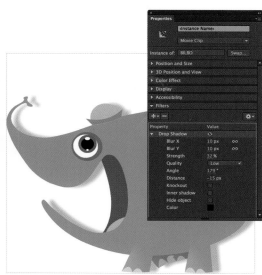

3 Drag an instance of this Movie Clip to a new layer on the main Timeline. Delete all the original frames and layers as they are no longer needed. Select your new Movie Clip instance and from the Properties panel select the Drop Shadow filter from the Filters section.

4 Adjust the amount of blur, opacity, angle and distance to achieve your desired results. You can also select the color of the shadow by clicking on the swatch color.

HOT TIP

Adjust the strength of the shadow to suggest more or less contrast between our character and wall. Less strength (less opacity) will suggest a softer light, such as an overcast day. Higher strength (more opacity) will suggest a stronger light, such as a very sunny day.

6 Select the Hide object feature to hide the Movie Clip. The drop shadow will remain on stage. Test your movie to see just the shadow animation. Experiment with some of the other options, such as Knockout and Inner shadow. You can also click the little lock icon next to blur to remove the X and Y constraint. Apply more blur to X or Y for even more interesting results.

Perspective shadow

S O FAR WE'VE LOOKED at how to add a Drop Shadow filter to an animated character using a Movie Clip and the Filters feature. But the Drop Shadow can be a little limiting in some situations. To place a character in an environment that has more depth and perspective, the Drop Shadow will not work very well since it tends to flatten the perspective. You may need a shadow that provides the illusion of perspective and depth.

1 Select your Movie Clip instance and copy it using ⌘ C ctrl C. Create a new layer below it and paste it in place using ⌘ Shift V ctrl Shift V.

2 Lock the top layer to avoid editing it. Select the instance in the layer below it, and using the Free Transform tool Q, edit its center point so that it is positioned on the bottom edge.

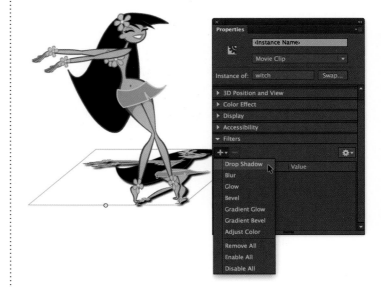

5 With the symbol still selected, apply a Drop Shadow filter to it.

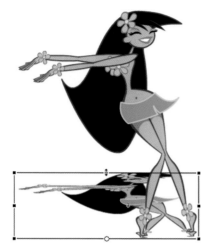

HOT TIP

Filters were introduced in Flash 8. Therefore the oldest player version to support filters is Flash Player version 8. You cannot publish to Flash Player version 7 or older and expect any filter effects to be included. Flash will warn you if your publish settings are set to a player that does not support filters. Plan ahead as much as you can. If your client requires an older player, then avoid filters.

3 Scale the symbol downward by dragging the handle in the top center. Notice that the center point positioned on the bottom edge limits that edge from scaling.

4 Next, skew the symbol by dragging in between the handles outside the top edge.

6 The "cheat" to this technique is to select the Hide object feature. Now all you'll see is the Shadow filter itself.

7 Play around with the options provided. You can adjust the amount of blur, opacity, quality, angle and distance. You can even change the overall color of the filter itself.

145

Flying text

R EMEMBER THE FIRST time you learned to use a mouse? Or tie your shoes? These tasks seem so simple now, but some things are just plain easier after someone shows you how. It's the "not knowing where to start" that can be frustrating.

Well, consider this your start. I'm going to show you how simple it is to achieve some basic, cool motion effects in Flash CC — effects that look really difficult to build, but are not so hard to create once you know how. Specifically, you'll make objects appear to move very fast using an animation effect known as Motion blur. This blur is not the same filter effect as shown in the previous example, but rather a simple use of a linear gradient.

1 First, you need to create the two objects used for this effect: text and a linear gradient. The linear gradient should have at least three colors; the middle color should be a value similar to the main color of the object and the left and right colors should be the same color as your background. If you have a complex background, mix these two colors with 0% alpha so that the blur blends into the background.

3 About three to five frames down your Timeline, add a new keyframe (F6). Holding down the Shift key, use the right arrow key to move the gradient across the stage. Position it wherever you like; just make sure it remains on the stage entirely (do not position it off the stage).

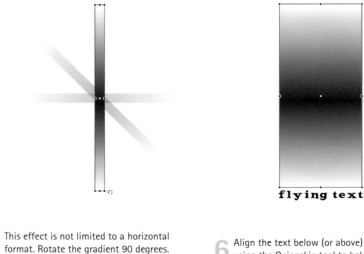

flying text

5 This effect is not limited to a horizontal format. Rotate the gradient 90 degrees.

6 Align the text below (or above) the gradient using the Onionskin tool to help guide you.

2 To create the animation for this effect, convert the linear gradient to a symbol and place it about halfway off one side of your stage. You might want to start the animation on a frame other than frame 1 to provide a moment for the viewer to anticipate the action.

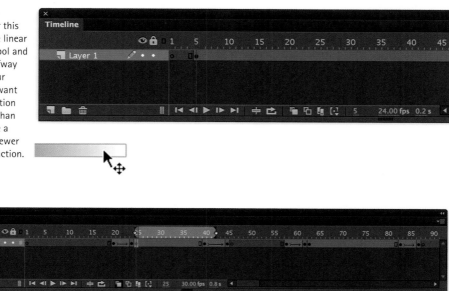

HOT TIP

This technique works quite well with objects other than text. Balls, bullets, superheroes, cars, just about any object in action that requires a high rate of speed will work with this effect. You will likely want to play around with a combination of frame rate and the length of your Motion tweens depending on your project. The advantage with this effect is you do not need a very fast frame rate (although it does help). You can achieve the same results with a lower frame rate as long as the number of frames in the Motion tweens are fewer than compared to a higher frame rate.

4 Apply a Motion tween to make the gradient symbol move across the stage. Next, create a blank keyframe in the frame after your second keyframe and drag your text symbol to the stage from the Library panel ⌘ C L.

Turn on the Onionskin tool, so you can see the previous frame and where the linear gradient is positioned. Align your text to the right of the gradient. Play back your animation.

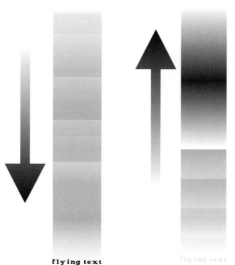

7 Repeat the same procedure as you did for the horizontal effect. Motion tween the gradient vertically from outside the viewable stage area. Then, in the frame after the tween, add a blank keyframe and position and align the text below the gradient. Reverse the procedure to make the text fly out and off the stage. I'm sure you will have a lot of fun with this effect as it is one of the easiest to master, yet it looks so good!

Combining effects

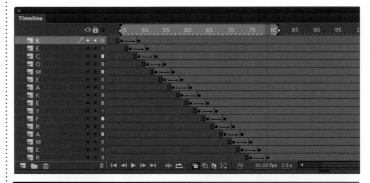

BECOME A KEYFRAMER

1 Type out your text using the Text tool **T**. This particular font is pretty complex and already suggests movement. Your text, however, can be hand-drawn graphics depending on the style of project you might have.

3 With every letter still selected, right-click over one of them and select Distribute to Layers which will create a new layer for every letter, and each letter will be placed into its own layer for you. A true time saver if ever there was one. Now is a good time to convert each letter to a Graphic symbol.

THERE ARE SOME ANIMATED EFFECTS that look so advanced it's difficult to determine how they were actually made. It is often assumed the skill level necessary to create such advanced motion graphics is well out of reach for the average Flash user.

Not true in most cases. When we watch animated motion graphics, if the frame rate is fast enough, the human eye may not be able to see everything that is happening. As a result, our mind fills in what may not even be there. The good news is, we can use this natural shortcoming of the human eye to our own advantage when creating "advanced" motion effects. In my experience I have discovered that the most visually appealing animations are a combination of multiple techniques happening at the same time.

5 Next, to create the effect of each letter fading in one after the other, you will stagger each Motion tween to overlap the one below it. Starting with your second letter, select the range of frames in the Motion tween, then drag them down the Timeline a few frames. You can also select a frame before the tween and press F5 (Insert Frames) to push each Motion tween down the Timeline.

BECOME A KEYFRAMER

2 With the text field still selected, break it apart using ⌘ C *ctrl* C once. Applying one break will split the text field into individual text fields per letter. One break retains the properties of the font, and you have the ability to edit each letter as such. If you wish, you can break it apart one more time to convert the font into raw vector shapes.

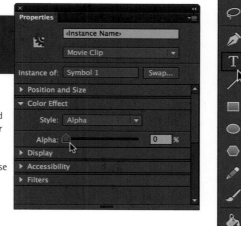

4 On each layer, add a keyframe about three to four frames down the Timeline. Now go back to the first keyframe containing your letter, select the letter symbol on the stage and apply some alpha via the Properties panel. Drag the alpha slider all the way down to 0%. Repeat this procedure for every letter. Apply a classic Motion tween for every letter so that they all fade in when you play back your Timeline. You can choose to use the new Motion tween for this effect if you prefer.

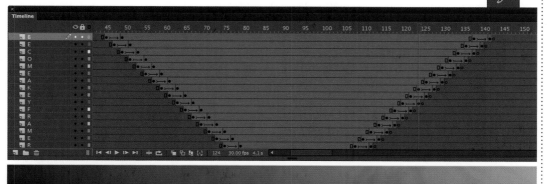

BECOME A K E

6 The final step is to select the first frame of each animation and use Shift while pressing the left arrow key to position each letter with 0% alpha to the left and on playback will create the motion of each letter flying into position while fading in at the same time. Once again, there is nothing particularly difficult about this effect. All you have done is use Motion tweens with some alpha fades. This is still a very basic Flash animation technique. The only difference is the timing of each letter relative to each other. Throw in a slight amount of movement, and suddenly you have what looks like an advanced animated text effect.

Blur filter (text)

SOMETIMES YOU MAY NEED a blur effect that is more realistic than the linear gradient method. The Blur filter is perfect for creating realistic blurs, even animated ones. Filters were introduced in Flash 8, and to create the same blur effect in older versions we had to export the object from Flash as a PNG file, open it in Photoshop (or any graphics editor of choice) and apply the Motion blur. Then we would have to export from Photoshop as a PNG file and import back into Flash. Thankfully, those days are long gone with the ability to not only apply filters, but to animate them as well.

1 It is usually a good idea when creating animated effects to work backwards. Start with the final frame, insert frames to extend your entire Timeline and then add keyframes to the last frame.

3 In frame 1, select a Movie Clip symbol on the stage and apply a Blur filter from the Filters panel. Click on the small black chain icon to unlock the blur constraint. Use the slider to adjust the amount of blur for the X axis only.

5 For objects that fly in vertically, limit the amount of blur to the Y axis. Remember to use your Shift and arrow keys to maintain alignment between keyframes, unless of course you want to have your object travel at an angle.

2 Go back to frame 1 and begin the animation process by positioning the objects that will animate into view off the stage. Hold down the **Shift** key while pressing the arrow keys to maintain alignment and move the object incrementally ten frames.

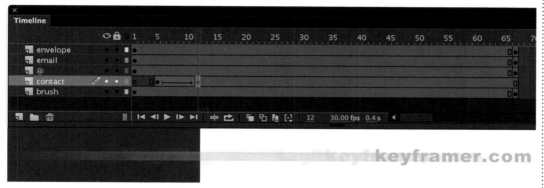

4 Drag the keyframe in your last frame closer to the first keyframe and apply a Motion tween. The symbol will animate from outside the stage into its original position. The Blur filter will also be motion tweened from the amount of blur in the first frame to no blur in the last frame.

6 Objects that appear as if being focused from thin air use an equal amount of blurring for both the X and Y axis. Did you know you can set a blur amount beyond what the slider allows? The slider taps out at a value of 100, but you can type in your own value up to 255.

Background blurring

I F YOU WATCH ANIMATED shows on television, then I'm sure you've seen the Motion blur technique, where the characters remain relatively still while the background is being blurred. These streaks provide the illusion that the characters are flying through the air at an incredible speed. Visually it's a very dramatic effect and can be used in a myriad of ways during an action sequence.

The illusion here is that the background is actually moving through the shot, but in fact it doesn't have to be. In this example the shapes that represent the motion simply wiggle slightly in a very short loop. What makes this effect convincing is a combination of color, line work and of course the character itself.

1 Start with a radial gradient as the undertone of your shot. Use the Gradient Transform tool **F** to position the gradient in the lower left corner. It is where the character will fly in from and helps provide some needed depth to the scene.

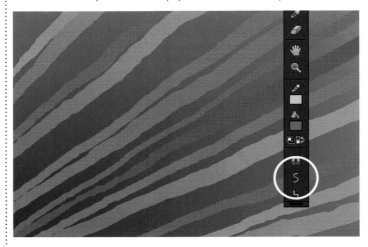

4 Select all lines and convert them to a Graphic symbol. Edit this symbol by adding several keyframes on the same layer. Each new keyframe will duplicate the lines for each added keyframe. Select all lines in each keyframe and click the "Smooth" tool (Brush subselection tool) a few times. Make sure the amount of smoothing is different for each keyframe. The idea is to create an oscillation between frames.

2 Create a new layer and use the Line tool **N** with a stroke color high in contrast to your gradient colors. Draw some lines to use as directional guides.

3 Create a new layer above your guidelines and using the Brush tool **B** and a large brush size, hand draw some thick lines that taper slightly towards the lower left corner.

5 On the main Timeline I added some random shapes flying through the shot in the same direction as the background lines. These shapes help emphasize the speed and direction the character is moving.

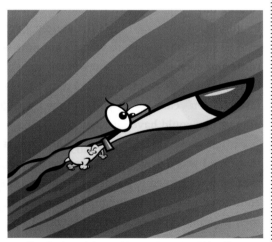

6 The final touch is to add your character. This effect works best when your character is drawn in a way that reflects the speed and wind resistance they would encounter.

HOT TIP

With the background as a nested looping animation, you can easily reuse it for other similar shots that need to imply very fast motion. As a symbol, it can be transformed by scaling, skewing and even tinting it based on the design of your shot.

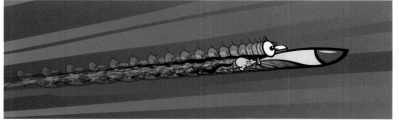

7 You can emphasize the dramatic effect by motion tweening the character from off the stage into its final position. Combine this effect with some of the Motion blur effects previously learned in this chapter, and you'll have a killer action sequence.

155

Aside from populating the online Flash forum with technical answers, I found myself delivering live Flash technical presentations via Adobe Connect and what is commonly referred to as "Tech Wednesdays." One such presentation has been overwhelmingly popular (http://my.adobe.acrobat.com/p46515568/). This demo was my very first recorded Breeze presentation, and it has been one of the most popular resources for Flash character design and animation on the Web. Funny thing is, I was merely filling for the original presenter who had to cancel last minute. With no time to prepare anything, I simply demonstrated what I do on a daily basis for clients and sometimes for self-amusement. Due to its popularity I was asked to host more online presentations, all of which were recorded and featured on Adobe's website. These are my most rewarding community experiences due to the number of users who continue to benefit from these recordings.

Ask me how I ended up here, and I will tell you it was the result of hard work, a little luck and the generosity of the Flash community. Ask me why I volunteer so much of my time to the Flash community, and I will tell you it's because I remember how precious the help was from them when I needed it most. Flash is just a tool, but it's the community that surrounds this tool that transforms it into a culture.

http://www.adobe.com/devnet/author_bios/chris_georgenes.html
http://www.adobe.com/devnet/flash/articles/design_character_pt1.html
http://www.adobe.com/devnet/flash/articles/design_character_pt2.html
http://my.adobe.acrobat.com/p46515568/

■ From concept sketch to finalized animated body parts, just how does a Flash animator get from point A to point B? What is the workflow when it comes to animating characters in Flash? This chapter looks at several real world examples of actual characters, how they were built and why.

Character animation

IT'S TIME TO GET DOWN AND DIRTY. IN PREVIOUS chapters we looked at how to achieve a wide variety of design styles, transformations and motion effects. But the concept of how to bring all these techniques together to create a successfully animated character can remain a mystery. When is it advantageous to nest certain animations and why? How can swapping symbols be effective? What exactly does the Sync feature do? What is the most effective way to synchronize a character's mouth and lips to a voice-over soundtrack?

These questions and more are explained in the following pages. So roll up your sleeves and get ready for a fun ride into the world of Flash character animation.

2.5D basics

TWEENING IS A GREAT WAY TO ADD A QUICK SIMPLE animation to your Flash movie. But what if you could push the tweening method to its limits and give more realism to your character? What if you could harness its simplicity and make it work in ways not too many other Flash users have considered? What if you have learned everything there is to know about tweening, go back to the first 10% of that knowledge and take a left turn? Where would that take you?

In this example, I'm going to reveal a truly killer Flash animation technique that will actually create a 3D optical illusion known to fool even the most discerning eye. The cool thing is you never leave the Flash environment and remain in the 2D realm. You are now in a dimensional limbo. If it's still 2D but looks like 3D, then what exactly is it? Welcome to what is commonly referred to as "2.5D animation."

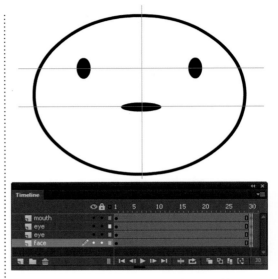

1 Let's start with a few basic shapes that resemble eyes and a mouth on a face. You can add some horizontal and vertical guides to help keep these objects aligned with each other. Before you start editing these shapes, insert keyframes a few frames down the Timeline across all layers. You will see why this extra time is useful later.

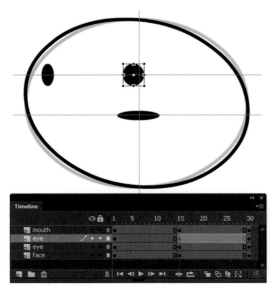

4 Move the other eye over as well but scale it slightly wider as it gets closer to the middle of the head. At this rotation, if it were truly mapped to the surface of a three-dimensional sphere, it would be at its widest at the point where it is closest to us.

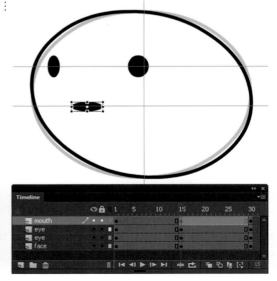

5 Next, move the mouth over in the same direction and scale its width slightly smaller like you did for the first eye. You might want to push the mouth closer to the left edge to provide more space between the mouth and the right eye. This trick will help make it feel as if the mouth is truly wrapping around the head like the left eye is starting to do.

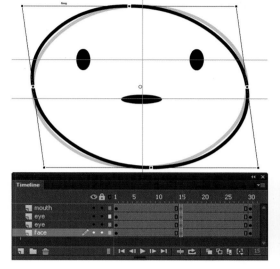

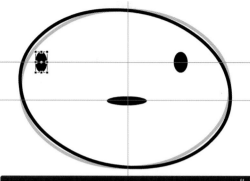

2 Insert keyframes across all layers between the first and last frames of your Timeline. Start with the head symbol by skewing it with the Free Transform tool **Q**. Since you will be creating the illusion of the head turning to the left, skew this shape by clicking and dragging just outside the bounding box in this direction.

3 Next, select the left eye symbol and position it close to the left edge of the head shape. Use the Free Transform tool to reduce its width slightly, creating the illusion of the eye moving away from us around the surface of the head.

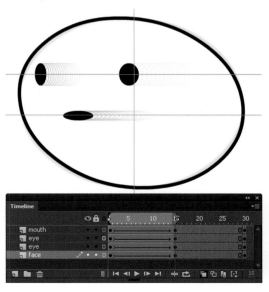

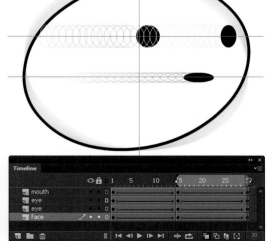

6 Now all you have to do is apply Classic tweens to all the layers. Drag across all layers to select them and apply a Classic tween from the context menu or Properties panel. Remember when you added keyframes to the final frame in step 1? Now all you need to do is apply Classic tweens to the latter half of your Timeline to return the head to its original position.

7 Repeat the same procedure but in the opposite direction to make the head appear to turn to the right. Experiment by making the head move from left to right by removing the keyframes in the middle of the Timeline.

2.5D advanced

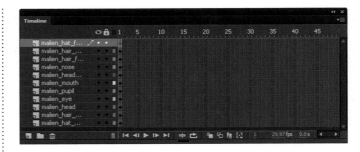

L ET'S APPLY THE SAME technique as explained in the previous example to a more sophisticated character. This character is comprised of several individual objects, all of which were designed and composed with this animation technique in mind. The spacial relationship of each object to each other is important as they will all need to move, skew and scale together but at varied amounts. The effect is based on the whole being greater than the sum of its parts. There's nothing overly sophisticated about creating this technique, but the result can look very complex on the surface.

1 The first step is to make sure all objects have been converted to symbols and you have edited their center point to your desired location this technique to be successful, it's often useful to design your characters in three-quarter view as opposed to a profile view or facing us directly.

4 Next, skew the hair to the right from its bottom edge. Since you want to convey this object coming around the front of the character's face, move it over to the right and scale it horizontally to make it slightly wider than it is in the first frame. Moving and scaling horizontally creates the illusion that it is moving not only across the face, but also slightly towards us as well.

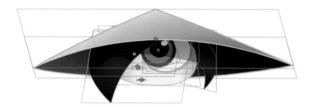

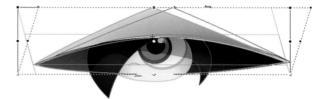

2 If you want to create a seamless loop by making the head eventually return to this same exact position, select a frame (across all layers) somewhere down the Timeline and add a keyframe (F6). It pays to think ahead because you have avoided having to copy and paste the keyframes from frame 1 later. Select another frame (across all layers) an equal distance between your first and last keyframes.

3 This middle frame is where you will edit your character. Start by using the Free Transform tool **Q** to skew the symbol instances. Here I have skewed the hat, which is comprised of two separate symbols, a front and a back. Selecting and skewing them together ensures that they remain aligned which each other. It's helpful to lock all other layers temporarily while you apply the transformations.

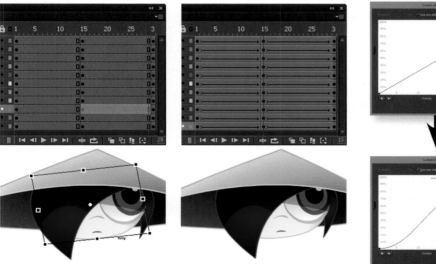

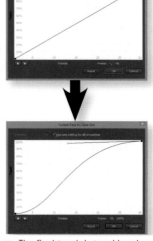

5 Repeat this process for each object, combining various amounts of skewing, scaling and positioning. The smaller symbol representing the hair on the right side is the only symbol in this example that gets positioned to the left. Moving it behind the head emphasizes the illusion that the head is a sphere that objects can seemingly "wrap" around.

6 The final touch is to add easing using the Custom Ease panel. The straight path represents no easing. The "S"-shaped path represents easing in and out within a single tween.

HOT TIP

Character design is critical for this effect to be successful. Keep it simple and stylized because the more anatomically correct your character is, the harder it will be to animate in this style.

2.5D monkey

T HE KEY TO REALISM LIES WITHIN THE shading. The same 2.5D animation technique is being used here, but this time the graphics are drawn using gradients to promote an even more convincing faux three-dimensional effect.

1 Start with the character at a three-quarter angle in frame 1. Let's call this "point A."

2 In your last frame, create what we'll call "point B." The challenge is getting from point A to point B through the use of tweens.

6 The ears play a pivotal role in this effect. At this new angle, we can see more of the left ear and less of the right ear.

7 Once the head symbols are transformed and positioned where you want them, lock their layers, select all the body parts and rotate them.

8 Next, adjust the legs and tail individually by selecting and rotating them.

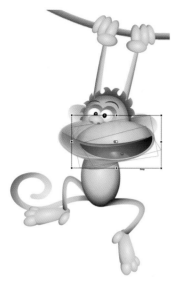

HOT TIP

Check out the "Using Gradients" topic in Chapter 2 to learn how to create and edit the radial gradients used in this example.

3 Using the Free Transform tool **Q**, rotate, skew and move each symbol into its "point B" position. Here the mouth symbols are transformed first.

4 Next, transform the nose, eyes, pupils and eyebrows. Pay close attention to the spacial relationship between each of these objects and our perspective at this new angle.

5 The head and hair symbols are rotated and positioned accordingly. At this angle, we see more of the hair from the left side and less on the right.

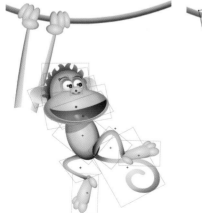

9 Select everything except the arms and hands and move the monkey over using the right arrow key. Hold down *Shift* to move in ten-pixel increments.

10 Rotate the arms so that they align with the monkey's new position. Their center point is positioned where the hands grab the vine to make the rotation even easier.

11 Apply motion tweens to each layer and play back your animation. Final adjustments are usually necessary at this stage.

6

Lip syncing (swap method)

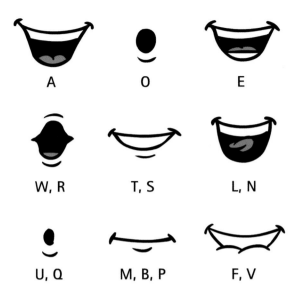

1 Here are the standard mouth shapes to use as a guide. Each shape corresponds to a specific sound or range of sounds. Each sound is noted below each shape. For most animation styles, you do not need to create a different mouth for each letter of the alphabet. In most situations, certain mouths can be reused for a variety of sounds.

LIP SYNCING IS AN ART FORM in its own right. It is the art of making a character speak to a pre-recorded vocal soundtrack. This technique involves the creation of various mouth shapes and matching them to the appropriate dialog. This technique can also be very time-consuming, especially if your dialog is very long. You can be as simple or as complex as you want. There's a big difference between *South Park* and Disney-style animation when it comes to matching mouths to sounds. There are two basic methods of lip syncing in Flash, which we will look at here.

4 The next step is to import your sound into Flash. Sound formats supported are WAV, MP3, AIFF and AU. Go to File > Import to Stage and locate the sound file on your hard drive. Once the sound is imported, create a new layer in your Timeline and select a frame. Using the Sound drop-down menu in the Properties panel, select the sound you just imported. Next, set the sound from the default "Event" to "Stream."

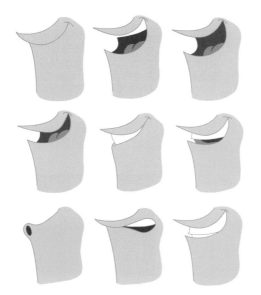

2 Using the standard mouth shapes as your guide, draw your character's mouth shapes, taking into consideration the design and angle of your character. After drawing each mouth, convert each one into a Graphic symbol.

3 Based on the design of your character, your next step will likely be to put the mouth symbol on its own layer making it easier to edit for animation.

5 On the main Timeline where your character resides you can animate the mouth talking by creating keyframes and using the "Swap Symbols" method via the Properties Inspector. The Swap Symbol panel will open, allowing you to scroll through your Library.

6 Click once to preview each Library item and click OK to replace the instance on the stage with this symbol. It helps to name your mouth symbols starting with the same three letters as they will be sorted by name in the Swap Symbol panel, making it easier to find the mouth you want.

7 Click OK to swap the symbol instance on the stage with this new symbol from the Library.

169

Lip syncing (nesting method)

THROUGH YEARS OF ANIMATING IN Flash, I have developed what I think is an even better and faster way to lip sync a character. A few years ago I was working in a full production environment with teams of animators producing several series for television and the Web. Most of these episodes were 22 minutes in length with several characters and plenty of dialog. Lip syncing quickly became the most dreaded of tasks. Using the Swap Symbols method is certainly a useful approach, but when you have 22 minutes of lip syncing to do and only two days to finish it, finding a faster method becomes a production necessity.

The Swap Symbols method requires a minimum of four mouse clicks for each swap.

1. Select the symbol instance.
2. Click the "Swap" button.
3. Select the new symbol.
4. Click "OK."

Over the course of thousands of frames and symbol swaps, those clicks can add up to an enormous amount. Shaving off just one click per mouth shape can, over time, save valuable production costs (not to mention an animator's sanity).

These situations are when "nesting" really shows its strength and versatility. By nesting all your individual mouths into a single symbol, you can control the instance of this symbol with the Properties panel. This method eliminates the need to swap symbols and also saves time.

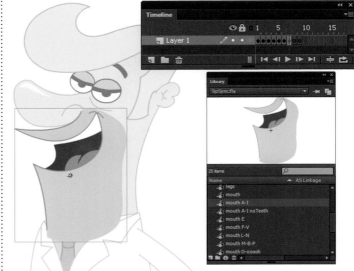

1 The first step is to place all your mouth shapes into a Graphic symbol. I recommend editing an existing symbol on the stage to help you align your additional mouths to the character on the main Timeline. Double-click the mouth symbol on the stage to enter Edit Mode. Create a blank keyframe for each additional mouth. If your mouths already exist as symbols, open your Library ⌘ L ctrl L and drag each mouth to its own keyframe. Use the Onionskin tool to help align each one.

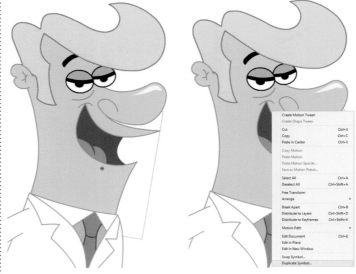

5 The convenience of nesting is obvious when you transform (rotate, scale, flip horizontally or vertically, etc.) your character; all nested assets are transformed as well.

6 Often you may need a custom mouth animation; for example, a mouth that whistles. Right-click over your mouth and select Duplicate Symbol. Give it a descriptive name.

2 Back on the main Timeline, open the Properties panel and select your "mouth" symbol containing all of your mouth shapes. As a Graphic symbol, the Properties panel will allow you options to control the instance.

3 Add a keyframe to the mouth layer, select the mouth instance and in the Properties panel select Single Frame. In the Frame input box, type in the frame number that corresponds to the mouth shape needed based on the sound at that keyframe.

4 Scrub the Timeline (drag the playhead back and forth) to hear the next sound. Repeat the same process by adding keyframes, and typing in the corresponding frame number for the mouth shape needed.

7 Remove the unneeded symbols by selecting them and choosing "Remove Frames" from the right-click context menu. Keep the symbol that closely represents a whistle shape.

8 Animate the whistling mouth as a short loop. Here I used the Envelope tool to distort my original mouth shape after breaking it apart.

9 On the main Timeline, add a keyframe and select the "whistle" symbol containing your new animation. In the Properties panel select "Loop" from the drop-down menu.

171

To sync or not to sync

TO SYNCHRONIZE A NESTED ANIMATION inside a Graphic symbol with the main Timeline, select the Sync option in the Property Inspector. Sync is a feature that is available when a Motion tween is applied. Select a keyframe with a Motion tween to find the Sync option in the Properties panel. What Sync means for nested animations is that the nested frames will be synchronized with the main Timeline.

In Flash CS3, Sync was inconsistently on or off depending on how you applied a Classic tween; if you applied a tween from the drop-down menu in the Properties panel, then Sync was UNCHECKED. If you applied a Classic tween via the right-click context menu, then Sync was CHECKED. The Sync feature was indicated on the Timeline when a keyframe is followed by a vertical line.

Flash CC consistently turns on the Sync feature by default no matter how the Motion tween is applied. So when would you use Sync? When would you want to avoid it? Let's first take a look at a situation where Sync would not be useful.

1 In order for you to see the effectiveness of the Sync feature, you need to work with a nested animation. A mouth symbol with several mouths on diferent keyframes will do just fine. Thumbnail views of each frame were displayed using the Frame View drop-down menu in the upper-right corner of the Timeline panel (to the right of the frame numbers) to select Previews. This view is a handy way to see the contents of each frame

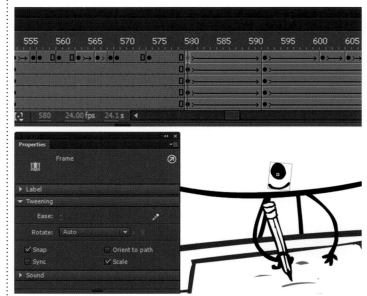

5 When you apply a Classic tween and want the ability to control the frames nested inside graphic symbols, select a keyframe in the tween and turn off the Sync feature via the Properties panel. Note that this only applies to Classic tweens in CS4+ and not the Motion Model.

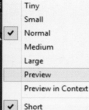

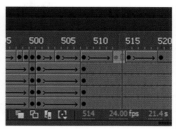

2 The Frame View drop-down menu offers several choices for you to customize the way your Timeline looks. My personal favorite is the "Short" setting, which lowers the overall height of each layer.

3 You can take lip syncing a bit further by tweening the mouth on the main Timeline. Tweening on the parent level adds a second layer of animation since this mouth symbol contains nested mouths as well.

4 Using the Free Transform tool **Q**, scale and/or skew the mouth depending on the vocal sound and apply a Classic tween. Sync is an option when Classic tweens are applied as shown in the next step.

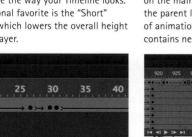

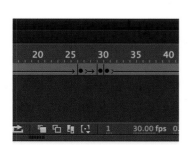

6 In the Timeline, the top image indicates a keyframe with Sync turned on. The bottom image indicates a keyframe with Sync turned off.

7 Having the ability to assign a specific frame number is critical for lip syncing. If Sync is selected, you will not be able to edit the current frame number. Once Sync is turned off, then you are free to change the frame number pertaining to the nested animation.

173

Sync (Classic tweens)

ONE DAY THE CLIENT ASKS FOR you to animate their company's character logo across their website splash page. You use several keyframes and Motion tweens to animate their character (nested inside a symbol) along a motion guide and deliver the final version to your client and await their feedback. Unfortunately the client changes their mind and asks if you could change the bee character to a dog with a jet pack instead. Do you have to do the entire animation over again? No, because you can always swap out the bee symbol for another symbol. But you have to swap out each instance of the bee for every keyframe you made in the animation. What a drag! The more keyframes on the Timeline, the more monotonous and frustrating this task can be.

Sync to the rescue!

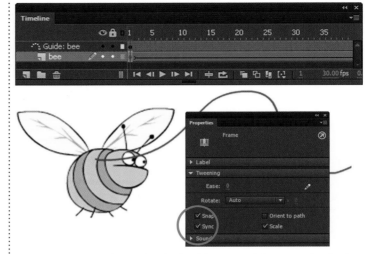

1 Let's start with a simple animation involving a nested character animation in a Graphic symbol motion tweened along a guided path. Apply a Classic tween by right-clicking over the keyframe in frame 1 and selecting Create Classic Tween. Select frame 1 and turn on the Sync option in the Properties panel.

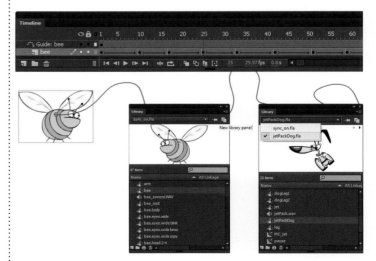

4 You just about finish the animation when the phone rings and your client informs you that they want to change the bee to a totally different character. Thanks to Sync, your time and hard work will not be wasted. Go to File > Import > Open External Library and navigate to an FLA containing the replacement symbol and click Open. You can also click the New Library panel button to open the Library of an FLA already open in Flash. A new Library panel will open displaying the symbols and assets contained in the selected FLA. Click and drag the preferred symbol from the external Library to the Library of your current document.

HOT TIP

Use the Sync option to control different symbols within the same Classic tween. Turn off Sync for certain keyframes if you want to swap to another symbol for that keyframe. Turn on Sync to keep the same symbol in sync with the main Timeline. This method will not work with Movie Clip symbols. Use only Graphic symbols because only Graphic symbols can be synced to other Timelines using the Sync feature. Movie Clips have Timelines that are independent of all other Timelines and need ActionScript to be synced to other Timelines.

2 Insert a keyframe somewhere in the Classic tween. Use the Free Transform tool **Q** to rotate the symbol. Feel free to scale or skew the symbol as well. Because the first keyframe is "Synced," all subsequent keyframes will have Sync turned on by default as well.

3 Continue to insert keyframes every few frames and transform your symbol by rotating and scaling. The idea here is to make this simple Classic tween relatively complex for the example purposes.

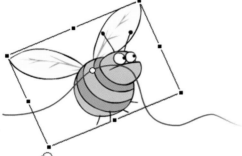

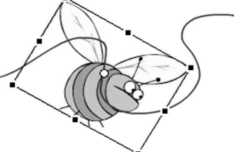

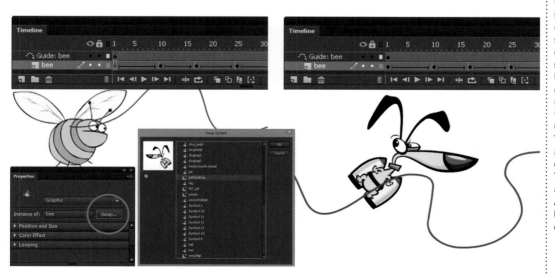

5 Select the bee character in the first frame of your Classic tween. In the Properties panel click the Swap button and locate the new symbol you just added to your Library and click OK.

6 Since every keyframe in the Classic tween has the Sync option selected, your entire animation will be updated across all keyframes. Crisis averted, go and make yourself another cup of coffee, catch up on your email overflow and get back to your client in a little while. Make sure to sound out of breath when you call them to tell them the changes have been made (just kidding).

175

Sync (Motion tweens)

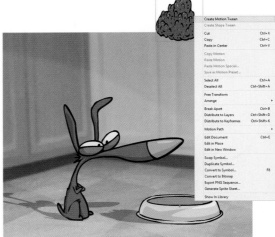

T HE MOTION TWEEN CHANGES EVERYTHING when it comes to tweens and what we can do with them. If you remember 1 thing about them, remember this: the Motion tween is *object-based* while the Classic tween is *frame-based* which means much of what we used to do in previous versions was in the Timeline when it involved animation: creating and removing keyframes, applying tweens, creating and applying motion guides, copying and pasting frames, etc.

With Motion tweens, most tasks are applied to the object on the stage while Flash does most of the work for us. For this particular animation, the joke is always on the dog. Each of his meals are dropped into his dish and each time the meal is different (as well as revolting and inedible). I knew this scene will be reused, so it was critical to build it in a way that made it easy to swap out the object that falls into the bowl. If you thought using the Sync feature to swap symbols across animations couldn't be easier, think again.

1 The first step is to draw the object that is to land in the bowl and convert it to a symbol. Position the symbol above the bowl and almost off the top edge of the stage. Since the Motion tween is *object*-based, right-click over the symbol and select "Create Motion Tween." Flash will automatically create a motion span in this layer and insert a duration of frames equal to a full second based on the document's frame rate which will likely be plenty of time as this animation won't last beyond 1 second.

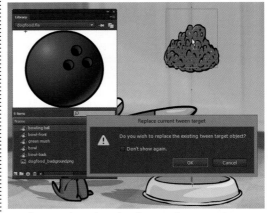

4 Once you have the animation complete, swapping out the current symbol for an alternative symbol is surprisingly easier than using the Sync method from previous examples. Thanks to the Motion tween, all you need to do is open the Library panel, find the symbol you wish to use in place of the current symbol and drag it to the stage (make sure the layer with the motion span is selected). Flash will prompt you to confirm that you want to replace the existing tween target object. Click OK.

2 Insert some time before the animation actually starts, which was always a bit cumbersome when using Classic tweens. With the Motion tween all you need to do is click and drag the left edge of the motion span and drag it to a new frame. Position the frame indicator somewhere around frame 15, hold down the *Shift* key and drag the symbol vertically so that it ends up inside the dog bowl.

3 To provide the illusion of weight to the dog food, additional keyframes and positions were added as well as some squashing and stretching. To make the effect even more convincing, the dog bowl itself can be animated as if it is reacting to the impact of the food.

To remove frames or cut frames from within a span, Ctrl-drag (Windows) or Command-drag (Macintosh) to select the frames and choose Remove Frames or Cut Frames from the span context menu.

5 Your new object has now been applied to the entire motion span, replacing the original object across all keyframes and properties. Using this technique has obvious advantages over the Sync method; instead of selecting the first keyframe in a Classic tween and swapping out the symbol from the Library, the Motion tween method is a simple case of dragging a new object to the stage containing the animation.

6 You can even select the span and press the *Delete* key to remove the object entirely from the animation. All of the Motion tween data is retained, allowing you to drag a new object to the stage or copy and paste a new object into the existing span.

To extend the presence of a tweened object on stage beyond either end of its tween, Shift-drag either end frame of its tween span. Flash adds frames to the end of the span without tweening those frames.

Hinging body parts

WITH FREE TRANSFORM, we can edit the center point of a symbol instance, thus editing the point on which the symbol rotates or "hinges" itself. Any simulation to inverse kinematics is purely coincidental. This technique does not allow you to link objects together in a chain like the Bones tool does but can be useful for manipulating objects individually.

1 Select the Free Transform tool **Q** and then click on one of your symbols on your stage. The center point of the symbol is now represented by a solid white circle. Simply click and drag this circle to a new location. In my example, I moved the center point of the arm to where the shoulder is (approximately).

4 You can select multiple symbols across multiple layers and hinge them as if they were one single object. With the Free Transform tool still selected, hold down the **Shift** key and click on multiple symbols on the stage. The center point will now be relative to the center point of all the symbols selected.

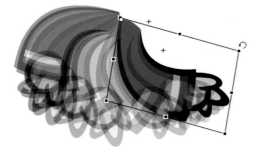

2 With the same tool rotate the arm symbol. It will hinge based on its new center point, making it easier to position each arm movement in relation to the body symbol.

3 Repeat this process for each body part you want hinged. As you can see I even hinged the ear symbol as well. Now you can start animating by creating additional keyframes and apply Motion tweens throughout your Timeline.

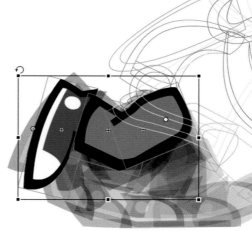

5 This technique can be very useful for hinging the head of a character which may contain multiple symbols (eyes, mouth, nose, hair, etc.).

6 The center point for each individual symbol will be retained, but the center point representing multiple selected symbols will not be remembered once they are deselected.

HOT TIP

To select multiple objects, it is often easier to click and drag with the Selection tool across the objects on stage. Make sure you set the center point for each symbol on frame 1 of your Timeline. If the center point is different between keyframes where a Motion tween is applied, your symbol will drift unexpectedly.

Closing the gaps

1 The Evil Mime character for the Yahoo! Super Messengers project was designed in a very anatomically correct style. This style caused some problems during the animation process, specifically the joints between limbs. When the arms or legs are in their original positions (as they were drawn originally), there's no gap.

FORM FOLLOWS FUNCTION IN Flash. The more stylized the design, the more flexibility you will have when it comes to adding motion. On the other hand, the more anatomically correct your character is designed, the less you can get away with when the time comes to animate it.

Sometimes a project comes along where the design style demands realism. As a result, the animation technique demands attention to detail, which can be limiting to a certain degree. One particular issue is the unsightly gap that is often created when bending arms and legs at their respective joints. The solution: "caps." At least that's what I like to call them. An elbow cap for the arms and a knee cap for the legs can solve the dreaded gap problem.

5 The leg, like the arm, works quite well when in a straight position. The upper thigh blends perfectly into the calf and shin.

6 The problem arises when these body parts are pushed to their anatomical limit when rotated and bent at the knee (or lack thereof).

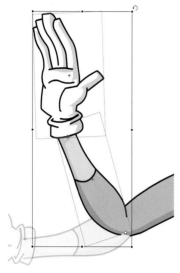

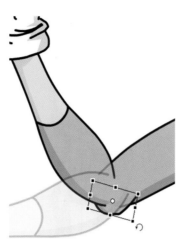

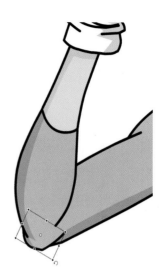

2 Once the arm is bent, the gap appears between the forearm and upper arm symbols. The gap is a problem inherent with this style of line work.

3 The solution is to add a new symbol in the form of an elbow. This new cap can be used as filler to hide that ugly gap between limbs when rotating.

4 Use the Free Transform tool **Q** to skew the cap symbol, so it aligns with both arm symbols bridging the gap between them, so to speak.

HOT TIP

Cut-out style characters like this one are perfect for animating when linked together in a chain-like fashion.

7 Once again, adding a knee cap symbol solves this problem quite nicely.

8 Position the knee cap in between the upper and lower leg symbols and align as necessary. Use the Free Transform tool **Q** to skew and scale the knee so that it fits properly.

9 It may seem like a lot of work to add elbow and knee caps, and subsequently more layers to your Flash document. But in the end, the results of your hard work and attention to detail will not go unnoticed.

6

Bitmap animation (Jib Jab)

JIB JAB MEDIA GAINED WIDESPREAD notoriety for its election year shorts "This Land" and "Good to be in DC," which featured George W. Bush and John Kerry during the 2004 Presidential campaign and were viewed online more than 80 million times.

The Jib Jab team uses both Photoshop and Flash to create the majority of their animation, and the process involves sketching, photography, Photoshop collage and, of course, Flash animation.

In this tutorial, you'll be instructed on how to make a President Bush dance cycle. You'll need a photo of President Bush's head, a camera and an understanding of tweens, guide layers and the basics of character animation.

Special thanks to Aaron Simpson (www.coldhardflash.com), and Gregg and Evan Spiridellis (www.jibjab.com) for their generous contribution to this book. This is Flash animation gold.

1 For this type of animation, you should define the proportions and the action your character will be executing. Start by drawing the first pose for your character.

2 Sketch the second pose and when you're finished, you should have a clear idea of the photos you'll need to animate.

6 You should only build one arm, as we'll flip these assets and reuse them on the opposite side. Here the arm was cut out using another Quick Mask.

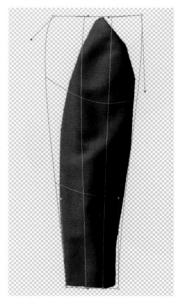

7 The arm looks too thin on the shoulder area. Press ⌘ ctrl T to enter Transform mode and click the Warp icon, then manipulate the Bezier handles to give it a cylindrical shape.

3 Photograph a front view of a jacket, shirt and tie and then a separate photo of a fist. In this situation, you can reuse the arms as legs, and create a vector foot.

4 Open your photograph file in Photoshop. Press **Q** to enter Quick Mask mode and using a hard edge brush, select the area you want to animate separately.

5 Here's the body section after cutting it out with the Quick Mask feature. Make sure the background is transparent.

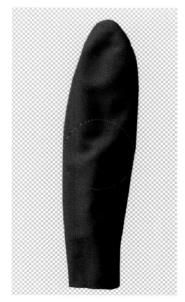

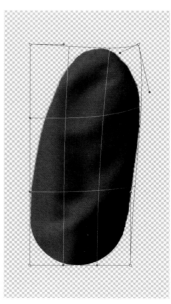

8 Next, select a circle where you want the elbow joint to be and save that selection in a new channel.

9 Here is the lower arm graphic after being cut out from the overall arm.

10 Here the upper arm receives a little more transforming with the Warp tool for good measure.

HOT TIP

Check out Steve Caplin's *How to Cheat in Photoshop* for some of the best tips and tricks for how to extend your Photoshop knowledge. It's a great companion book to have next to this one.

183

PSD Importer (Jib Jab)

H ERE WE SEE how the PSD Importer has evolved in Flash CC. You have the ability to import PSD files straight into Flash! This feature is great at integrating Photoshop and Flash seamlessly.

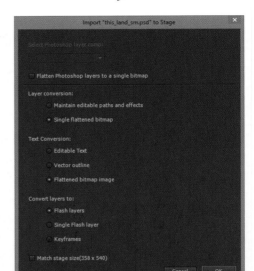

1 Here is how the layers look in the Photoshop file. Many of the images have transparent backgrounds. Transparency is one of the many features preserved when importing.

2 In Flash go to File > Import and navigate to your PSD file. The PSD Importer wizard will launch automatically. Your options include the ability to flatten the PSD to a single bitmap, convert layers as single flattened bitmaps or retain editability of any paths or effects, convert text fields to vector outlines or flattened bitmaps and convert layers to Flash layers or keyframes.

6 The image of President Bush is easily found by doing an image search on the web. Assets like the hands can be shot with your own camera and edited in Photoshop.

7 Reuse the arm assets for the legs by copying and pasting them to new layers. Then scale and stretch the copied version and align it to your character as the thigh and calf.

3 You may prefer to convert your images to symbols after importing. Keep your Library organized by using symbol names the same as the names of your images.

4 Edit the center point of each symbol using the Free Transform tool **Q**.

5 The shoulder should rotate where it meets the torso, and the forearm should rotate at the elbow.

HOT TIP

Besides File > Import, you can also drag and drop a PSD file onto the Flash stage to invoke the PSD Importer wizard. Always maintain RGB color values in Photoshop to preserve their consistency when importing into Flash.

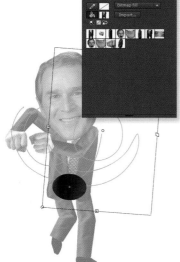

8 The pelvis area was created with a shape and a bitmap fill from one of the imported bitmap images. Use the Gradient Transform tool **F** to scale it to show only the blue fabric.

9 In frame 1, pose your character based on your initial sketch. You can choose to have your sketch to the side or directly underneath your symbols. Whichever way you prefer, the main objective is to position your character in this same gesture. In your second keyframe, pose your character in its final state using your sketch as a guide. You can't flip your symbols horizontally or you will ruin the Motion tween.

185

Motion guides (Jib Jab)

MOTION GUIDE LAYERS let you create paths along which you can tween instances of symbols, grouped objects or text blocks. You can link as many layers as you want to a Motion Guide layer and have multiple objects follow the same path. A normal layer that is linked to a Motion Guide layer becomes a guided layer.

Motion guides are useful because, without them, a normal Motion tween is linear, meaning it moves in a straight line only. If your object needs to move along a curve, a Motion Guide is necessary.

1 Create a Motion Guide layer by adding a normal layer, right-clicking over it and then selecting Guide from the context menu.

2 Drag the layer you want to be guided to the Guide layer to link it. The layer icon will now be offset.

6 Add a Motion guide for each additional object you need to animate along an arc and draw the appropriate path needed.

7 Using a combination of Motion guides, paths, transformation and tweens, you can animate any object along in any direction you prefer.

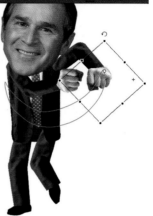

3 Make sure Snap is selected (magnet icon) and drag your symbol until it snaps to your Motion guide.

4 Add additional keyframes as necessary and snap your object to the path. Use the Free Transform tool ⓠ to rotate your symbol as well.

5 In your last frame, snap your symbol to the end of your Motion guide and add your final transformation.

HOT TIP

Test your work often by using Ctrl + Enter. Flash will generate an SWF file and play it for you within the Flash authoring environment. This SWF can be found in the same directory where you saved your FLA file.

8 The legs and feet do not need to be guided along a Motion path since they only move in linear directions.

9 The final step is to place your character in its intended environment by adding a background. The American flag shown here was edited in Photoshop and imported into a layer below all the other layers.

187

Character animation

Walk cycle

L ET'S FACE IT, AS AN ANIMATOR YOU ARE eventually going to be faced with the task of making somebody or something walk. For whatever reason, newcomers to animation regard walk cycles as extremely difficult. Why? I won't lie to you, they are. Well, in an anatomically accurate way they can be very challenging. As an animator, you will find it nearly impossible to avoid the walk cycle, so it may be best to face your fear head-on right now. You just might learn that walk cycles aren't all that difficult to accomplish. There are several ways to make the task of animating a walk cycle very difficult or relatively easy. Let's examine the easy way.

The best way to create a walk cycle in Flash is to animate the character walking in place, as if on a conveyor belt. The main idea here is to drag an instance of this looping walk cycle animation to the stage and use a Motion tween to animate the character walking across the scene. We'll get more into that after we tackle the actual walk cycle.

1 Design your character in three-quarter view. At this angle the character is simply easier to animate, especially when it comes to walk cycle animations. Next, convert your entire character and all its parts into a Graphic symbol. You will be working entirely inside this symbol to create your walk cycle.

2 Let's concentrate on just one leg for now. In fact, turn all other layers off so that only one leg of your character is visible. This character's leg is made up of three different symbols: an upper thigh, a lower leg and a sneaker. This straightforward setup is flexibility enough for a simple walk cycle.

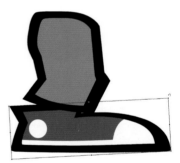

4 Notice that I didn't use the same sneaker for every frame. Depending on the position of the leg, I duplicated the original symbol, gave it a new name and edited its shape to reflect its new position. This type of detail is what I love to add to my animations and I really feel, as subtle as it may be, it adds a lot to the overall look and feel of the character's movements.

8 Feel free to experiment with the amount of frames between each of your leg positions. You can have more frames for when the foot is sliding back along the ground (so it travels more slowly) and fewer frames while the leg is off the ground (so it travels more quickly), returning it quickly to its initial position. This change in speed can create the illusion that the character is heavy, or perhaps carrying something heavy. If you do the opposite and have the foot slide quickly across the ground and slowly when off the ground, it may suggest your character is on a slippery surface, such as ice.

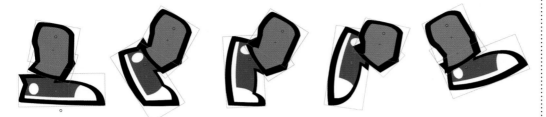

3 Position the leg into several major walk positions using keyframes. Start with the leg planted firmly on the ground. The next position is the foot still on the ground but bent so that the heel is up off the ground. Then create another keyframe and position the leg just before it is lifted off the ground. Next, position the leg completely off the ground and in its most rearward position. The final keyframe shows the leg is in its most forward position off the ground. Use the Free Transform **Q** tool to rotate each leg symbol

until it is in the desired position. Notice there are several slightly different shapes to his sneaker based on the amount of weight (or lack of) being placed upon it. When it is fully compressed on the ground its bottom edge is flat. Just before it's lifted off the ground, it is bent just after the toe. When it is entirely off the ground, its bottom edge is slightly rounded. These may seem like very insignificant details, but in the grand scheme of things, they can make all the difference.

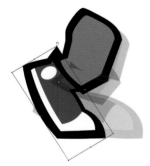

5 Turn on the Onionskin tool and adjust the playhead brackets, so you can use your established leg positions as references. Create keyframes across all layers that contain your leg symbols.

6 Use the Free Transform tool **Q** to rotate and move each leg symbol into an intermediate position relative to the keyframes you already created. The number of frames between the major leg positions will determine the characteristics of the walk cycle.

7 Experiment with the frames between each leg position. Adding more frames when the foot is sliding back along the ground will create the effect of the character gripping the surface. Add fewer frames while the leg is returning to its initial position.

9 Play back your animation constantly, so you can get real-time visual feedback as to your process. This type of animation work is trial and error and depends on your personal animation style to get the walk cycle to look and feel good to you. Don't get frustrated; it simply takes practice. Sometimes it helps to not think of it as an actual leg. Try to imagine it's not a leg at all but some kind of mechanical assembly like a basic pulley or lever system. This thought process can make animating less daunting and a lot more fun. Open the "leg_simulation.fla" from the downloaded source ZIP file. This FLA contains an example of a walk cycle experiment. I made it to show how a walk cycle can be thought of in mechanical terms. It was a fun experiment because it removes the intimidation factor that is associated with animating a walk cycle.

Continued...

189

ONCE YOU ARE FINISHED creating enough keyframes and leg positions, and you are satisfied with the movement of your leg, we can now move on to the other leg. Since you already animated one leg, there is no reason to start from scratch with the second leg (unless the other leg is designed differently). Therefore, delete the other leg entirely from the stage. Seriously, go ahead and delete it. We don't need it any more. Trust me.

10 Hold down the *Shift* key to select multiple layers and drag them to the trashcan icon or click on the trashcan icon to delete them from the Timeline.

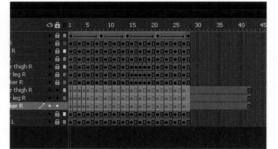

11 Select the entire range of frames and layers of the leg you previously animated. Right-click (Control + click) over the highlighted area and select "Copy Frames" from the context menu.

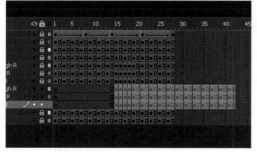

15 Select this entire range of frames and layers by clicking and dragging across all of them.

16 Click and drag this entire range of frames and layers to the left until they start on frame 1. Remove the residual frames by selecting them and "Removing" them from the right-click context menu.

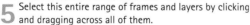

20 As we did with the leg animations, animate just one of your character's arms and then copy and paste its keyframes into a new layer(s) to achieve the second arm. Select the first half of your arm/hand animation and place it after the latter half of the animation.

21 Select and drag the entire arm/hand animation, so it starts again on frame 1 and remove the residual frames that are left behind.

12 Add a new layer below your existing leg, select the entire range of frames, right-click over them and select "Paste Frames" from the context menu.

13 Lock all layers except these three you just copied and pasted. Select the first half of this duplicated leg animation by clicking and dragging across layers and frames.

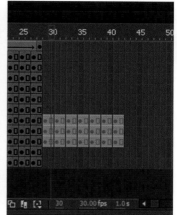

14 Click and drag the entire section of highlighted frames down the Timeline and place it after the latter half of the animation.

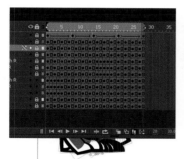

17 Using Edit Multiple Frames, select the new leg symbols and use the arrow keys to nudge them to the right and up slightly. Nudging will help separate the two leg assemblies.

18 Apply a color tint to the leg symbols using black with about 30% strength. The tint gives the illusion the back leg is in shadow and helps create a sense of depth.

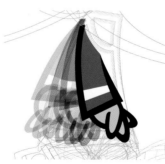

19 Animate the arm and hands by rocking them back and forth. You can use frame-by-frame or Motion tweens depending on your needs.

22 Turn on Edit Multiple Frames again and select this entire range of arm/hand symbols. Click on them once with the Selection tool and apply the same color tint as the legs.

23 With Edit Multiple Frames still turned on, use the arrow keys to nudge them up and to the right slightly.

24 You can add to your walk cycle animation by adding some motion to its head and body. It comes down to personal preference and your individual animation style.

HOT TIP

Be careful when using the Edit Multiple Frames feature. Make sure only the layers you want to edit are unlocked and all other layers are locked to avoid accidents.

191

Advanced walk cycle

Contributed by Ben Palczynski
www.hiylea.com

1 Pick a starting point to draw. The initial step as the front foot contacts the ground will do. It helps to use a horizontal guide to help keep things aligned and level.

2 Now draw the halfway position where the standing leg is straight and central. Turn on the Onionskin tool to use the previous drawing as your reference for scale and alignment.

5 Turn Onionskin on over the whole animation, so you can look for the arcs of motion to check that things are generally lined up. If something is jittering in your animation, having Onionskin on can help you spot where the problem is.

THIS EXAMPLE SHOWS A traditional walk cycle animation where each frame is drawn completely by hand. What makes this particular animation advanced is that it requires not only drawing skills, but a sense of rhythm and timing. Ben makes it look easy, but with some dedication and practice, you can achieve great results.

One of the most well-known and highly-praised resources for character animation is *The Animator's Survival Kit* (Richard Williams). Williams explains everything you could ever want to know about all kinds of walk cycles, and it's a reference no animator should be without.

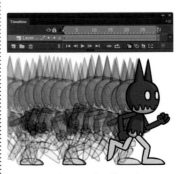

8 Drag this nested walk cycle to a new layer on the main Timeline and Motion tween it across the stage.

9 The head "turn" uses the same "globe" technique as shown in Chapter 4.

3 Continue drawing the key main poses using the Onionskin tool to reference your previous keyframes.

4 Now do the poses in between these positions. The more keyframes and poses you add, the smoother and slower your animation will be. Experiment with frame rate and number of keyframes for your walk cycle.

6 Next, center the drawings so you can create a nested loop. Combine any layers you have for each frame, turn on Edit Multiple Frames and span all keyframes using the Frame Indicator brackets. Use the Align panel to center them all.

7 Place these keyframes in a symbol if they aren't already. Draw your character or drag pre-made body parts from the Library into a new layer above your walk cycle. Align each body part according to each sketch for each keyframe.

HOT TIP

When animating a walk cycle, it's sometimes a good idea to start off by animating the character literally walking across the screen, one image positioned after another like the thumbnails along the top and bottom of these pages. Lining them up might help you fine-tune the overall mechanics and the ryhthm of your walk cycle.

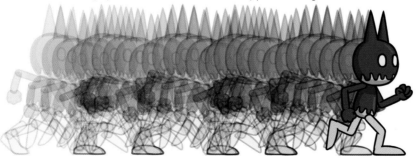

10 To prevent your character's feet from slipping along the surface as it walks across the stage, set the symbol to graphic and playback to loop. Turn on the Onionskin tool and make sure that the feet overlap fully when they're placed on the ground. The advantage of having the walk cycle nested in a single symbol is the ability to scale the walk cycle quickly and easily. You can also flip the walk cycle horizontally to make the character walk in either direction.

Walk cycle examples

Contributed by Colter Avara
www.tumblrdorfscastle.tumblr.com

COLTER AVARA IS A friend and talented designer. Recently he was experimenting with walk cycles and sent them to me for feedback. I loved them so much I asked if he'd let me provide them as examples. Colter's walk cycles are wonderful animations created in Flash using traditional frame-by-frame animation. He started with the initial contact pose, the passing position pose and then the ending contact pose. Then he worked backwards by drawing in the keyframes in between each of the key poses.

1 Timing is key! Most cartoony walks can be animated on 8's (a key pose on every 8th frame), which is actually 3 steps per second at 24 fps. Most people walk on 12's (a key pose on every 12th frame), which is 2 steps per second, but it varies. Everyone walks differently. Check your own walk sometime, and while you're at it study real people and try to observe as much from real life as possible. First you'll want to create keyframes 1, 5 and 9.

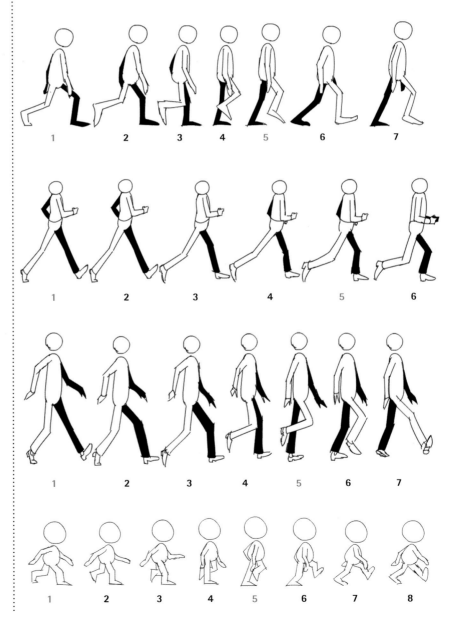

2 You'll then draw opposing contact poses on frames 1 and 9. Contact poses are points in a walk where your character's heel first makes contact with the ground. Once you've drawn in frames 1 and 9, you'll then draw a passing position on frame 5. Passing positions are mid-points where the stepping leg passes the balancing leg during a walk. These poses can really set the tone of a walk, so experiment!

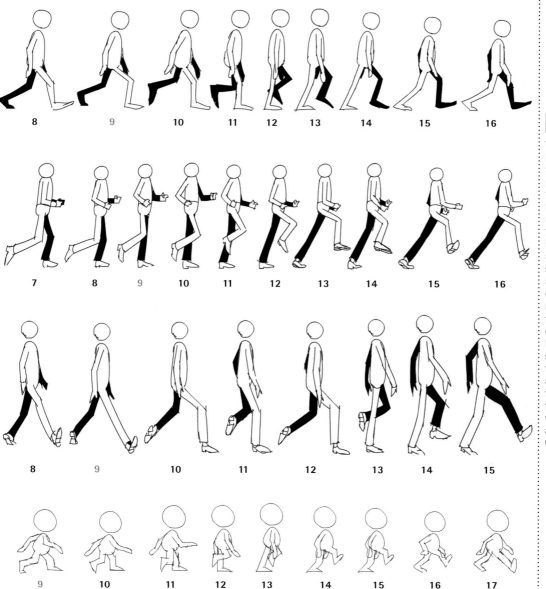

HOT TIP

The numbers below each of the walk cycle poses indicate the frames where each pose resides. The frame numbers in red indicate a key pose. In some cases the actual walk cycles contain more frames than could fit on these pages. Locate the source files for these examples and play the timeline to see the complete walk cycle animations as Colter intended.

195

Anticipation

1 Here the character is in its initial position. Not much going on in terms of action, but we can assume he might do something due to the slight tension in his stance and his hands being in close proximity to both holstered guns.

BY DEFINITION, ANTICIPATION IS THE preparation for a particular action or movement. It can also be used in animation to attract the viewer's attention to a specific event that is about to occur. An example of anticipation would be an archer pulling an arrow back along its bow or a baseball player raising his arm to throw a ball.

Anticipation can also be used to build suspense in a scene. It tells the viewer something is about to happen, and the longer the anticipation is, the more suspenseful it can be.

Anticipation is critical to making believable animation. Without anticipation, your animation may appear too abrupt and unnatural. It is important as an animator to study from life and notice how we move and react anatomically.

4 The first step shows the character still on one foot, but also leaning back a little further and crouching lower with all his weight on this one leg. This stance is obviously not a comfortable gesture that could be held for very long. Hence the anticipation that something is about to happen.

2 To anticipate the action, animate the cowboy in the opposite direction he will be moving. Make a new keyframe across all layers where the next position change will occur and use the Free Transform tool **Q** to rotate and position your character. Apply a Motion tween and some easing out to imply physical tension within our character.

3 Sometimes an animation requires more than one keyframe position to achieve the right movement and gesture. For this particular animation I used four different gestures for the anticipation animation, each with a Motion tween and some easing applied.

HOT TIP

Refer to the topic in this chapter on "Hinging body parts" to help you rotate symbols based on a customized center point.

5 Here I am pushing the envelope by adding even more tension in the character's overall gesture. There's no doubt he is about to react in a very physical way.

6 Sir Isaac Newton showed us for every action there is an opposite but equal reaction. In keeping with this law of motion, animate the character moving in the opposite direction and ultimately performing the anticipatory action.

Drawing upon oneself

Contributed by Laith Bahrani
www.monkeehub.com
www.lowmorale.co.uk
www.jcbsong.co.uk

THE MOST COMMON TECHNIQUE I use to make a character or an object appear as if it's drawing itself into the scene is purely frame-by-frame animation anyone can achieve. Although the effect can be quite labor intensive, it can also be visually effective if you want to achieve a very organic hand-drawn effect. The basic principle involves starting with a finished drawing; over a series of keyframes, cut away bits of the drawing with the Lasso tool. Work backwards starting on what will eventually be the end keyframe of the animation. When you play back the animation from frame 1, the drawing will appear to draw itself. The same effect can be achieved by using a mask to reveal the character or object. I find this works best on areas of color as opposed to lines. Let's look at how you can incorporate both techniques to animate a chicken character who appears to draw itself.

1 The first step to animating the chicken character is to spend decades studying and sketching this wonderful species of bird. As you can see I skipped this part and just scanned in the first chicken I drew. Resize the scanned sketch into a workable and desirable size in Photoshop and then import it into Flash.

2 With the scanned sketch imported and on the stage, convert it to a Movie Clip. The scanned sketch will be the drawing guide and drawing over it is how I do a lot of my characters. Adjust the alpha of this "guide" to about 50% so that the contrast of the lines you draw over it will be clearer.

6 Now lock all the layers except for the body outline layer; having all other layers locked helps ensure you only work on the appropriate area. Insert a keyframe in frame 2. Select the Lasso tool **L** and cut away a small portion of the line.

7 Repeat this procedure of adding keyframes and removing small portions of your line work until they are completely removed. Select the entire range of keyframes, right-click over them and select "Reverse Frames" from the context menu. Repeat this process for all other outline layers.

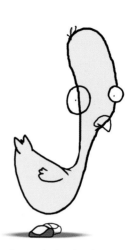

Instead of using the Lasso tool to select and delete a small portion of your line work, you may want to try using the Eraser tool or the pressure-sensitive eraser on the opposite end of your stylus (if you have one).
In terms of style and pacing it's worth keeping in mind that if you cut big pieces away at each keyframe the line will appear quickly and could look a bit jumpy.

3 Build the chicken character up in layers, keeping individual parts on separate layers. The techniques of splitting a character up are fairly universal and logical – head/body/arms/legs/eyes/mouth (or in this case beak). Create a new layer (above the guide) and using the Paintbrush tool, draw the outline of the chicken's body.

4 When you've drawn the body outline, fill it with a color. Next click on the filled color area to select it, cut it using ⌘ X ctrl X, create a new layer underneath the outline and paste the fill using ⌘ Shift V ctrl Shift V. Create one more layer, above the others, and draw the wing as an outline only. This process gives you three layers for the body: for the outline, for the fill and for the wing.

5 Create the head and other parts in the same manner. Add a new layer for each new body-errr-chicken part, keeping them all separate. Remember to cut and paste each color fill to individual layers as well. If you are familiar with character animation, then you are already used to working with multiple layers and layer folders.

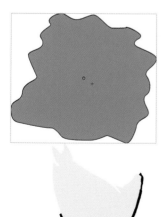

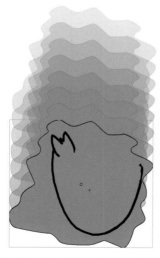

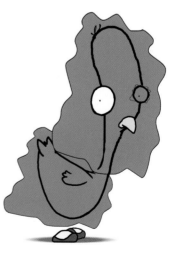

8 To create the effect of each color fill being "drawn" in, add a new layer above the body layer and convert it to a mask layer. In this layer create an irregular shape and convert it to a symbol.

9 Insert a keyframe in the mask layer in a frame at the end of your Timeline. Position the symbol containing your shape, so it completely covers your fill color for the chicken's body. Apply a Motion tween to animate the mask so it "reveals" this color fill.

10 Add a mask layer and create new mask shapes for each color fill. Motion tween each one into position to reveal each chicken part. Lock all layers or publish your movie to see your animation effect

Tradigital animation

THE FUSION OF TRADITIONAL AND DIGITAL animation has given us "tradigital" animation. I don't know who invented the term, but the effect was first shown to me by Ibis Fernandez (flashfilmmaker.com), a well known and talented animator who blew me away when he sent me a sample of this technique a few years ago. Up until that point in my career, I had been using Flash for four years and thought I knew every trick in the book. It was clear to me I had more to learn.

Tradigital animation is the result of traditional animation techniques translated by the use of digital tools. The end result may look traditional, but the process is very different and less time-consuming. When a client deadline is looming, traditional animation goes out the window. A common argument among traditionalists is that tweens are too easy to use and often become relied upon for every aspect of an animation. Dependence on tweens alone may result in your animation looking very mechanical and stiff. So where do you draw the line (sorry, bad pun)? What technique should you use? Motion tweens? Shape tweens? Frame by frame?

Answer: All of the above. Don't limit yourself to just one technique if you don't have to. Use the technique that the action calls for, even if it means combining two or more techniques. What is so impressive about this particular technique is the fluidity of the movement you can achieve. Draw image "A" and then image "B" with the Line (or Pencil) tool; then with each line segment on its own layer, shape tween from "A" to "B." Merge all your layers, clean up your lines, add some fills and shading – voila! You're a "tradigitalist."

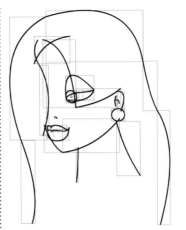

1 For this technique to be a success, you need two different drawings of your character or object. Object Drawing mode is highly recommended here as each stroke will remain as a separate object that can still be edited. It is also critical because you will later distribute each stroke to its own layer.

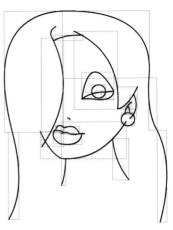

2 Insert a blank keyframe (F7) in a new frame (frame 30 will do), and draw the new angle of your character or object. The trick here is to use the same number of strokes as you did in the first drawing. You could also choose to insert a keyframe (F6) and edit the same strokes to reflect your new angle.

6 Make sure you have the Merge Layers extension installed (included with the downloaded example files). Make sure all layers and keyframes are selected and go to Commands > Merge Layers. This extension will run the JSFL command that will compress all keyframes and layers to one single layer for you.

7 You can delete all the old layers as they will all be empty after the merge. Go to File > Save As and save this file with a new name which is important because you may decide to make some changes to your image at some point in the future. After all layers are merged, making changes becomes very difficult.

3 For both drawings, select all of your strokes, right-click over them and select Distribute to Layers from the context menu. Since this process will create a whole new set of layers for each drawing, you will need to select all the keyframes for one drawing and drag them to the other drawing's layers.

4 Drag across all layers, right-click and select Create Shape Tween from the context menu. Previous versions of Flash didn't offer this option in the context menu. If you are using an older version of Flash, apply the Shape tween using the Properties panel or drop-down menus. Now is the time to add easing if preferred.

5 Next you need to prepare your layers for merging. Drag across all layers and frames, selecting them all in gold. Right-click over the highlighted area and select Convert to Frame-by-Frame Animation from the context menu to convert the entire animation to keyframes and remove the tween spans in a single command.

8 Next, you need to break apart strokes from the Object Drawing mode. Why? Because if you have overlapping strokes and want to add color fills to your image, it needs to be flattened one step further for editing. Turn on the Edit Multiple Frames feature and adjust the frame indicator brackets to span all keyframes. Break apart *ctrl* *B* to merge all strokes.

9 Use the Selection tool while holding down the Shift key to select all unwanted strokes and delete them. In this situation it is simply a fact of life that, as an animator, eventually you will have to perform the tedious chore of cleaning up after yourself or even worse, someone else's work.

10 As tedious as the last step was, here's your reward, a very slick looking animation that looks like it was made using three dimensions. But it gets even better when you add color and shading.

11 Once all your strokes are connected and cleaned up, mix your colors and start filling. You will need to apply all color fills across all keyframes by hand. Flash has no automatic way of doing this for you.

12 Occasionally you may find an area of your image will not accept the fill color. Usually the cause is a gap between strokes that is hard to see. Make sure Snap is turned on and use the Selection tool to drag their end points until they "snap" together.

13 Let's take this effect to the next level by adding shading. Add two new layers above your animation and draw two shapes in each new layer. Use the color black mixed with about 30% alpha. Make sure the brush has Smoothing set to 100. The fewer vector points the better.

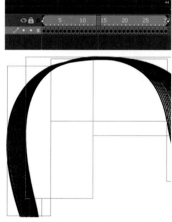

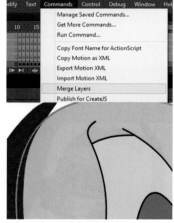

17 Turn on the Edit Multiple Frames feature and make sure the Frame Indicator brackets span all keyframes. Select all *ctrl* *A* and break apart *ctrl* *B* all Drawing Model objects to merge all the strokes together.

18 Copy all frames of your outline from the previous step and paste them into a new layer above your shading layers. Make sure all other layers are locked, turn on Edit Multiple Frames, select all strokes and change their color to bright red or something in contrast to the character itself.

19 Turn off Edit Multiple Frames, and unlock the two layers containing the shading animations. Select all frames across all three of these layers and go to Commands > Merge Layers to compress them down to one layer. Delete the remaining empty layers.

14 Insert a keyframe in both layers in your last frame of your animation. Move the left shape about 20 pixels to the left and the right shape the same distance to the right. Use the Selection tool to bend their outlines to reflect the new contour of your character and apply Shape tweens.

15 Remember the previously saved version of this animation? Open it and find the layers containing the outline strokes of your character. Select them and Copy/Paste Frames into a new document. You will use these strokes to "cut" away the shading you will not need.

16 Select all frames and layers, right-click over the highlighted area and select Convert to Frame-by-Frame Animation. Merge all layers using the Merge Layers JSFL extension (Commands > Merge Layers).

20 Use the Selection tool to click anywhere outside the shapes to deselect them. Select the shaded area outside of your character's outline and delete it. Repeat this procedure for every keyframe.

21 The final step is to double-click the red stroke (double-clicking selects all segments in the stroke), and delete it. Repeat this step for every keyframe until you are left with just the shading shapes inside the contours of the original character.

22 Next, test your movie and sit back to enjoy the fruits of your labor. This technique is great when you want to add some realism and drama to your shot. But remember to plan ahead carefully to avoid having to spend more time making revisions.

Brush animation

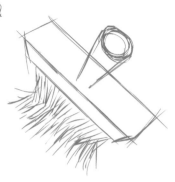

1 Coincidentally I used the Brush **B** tool to sketch the brush image at the angle shown above. At this stage I kept my drawings loose as I was only trying to achieve the basic motion of the brush.

2 With the Onionskin tool turned on I inserted a blank keyframe **F** **7** and sketched the brush at a slightly different angle. I started with circular butt end of the handle and continued drawing the rest of the brush.

ONE OF MY JOB RESPONSIBILITIES AS a Creative Director for GSN Games is creating Flash animations for our Flash game titles. For some of these animations I have created ambient effects such as explosions, flying birds, floating clouds and rolling fog to name a few. This example deconstructs the creation of a very specific effect animation for a solitaire game where a brush is needed to provide the transition effect for the game cards. As the game is launched and the cards are dealt across the screen, the brush is programmatically moved across the screen to "dust off" the back of the cards to reveal their face value. The original brush reference was drawn at a single angle and sent to me by our staff illustrator in the form of a layered Adobe Photoshop file. It was my job to envision the brush at a different angle and animate it as if it were directly in front of the user. This animation was one of the more complicated effects for me to create because it required several hours of hand-drawn animation combined with a little Flash ingenuity.

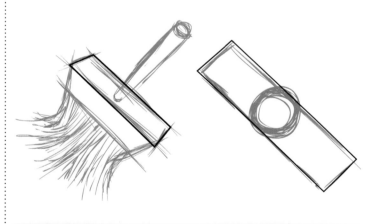

6 With the animatic stage completed I created a new layer. This next step borrows from the tradigital technique from the example on the previous pages. Concentrating on just one plane of the handle, I drew a rectangle using the Rectangle **R** tool with black as my stroke color and no color as my fill in frame 1. Using the Selection **V** tool, I clicked and dragged each corner of the rectangle to create the perspective using the sketch as my guide. In frame 10 I inserted a blank keyframe **F** **5** and drew another rectangle using just strokes in the shape of the plane with the sketch as a guide.

3 The next frame the brush was drawn at an angle where the butt-end of the handle is almost completely facing us. The top plane representing the body of the brush is almost facing us at a 90 degree angle.

4 Here the brush angle has rotated enough to see its opposite side.

5 The Onionskin tool is useful for making sure the alignment of the handle is in check during this phase. I used the circular end of the handle as my visual aid to keep the brush aligned throughout the rotation in each frame.

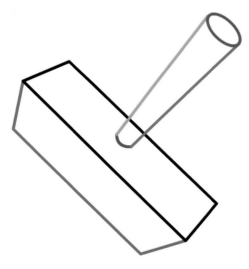

7 Repeat step 6 by inserting new layers for every new stroke or plane. To complete the body of the brush I used a total of 6 new layers. The different strokes for each layer are shown above in different colors for illustration purposes.

8 Here is how the timeline layers look at this stage of the process. Each layer contains a different segment of the brush. The reason for keeping the strokes on separate layers is to make it easy to animate each stroke using Shape Tweens in the following steps. In most cases a layer will contain more than 1 stroke segment which is OK. The idea is to limit the number of vector points to as few as possible to ensure the Shape tweens have a better chance of working in the next steps.

205

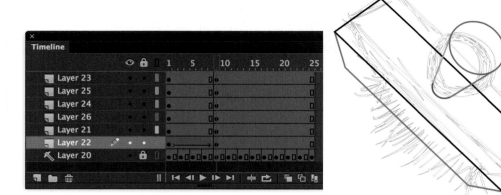

9 Keyframes are inserted across each layer on frame 9. This frame is where I want to have the tween span ultimately end. My decision to animate to this point is based on the angle of the brush in this frame. As seen above, the brush angle in the original sketch is at an angle right before it travels past its own axis. In the following frame we begin to see the opposite side of the brush as the handle moves past us down to the left. I know from experience that shape tweening vector points beyond this angle will be problematic. In an effort to worry about only the things I can control, I chose to animate the first half of the brush movement and worry about how to animate the latter half later.

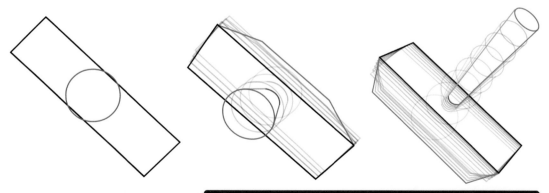

11 I continued the rest of the brush animation using the same process as described in the previous steps. Keyframes were inserted, lines were drawn and shape tweens were added using the original animatic as my guide. With the brush animation complete, my timeline consisted of mostly shape tweens and a few keyframes. Blank keyframes were the result of when the brush was at an angle where neither of its sides could be seen.

10 With each stroke in place on frame 10, apply shape tweens across each of the layers between the keyframes. Playback your animation to see the brush appear to change angle across a faux 3 dimensional space. At this point I chose to apply an easing in value of -100 to create a more realistic motion.

HOT TIP

I wasn't sure when I started this effect if it was going to work out or even look good. The important thing is to start somewhere and keep it simple. I enjoy challenging myself because with failure or success comes learning, either way.

12 The next step was to merge all the layers down to a single layer. The reason for merging is to have each stroke on the same layer so that the Fill **K** tool can be used to fill the closed shapes. To merge all keyframes across all layers manually would be painfully redundant work. Since Flash doesn't have a native feature for this specific task, we luckily have David Wolfe to thank for his handy Merge Layers extension that is available on his website *toonmonkey.com/extensions.html*. With the extension installed it can be accessed from the Commands menu. Select the entire range of frames and layers and then choose Commands > Merge Layers.

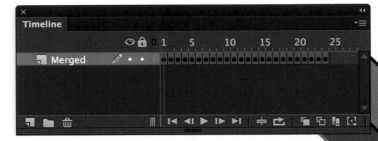

13 With all of the strokes merged into a single layer, I could now use the Fill **K** tool to add color to the brush handle. Here I mixed a couple of brown colors to add shading as well as a linear gradient for the handle to create the illusion of it being round. I manually added color to the brush on every keyframe.

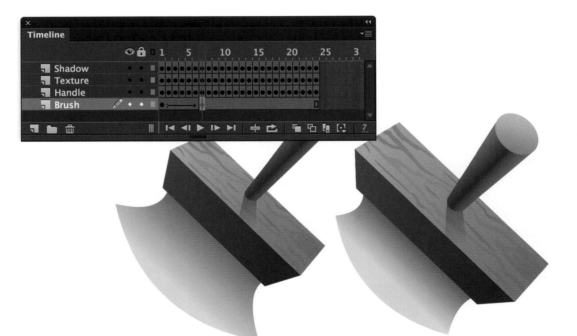

16 The next challenge was to create and animate the bristles of the brush. In an effort to keep things simple, I used the Rectangle **R** tool to draw a simple square fill. I then used the Selection **V** tool to manipulate the corners and sides to look like the shape in the image above. I inserted a keyframe **F 6** in frame 7 and using the Selection tool again I manipulated the shape as seen in the 2nd image above. I then applied a Shape Tween to these frames to animate the shape. The reason I limited the animation to 7 frames was to help prevent the shape tween from breaking apart which can happen when the shape is transformed too much from one frame to the next. The remaining bristles animation was created the same way using shape tweens across short sequences of frames.

14 Using the Selection **V** tool, I manually selected the strokes from each frame and deleted them, leaving behind just the fill colors.

15 Here I added some texture to simulate wood and a small shadow being cast by the handle to create a stronger illusion of this being a 3D object. This step was not necessary, but I like going the extra mile to take my animations to the next level.

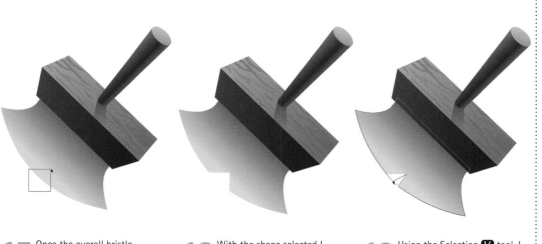

17 Once the overall bristle animation was complete, I selected all the frames in the layer across all the shape tweens and converted them to keyframes. Next I used the Selection **V** tool and selected a small portion of the shape.

18 With the shape selected I pressed the *Delete* key to create a notch in the shape allowing me to now manipulate it further.

19 Using the Selection **V** tool, I dragged the corners to create a thin notch as shown above.

20 Repeat steps 18 and 19 to add additional notches in the shape to create the illusion of bristles.

21 Go to the next keyframe in the timeline and repeat steps 18-20, but in this keyframe the notches should be slightly thinner.

22 In the next keyframe the same steps are applied, but the notches should be smaller and fewer in number. The idea is that the bristles are coming together and the spaces between them are going away over time.

26 The final step was to add the dust animation. Using the Brush **B** tool, I drew the dust as solid shapes using the brown color as seen above.

27 With each keyframe I drew the dust over again using the Onionskin tool as my guide. In this keyframe the dust is slightly smaller in volume

28 Over time the dust begins to disappear. The trick to making dust look real is to slowly animate the edge of the dust closest to the brush faster than the leading edge of the dust.

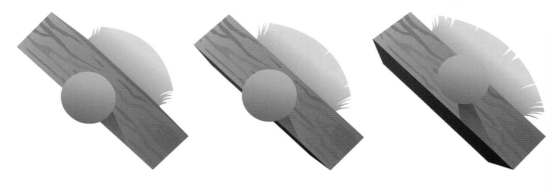

23 As the brush changes direction, so do the bristles. As the bristles extend away from the brush handle, the notches begin to appear. Repeat steps 18-20 to create the illusion of bristles once again.

24 In this keyframe I only needed to add a small number of notches. The animation is very quick during playback, and not much detail can be discerned by the human eye.

25 Here is the keyframe where the bristles are spread out the most. This frame contains the biggest notches and the largest number of them as well.

HOT TIP

Keep it simple! I was unsure how to animate the bristles and decided to start with a basic rectangle shape to make the animation process much simpler. Having drawn and animated each individual bristle would look realistic but is not necessary. The dust animation was also not very difficult because I kept it as simple solid shapes drawn with the Brush tool. The trick here was to not overthink the design.

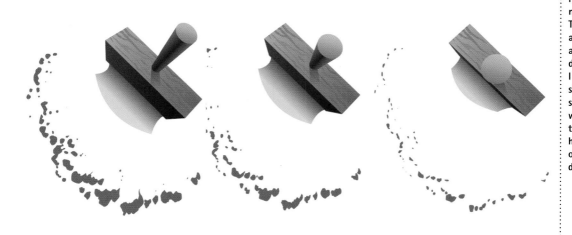

29 With the trailing edge of the dust moving faster, more of the dust particles break apart and start to disappear from the direction where they are originating from.

31 Here the dust is mostly small blobs, continually getting smaller and breaking apart.

32 In the final keyframe the dust is almost completely gone. Open the example file if you haven't done so already, and in the last scene you will find the dust animation.

Embracing challenges

"Absolutely! That shouldn't be a problem. I'll get started right away."

I was totally lying.

That's how I ended many phone conversations at the start of a new client project. I remember sounding very confident and convincing. I even made myself believe in me. But in full disclosure, I often had absolutely no idea how I was going to execute what the client wanted. Upon hanging up the phone I would enter panic mode. What the client asked for and how I was going to create it was a complete mystery to me. I couldn't fathom how to draw a straight line from concept to final execution and do so within a specified duration of time as requested. I was in way over my head with multiple clients throughout a large portion of my design and animation career.

This was exactly where I wanted to be.

I'm not sure why I enjoyed this masochistic approach to my design career. Common sense should have prevailed as I could have politefully declined these jobs and perhaps even helped each client by referring someone else more capable. It was arguably an irresponsible act accepting a client job as it could've hurt my career and reputation if I was unable to deliver what the client expected of me. It was, for all intents and purposes a selfdestructive work style.

But I became a better designer and animator because of it. Somehow I found ways to complete each project successfully and meet the clients' expectations, if not exceed them. Taking on these kinds of challenges forced me to push myself beyond my comfort zone. I had to be inventive and take risks.

I'm no athlete, but I do recognize that athletes perform better as a result of pushing themselves beyond their limits. A long distance runner starts his journey one mile at a time. The only way to complete a marathon is to push the limits of how far he can run which was also my approach as a designer and animator. I never accepted complacency because it was boring. Playing it safe was a dull place to be. Taking on design challenges that were seemingly impossible was like inspirational fuel. It was exciting and scary all rolled up into a ball of determination that kept me focused and above all, challenged.

The best way to improve your skills as artists, designers and animators is to push yourself beyond what you think you are capable of. Failure is always a possibility, but we learn from our mistakes. I know my limitations, and I have many. But I used these limitations to push myself by finding different ways to solve problems.

■ Surprisingly, the most impressive of Flash effects are often the simplest to create. The above characters are animated running in place as a looped sequence. It looks cool as it is but if you copy and paste an instance of it, flip it vertically and lower its opacity, you can achieve the sense that the surface they are running on is reflective and maybe even a bit slippery.

Animation examples

I HAVE SPENT MY FAIR SHARE OF TIME ON VARIOUS
Flash online forums, reading, learning and providing
my own perspective when needed. As a result, I've seen
what animation techniques and examples Flash users are
always requesting. I will often create a sample FLA and
make it available for everyone to download and dissect
for themselves. It's very difficult to teach design and
animation in text format and, often, a simple FLA can
make all the difference.

This chapter contains some of the most popular "How
do I..." animation requests from Flash users as far back
as Flash version 4. If this chapter teaches you one thing,
I hope that it teaches you how to think differently about
how you approach Flash as a tool.

Super text effect

S O OFTEN THE SIMPLEST
animation technique is the
most effective visually. Take this
website introduction for Superbusy
Records as an example of simplicity
at its finest and how to get the most
bang for your buck with the basics of
Flash animation. The text animation
is comprised of basic Motion tweens
and scaling, and the bee animation
takes advantage of some old-school
blurring with a linear gradient. Timing
is everything and the fast-paced
editing of this animation makes it
look more complicated than it truly is.

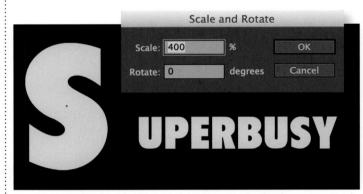

1 Start off with a text field set to Static and type in your text. Nothing fancy here, just some basic text to get you started.

Scale and Rotate

Scale: 400 %   OK

Rotate: 0 degrees   Cancel

4 Select all layers on a frame somewhere down the Timeline (frame 30 will do) and insert a keyframe for every layer by hitting the F6 key. Go back to frame 1 and select your first letter. Use the Scale and Rotate *ctrl* *alt* **S** to scale it to 400% or greater.

7 The bee graphic is introduced using a simple linear gradient first; then the bee "pops" into position.

2 Break apart the text field once using ⌘ B ctrl B and each letter will be broken apart but still editable. Break apart twice to convert your text to raw vector shapes. Your text will no longer be editable once broken down this far. You can choose to break apart only once if you think you might want to edit the text at a later time.

3 Select each letter individually and convert each to a Graphic symbol. Once all letters are converted, select them all, right-click over them and select Distribute to Layers from the context menu.

5 Apply a Motion tween to animate this letter scale from 400% to 100%. Select the keyframe in frame 30 and move it to around frame 5. Play back to test the speed based on your frame rate. Adjust the tempo as necessary by adding or removing frames in the Motion tween.

6 Repeat this procedure for each letter. Then stagger each letter's animation by sliding the Motion tween down the Timeline so each letter animates into place one after the other. Your Timeline tweens should resemble a staircase.

8 The bee is a Movie Clip containing a very simple, two-framed animation of the wings. The original wing is replaced with a radial to provide the illusion that it is blurred because it is moving faster than our eye can see.

9 The blur animation is comprised of only two frames with the radial gradient slightly rotated between them. The looping of these two frames at 30 frames per second is enough to convince us that they are oscillating at a very high speed. Adding the appropriate sound effect makes it even more convincing.

217

Page turn

1 Start with a simple rectangle with a linear gradient fill or your own color fill preference. Convert it to a Movie Clip symbol and apply a drop shadow filter to add a little depth.

2 Duplicate the cover symbol, and place it on a new layer above the original. Edit the graphic inside by filling it with a different color. Add some text or an image of your choice.

PAGES THAT CURL UP AND AWAY to reveal more pages are always an appealing effect (see what I did there?) for introducing content on your website or as buttons to other web pages. There are variations created entirely with ActionScript, but my AS skills are not anywhere near the level required to generate this effect dynamically. But that doesn't mean you can't add some interactivity by placing this animation in a Movie Clip and controlling its playback when the mouse rolls over it. For more robust and dynamically controlled page flip effects, check out:

http://page-flip.com/

http://www.flashpageflip.com/

http://www.pixelwit.com/blog/page-flip/

6 Insert a new layer and create a triangular shape that resembles a page curl similar to the example above. The easiest way to make this shape is to start with a rectangle. Turn on the Snap tool and drag one corner until it snaps to another corner. Now that you have made a triangle, move the remaining three corners into the positions as seen in the above example.

7 Mix a linear gradient using three colors. The first and last color swatches should be the brightest and similar in value. The middle swatch should be the same color but darker in value. Fill the curl shape and use the Gradient Transform tool **F** to rotate and position the gradient so its bottom edge shows a slight amount of the lightest value.

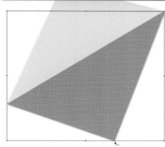

3 Insert a new layer again above your existing layers. Convert it to a mask layer and draw a shape that spans the lower right corner. Insert a keyframe in frame 30 so that a duplicate of this shape is created.

4 Select the shape in frame 1. With the Free Transform tool **Q**, position the center point at the bottom corner. Hold down **⌥ alt** and scale the shape until it is very small.

5 Holding down **⌥ alt** will constrain the shape based on its center point. Apply a Shape tween so the shape grows from small to large. This animation will reveal the content page.

HOT TIP

You can duplicate this effect to create additional page curls, allowing the user to turn more pages to reveal more content. Nest the page curl animation into a Movie Clip symbol and drag multiple instances of it to individual layers. With some basic ActionScript, you can control the page turns during runtime in the Flash player.

8 Convert the shape from step 7 to a Graphic symbol and double-click it and add a new layer inside this new symbol. Create another shape in this new layer using the rectangle tool for the shadow created by the page curl. This shadow will be cast onto the page below, so draw the shape to span only the area necessary inside the content page.

9 Fill this shape with a linear gradient consisting of two colors. Mix about 50% alpha into the first color and 0% alpha into the second color. Use the Gradient Transform tool **F** to rotate the shadow so that it fades away from the curl. Convert both shapes to a Graphic symbol.

10 Animate the curl just as you animated the mask in steps 4 and 5. Insert a second keyframe in frame thirty and select the curl graphic in frame 1. With the Free Transform tool, move the center point to the lower corner, hold down **⌥ alt** and scale it until it is the same size as the mask shape in this frame. Apply a Motion tween.

219

Smoke with gradients

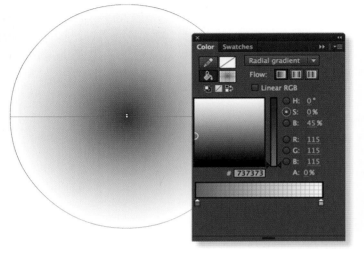

THERE ARE SEVERAL WAYS TO animate smoke and each technique is based on the style of the smoke itself. Do you need your smoke to be a cartoon style smoke cloud? Maybe you want a more realistic billowing of soft puffy clouds? How about a very stylized smoke effect with curling hard-edged shapes simulating the basic movement of smoke? There are many different ways to achieve the same results in Flash, whether it's with ActionScript or animation. Flash has always been a blank canvas for us to express ourselves. Let's take a look at a few ways to approach the dynamics of the smoke cloud.

1 Create a radial gradient with a dark gray center and the outer color mixed with 0% alpha. Create a circle with the Oval tool ⬤ with this gradient as your fill color (no stroke). Convert this shape to a Graphic symbol.

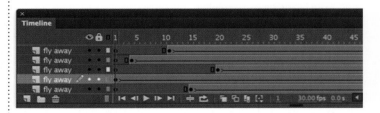

4 Select the entire Motion tween, copy all frames and keyframes, insert a new layer and paste all frames into it. Select the graphic in the first frame and move it a few pixels in any direction. Do the same for the Graphic symbol in the last keyframe. Select the entire Motion tween and drag it down the Timeline a few frames. Repeat this procedure until you have several layers of slightly different animations of your gradient starting small and rising while fading out completely.

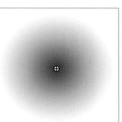

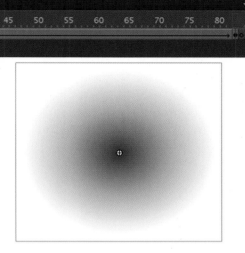

2 Select the Graphic symbol and convert it to a Movie Clip symbol. Double-click this Movie Clip to enter edit mode. This is where the animation will take place.

3 Insert a second keyframe several frames down the Timeline. Scale the Graphic symbol to about 200% and move it up about 75 pixels. Apply a Motion tween.

HOT TIP

The Blur filter, when used excessively, can cause potential performance issues during playback. Test your animation frequently to avoid causing a processor intensive animation. Remember, the Flash player is not like pre-rendered video format. Flash renders on the fly in the Flash player, so too high a frame rate combined with complex animations can demand too much from the player. Optimize your shapes whenever possible and use a realistic frame rate.

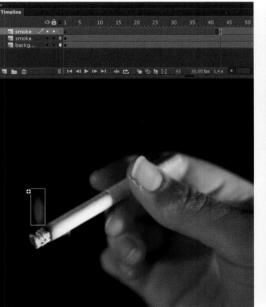

5 On the main Timeline, copy and paste the Movie Clip containing your "smoke" animations to a new layer. Drag the keyframe to a frame later in the Timeline; frame 25 will work fine. Select the instance and flip it horizontally to help change its appearance from the original.

6 Since the animation is inside a Movie Clip, it is best to stop the Timeline once the second instance is introduced on the Timeline by adding a stop action. The Movie Clip instances will continue to play and loop. Since they start on different frames, they will overlap to produce a constant flow of smoke.

221

Smoke stylized

1 The easiest way to start is with the final shape you will want as your stylized smoke shape. This shape can be drawn with any of Flash's drawing tools. I recommend no outlines stroke.

2 Insert a keyframe (F6) in frame 2 and, with the Lasso tool, select a small section at the top end of the smoke shape and delete it.

STYLE WILL ALMOST ALWAYS DICTATE THE animation technique. Often the client will request a specific artistic style based on a pre-existing logo or company identity. The challenge here is to be consistent, not only with the artwork but also with the animation style. A realistic smoke animation would look nice but not match the client's style preference. It's time to be inventive and to create a smoke animation that is stylized, yet simple and effective. Oh, and the client needs it yesterday.

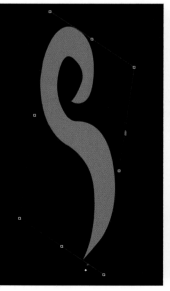

6 Copy and paste all frames into a Graphic symbol so it can be re-used later. Create a second keyframe down the Timeline and, with the Free Transform tool, skew it and move it up about 30 pixels.

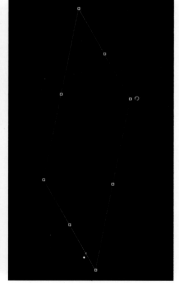

7 Create a third keyframe further down the Timeline and adjust the alpha to 0% so it fades out. Apply another Motion tween and maybe a little more skewing.

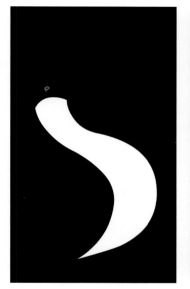

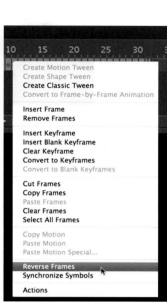

3 Repeat the process of inserting a keyframe and selecting a small section of your shape and deleting it. Use your keyboard shortcuts to make this task faster and easier.

4 Toggle between F6 and the Delete key while selecting sections of your shape until it has been completely removed from your stage.

5 Select the entire range of keyframes and then right-click over them to bring up the context menu. Select Reverse Frames. This will reveal your shape when you play back your animation.

HOT TIP

As you work through this example, you may realize at some point that you are creating a pretty sophisticated frame-by-frame animation sequence that looks like it was made by the hand of a very experienced animator. That's our little secret. You may choose to use the Eraser tool instead of the Lasso tool and avoid having to use the Delete key entirely. If you have a pressure-sensitive tablet and a stylus with an eraser on one end, you may have the fastest way to pull off this technique.

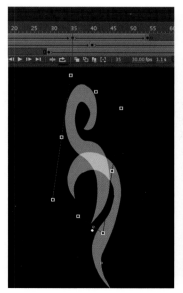

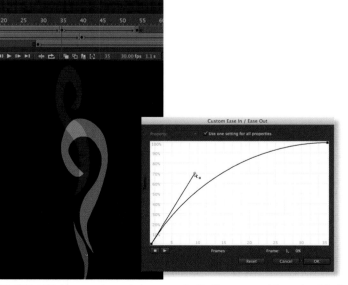

8 Add another layer and drag an instance of the same symbol (containing your animated shape) to the stage. Flip it horizontally and repeat steps 6 and 7.

9 Add a third layer and repeat steps 6 and 7 again. Play back your animation frequently and adjust the amount of skewing, tweening and the overall timing as necessary.

10 You may want to apply a bit of easing out to the symbols as they fade away. Although it may not be necessary, it might just add that final touch to your overall effect.

Full steam ahead

FILTERS ARE ANOTHER GREAT WAY to create realistic smoke or, in this example, steam. Since the image we are working with is an actual photograph, the animation needs to be just as convincing. Without the presence of steam, this cup of tea looks cold and somewhat unappealing. Not only can you use filters to blur objects in Flash, but you can also animate these filters.

1 Start off by drawing some simple shapes with the Brush tool. They should be random and abstract.

2 Select this shape (or shapes) and convert it to a Movie Clip symbol. With this symbol still selected, convert it to a Movie Clip once again so you end up with two Movie Clips, one nested inside the other.

6 Select the Movie Clip instance in the second keyframe and apply another Blur filter. Increase the amount of blurring so it is slightly more than the blurring in the first keyframe.

7 Select the Movie Clip instance in the third keyframe and apply another Blur filter. Increase the amount of blurring even more than you applied in the second keyframe.

3 Double-click the Movie Clip symbol on the main Timeline to edit it. Insert a second keyframe a few frames down the Timeline and scale the original Movie Clip symbol as shown above.

4 Insert a third keyframe down the Timeline and scale the Movie Clip even wider and position it a little higher.

5 Go back to the first keyframe and apply a Blur filter using the Filters panel (Window > Properties > Filters).

HOT TIP

Filters can only be applied to Movie Clip symbols and you must publish Flash Player version 8 or 9. Animated effects involving filters can be very processor intensive. Use them sparingly and test often to make sure playback performance remains acceptable.

8 Apply Motion tweens to all keyframes. Play back your animation and make adjustments as necessary. You may want to adjust the amount of blurring, alpha or transforming to your animation. You can also create a second steam animation by creating a new layer and drawing more shapes; convert them to a Movie Clip symbol and repeat steps 1 through 7. Then select and drag the entire range of keyframes and frames down the Timeline so they start after the original animation. This will help eliminate the repitition of one single looping steam effect.

Handwriting effect (frame-by-frame)

Flash

IN CHAPTER THREE I SHOWED YOU HOW to create the effect of text writing itself using a mask. While the mask technique yields a smaller file size, it doesn't look as realistic. At the expense of a few extra bytes, you can create a more realistic version of this effect with a little manual labor and patience.

1 The first step is to start with some text. You can either hand write this yourself using the Brush **B** tool or type some text using the Text **T** tool. This technique requires that the text be actual vector art. If you used the Text tool to type text into a text field, you will need to break it apart until it is actual vector art. To do this, select the text field and use **⌘ B** **ctrl B**.

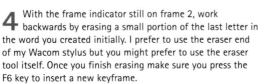

4 With the frame indicator still on frame 2, work backwards by erasing a small portion of the last letter in the word you created initially. I prefer to use the eraser end of my Wacom stylus but you might prefer to use the eraser tool itself. Once you finish erasing make sure you press the F6 key to insert a new keyframe.

5 Before moving on make sure you have inserted a new keyframe by pressing F6. I typically keep a finger at rest over the F6 key while I'm executing this technique. Make it a habit to erase, press the F6 key, erase more, press the F6 key and so on...

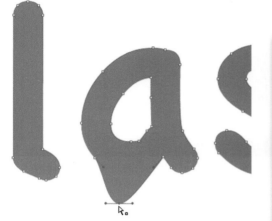

2 As you can see here, make sure your text field is broken apart until it is converted to vector art. Older versions of Flash required the text field be broken apart once while more recent versions require the text field be broken apart twice.

3 The next step is to insert a keyframe in the timeline on frame 2. Select this frame and press the F6 key. This is the frame where we will start animating.

HOT TIP

This technique can be very time consuming if you have a large block of text. It will also create a larger file size as each keyframe contains new artwork that will have to be loaded before it can be played if you are publishing to the web. Be aware of this and test your file often if bandwith issues are a concern. I also recommend working in a symbol or copy and paste this effect into a symbol so that it becomes a nested asset. Transforming an effect like this is best when it is contained inside a symbol.

Create Motion Tween
Create Shape Tween
Create Classic Tween
Convert to Frame-by-Frame Animation

Insert Frame
Remove Frames

Insert Keyframe
Insert Blank Keyframe
Clear Keyframe
Convert to Keyframes
Convert to Blank Keyframes

Cut Frames
Copy Frames
Paste Frames
Clear Frames
Select All Frames

Copy Motion
Paste Motion
Paste Motion Special...

Reverse Frames
Synchronize Symbols

Actions

6 Moving from right to left keyframing and erasing the text you will eventually get to the end where your text has been completely erased from the stage. If you scrub the Timeline from right to left you will see the effect take place.

7 The only thing left to do is select the entire range of keyframes, right click over them and select Reverse Frames from the context menu.

227

Fireworks

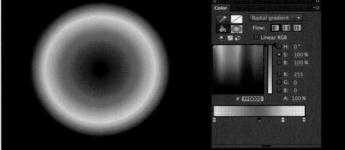

1 Start with a radial gradient with at least four colors. The middle and outer colors should be mixed with 0% alpha. The second and third colors are based on your own fireworks color scheme. Convert the gradient to a Graphic symbol.

EVERYBODY LOVES FIREWORKS. There's nothing like a warm summer night under the stars watching the skies light up with the brilliance of pyrotechnics. You can make every day the Fourth of July by animating your own fireworks display, and they'll be legal in every state. With some simple gradients, a little masking and some tweens, you'll be hearing "Oohs!" and "Ahhhs!" in no time.

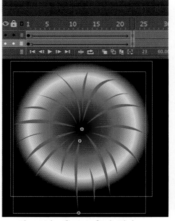

5 Insert keyframes for both layers somewhere down your Timeline and scale them both up about 300%. The gradient should be at least as big as the mask.

6 Insert two more keyframes much farther down the Timeline and scale both the mask and gradient about 125% more. Fade out the gradient to 0% alpha.

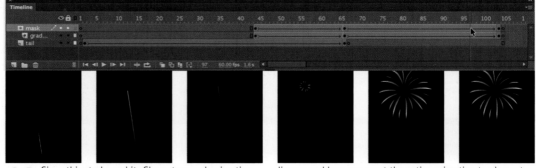

10 Since this stroke and its Shape tweened animation simulate the ascending explosive, you will need to slide the actual fireworks animation down the Timeline to make room for it. At this point, it comes down to artistic license and how you want the entire animation to play out. Here I have the ascent disapear just before the burst effect appears. The speed of the ascent can be adjusted by adding or removing frames during the Shape tween.

2 You need to create a mask that resembles the shape of exploding fireworks such as in this example. Convert it to a Graphic symbol.

3 Place the radial gradient in the masked layer so when the layers are locked, the gradient shows through the mask only.

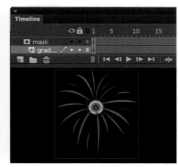

4 Scale both the mask and gradient in frame 1 so they are very small. Scale the gradient even smaller than the mask.

7 Lock both layers and play back or test your movie. You should have a pretty convincing fireworks explosion.

8 Draw a stroke and fill it with a linear gradient that contains two swatches mixed with 0% alpha at both ends.

9 Shape tween the gradient so it starts at the bottom of the stroke and ascends until it reaches the top and beyond so it disappears.

11 If you nest this animation in a symbol, you can duplicate it in the Library to create additional fireworks with different colors.

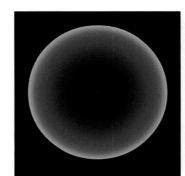

12 Edit the duplicate symbol(s) with a new radial gradient symbol. The darker the background, the more vivid the fireworks will be.

13 Drag multiple instances of your fireworks to the stage and start them on different frames to vary their timing.

Soft reveal

F LASH LACKS THE ABILITY to create masks with soft edges. When you use masks in Flash, you are limited to a hard edge, even if the mask contains a gradient with one color mixed with 0% alpha. Perhaps someday a future version of Flash will support masks with feathered edges. Until then, we need a workaround. So far the only solution I have been able to come up with is not even a mask at all. It's a simple gradient with at least one color mixed with 0% alpha. In the end, the effect is successful because it is what the viewer doesn't see that convinces them visually.

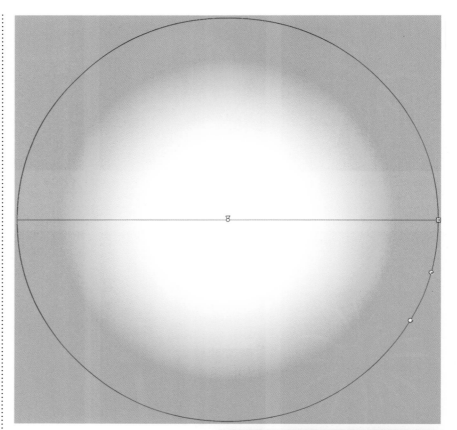

1 Start with a radial gradient (shown here with orange for clarity) with two colors. The outer color should match the solid color background which you will need for this effect to work. The middle color should be mixed with 0% alpha to make it completely transparent.

Use the Rectangle tool **R** to make a very large shape with this radial gradient as your fill color.

2 Convert this rectangle to a symbol and place it on a layer above the image you want to reveal. Scale the rectangle large enough so you can see the entire image through the middle color that you made transparent.

In frame 1, position the rectangle so that the image below it is completely obscured from view. This is if you want to start your animation by revealing the image over time.

HOT TIP

This effect can be achieved not only with a radial gradient, but also a linear gradient. It depends on your needs of course, but a feathered edge can always be achieved if your animation contains a solid color background.

3 Create a second keyframe somewhere down the Timeline and position the gradient so that the image below it is clearly seen through its transparent center. Apply a Motion tween and play back your animation.

Star Wars text

TEXT EFFECTS ARE ALWAYS a popular request among Flash users - specifically the "Star Wars" effect made famous during the opening scene in the original 1977 film. The effect is relatively simple to create but comes with a price: playback performance can suffer. Proceed with caution and test your animation often. Remember, the text must be legible without giving the reader a headache.

This is how to make a "Star Wars" style opening text effect. It ain't too hard once you know how. This is how to make a "Star Wars" style opening text effect. It ain't too hard once you know how. This is how to make a "Star Wars" style opening text effect. It ain't too hard once you know how. This is how to make a "Star Wars" style opening text effect. It ain't too hard once you know how. This is how to make a "Star Wars" style opening text effect. It ain't too hard once you know how. This is how to make a "Star Wars" style opening text effect. It ain't too hard once you know how. This is how to make a "Star Wars" style opening text effect. It ain't too hard once you know how. This is how to make a "Star Wars" style opening text effect. It ain't too hard once you know how. This is how to make a "Star Wars" style opening text effect. It ain't too hard once you know how. This is how to make a "Star Wars" style opening text effect. It ain't too hard once you know how. This is how to make a "Star Wars" style opening text effect. It ain't too hard once you know how. This is how to make a "Star Wars" style opening text effect. It ain't too hard once you know how.

1 Start by typing your block of text. Try to use a simple and bold font that is easy to read. You will be transforming this text and animating it. Since it will be constantly moving, priority should be making sure it is legible and easy to read for the viewer. Select your text field and break it apart until the text becomes raw vector shapes. The amount of vector information will be substantial and will most likely cause some performance issues during playback. This is another reason to choose a font that is as simple and clean as possible as it will produce fewer vector points.

3 Insert a new layer and convert it to a guide layer. Make sure the layer containing your text is not "guided" or linked to it. You can drag the guide layer below your text layer to prevent them from being linked together. Anything on a guide layer will not be included in the exported SWF. Flash CS5 offers a nice feature that provides the option to export or not export hidden layers. This option is accessible by going to File > Publish Settings > Flash tab. On this layer use the Line tool to draw a stroke at the same angle as your text field. Copy and paste it in place, flip it horizontally and position it on the opposite side of your block of text.

4 Add a second keyframe and scale your text until it fits inside your guides at their smallest point. You will need to insert several frames between these two keyframes and apply a Motion tween.

2 The next step is to simulate the perspective needed to provide the illusion that the text is receding. Select the Free Transform tool **Q** and then the Distort (subselection) tool. While holding down the **Shift** key, drag one of the upper corners horizontally towards the middle of the

text. Holding down the **Shift** key constrains the proportions of the transformation by distorting the adjacent corner in the opposite direction. Convert this block of text to a Graphic symbol. If you have several blocks of text, it might be best to keep them as smaller individual symbols.

5 The final step actually breaks the one and only perspective rule this animation relies on. I also think it is the most important step since it really helps provide the illusion of the text disappearing into infinity, yet it is so simple. In the very last frame of the tween, select the symbol containing the text field and, using the Free Transform tool, scale it vertically using one of the two middle handles along the top or bottom edge. In essence you will be squashing

the symbol to make it flatter (do not widen it). For smooth playback, you will need a combination of hundreds of frames and a high frame rate. The exact amount depends on the amount of text, the font style and how large (width and height) your movie is. The larger the movie, the more processor intensive it will be. Any animated effect that uses a combination of these factors can cause poor playback performance. Test often and know your target audience.

HOT TIP

You could try this effect with a block of text made in Photoshop that is distorted in the same perspective. Import the text as a bitmap with the same solid color background as your Flash movie. It may result in a more processor-friendly animation sequence but will suffer from loss of quality when scaled. Flash doesn't scale imported bitmaps very well and the results may not be visually appealing. The trade-off is using crisp vector text with some possible performance issues during playback. Testing often is your best defense.

Color adjustments

BEFORE FLASH 8 introduced filter effects, advanced bitmap effects meant having to spend time outside of Flash editing several duplicates of the original image. Depending on the desired effect(s), several different versions of the same image would have to be created and imported into Flash. With Flash CS3 - CS5 and now CC, this process is much easier. Using only one single bitmap image and the Adjust Color filter, you can create some striking color effects with minimal time and effort. The advantages of using this filter technique include smaller file sizes and faster results that can be mixed with any of the other filters.

1 To convert a full color image to grayscale, slide the Saturation slider all the way to the left.

2 Click the Reset button in the Filters panel to return each color setting to "0".

3 To adjust the overall color hue of your image, use the Hue slider. Here the Contrast and Saturation have been slightly adjusted as well.

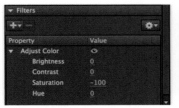

1 The imported image here has been blurred and adjusted using the Blur and Adjust Color filters.

2 Here the Saturation and Hue have been increased as well as the Contrast.

3 Here's the original image without any filtered effects.

4 Each of these color adjustments can be keyframed and Motion tweened to create smooth color transitions.

5 Any of these color effects can be visually effective when introducing images for a variety of uses.

6 You can also add some basic ActionScript to control color changes when the user rolls over various menu buttons.

Property	Value
▼ Adjust Color	⊙
Brightness	−38
Contrast	100
Saturation	100
Hue	52

Property	Value
▼ Adjust Color	⊙
Brightness	−34.6
Contrast	91.2
Saturation	91.2
Hue	−164.1

Property	Value
▼ Adjust Color	⊙
Brightness	−38
Contrast	56
Saturation	−75
Hue	−71

HOT TIP

You can copy a filter effect by clicking on the "Copy Filter" button in the Filter panel. Then you can paste it to another Movie Clip instance elsewhere in your Flash document.

235

Vertigo

CAUTION: THIS EFFECT may cause temporary headaches and possibly some minor nausea if stared at too long.

Well, perhaps it won't cause sickness, but it's a great effect for representing vertigo: a balance disorder that causes a spinning sensation. If you're familiar with Alfred Hitchcock's film *Vertigo* you will already be familiar with how this visual effect can be used to show something or someone spinning out of control. With animation, it can also represent time travel, a wormhole or even the beginning of a dream sequence or hallucination.

1 The success of this effect is in the one single graphic: the spiral. It was created in Adobe Illustrator using, you guessed it, the Spiral tool. Flash does not have a tool like this so Illustrator proved to be a huge time saver. Of course you can always draw this spiral graphic by hand using the support of a pressure-sensitive stylus, but that would certainly require a very skilled hand.

3 This is a great effect to place a character or an object on top of. Place the object in a Movie Clip symbol and rotate it in the opposite direction as your swirl. This will enhance the effect by providing the illusion of the object traveling through time or space and may even induce some minor headaches and nausea.

2 Convert your spiral graphic to a symbol. Insert a second keyframe about 100 frames from the first keyframe. Apply a Motion tween. Of course nothing will happen on playback because no change has been made to either instance of the spiral. Select a frame anywhere along the Motion tween and in the Rotate drop-down menu, select CW (clockwise) or CCW (counter-clockwise). Type in the number of rotations desired.

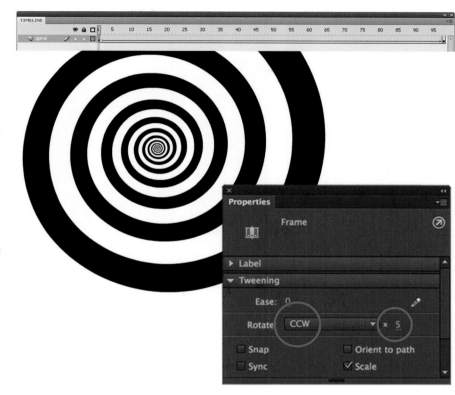

4 It's time to have some fun! Change the colors of your spiral and then select the character or object (make sure it is in a Movie Clip) and experiment with some of the Blend Modes available from the Properties panel. There are some interesting effects to play around with here that may provide some cool results.

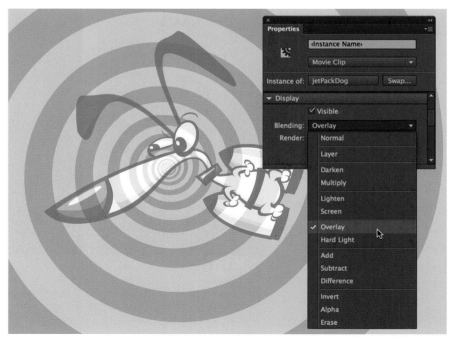

Let it rain

1 Use the Brush tool to draw your rain drop. Gravity suggests that the shape of the drop is thicker and rounder at its bottom. Fill your raindrop with a solid color or a radial gradient for some extra realism. This is a style choice for you to decide.

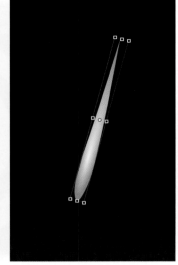

2 Convert your drop to a Graphic symbol and rotate it slightly. The amount of rotation is up to you based on how strong a rain storm you want to have. The more angle your rain has, the more wind is suggested.

THERE ARE SEVERAL WAYS TO APPROACH animating rain, probably because rain falls in several ways depending on wind conditions. I chose an average style of falling rain that can easily be expanded upon based on your own needs.

Rain, to our advantage as animators, is repetitive. Reusing assets is one of the strengths of Flash. You only need to animate one raindrop and then populate your scene with multiple instances of it. You can then control how your rain acts by adjusting the angle at which it falls, its speed and how many instances of it appear at any given time.

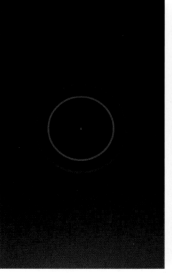

6 Copy all frames of your circle animation. Insert a new layer and paste the frames into it. Select all the frames in this new layer and drag them about five frames further down the Timeline.

7 Navigate back to the main Timeline and transform your water drop symbol (containing its animation) by dragging the middle handle along the top or bottom edge (Free Transform tool).

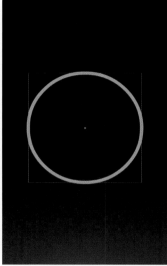

3 Insert a keyframe further down the Timeline. In frame 1, position the drop outside of the stage. In your second keyframe, position it near the bottom of your stage area. Apply a Motion tween.

4 Let's create a ripple effect for the raindrop after it reaches its destination. Using the Oval tool *O*, draw a circle with a stroke color only. Hold down *Shift* to constrain its proportions. Convert it to a Graphic symbol.

5 Convert it to a Graphic symbol again and double-click it to edit it. Insert a second keyframe and Motion tween it from small to large over approximately ten frames. Select the instance in the last frame and apply 0% alpha so it fades out completely.

HOT TIP

Nature isn't perfect. You simply can't find lines in nature that are exactly horizontal or vertical. Rain is the same way in the sense that it rarely falls perfectly straight down. Even a slight breeze will cause raindrops to fall at an angle. You can suggest stronger wind conditions by increasing the angle and speed of your rain drops. Decreasing the angle and speed of your rain animation will suggest a light shower.

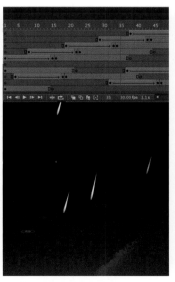

8 Place the symbol containing your ripple animation in a blank keyframe (F7) in the frame after your rain-drop animation. Position the ripple just below the raindrop in its last frame. Copy all frames in this layer.

9 Paste these frames into a new symbol. Add several layers and continue to paste your animation into each one. Select and drag each layer's animation so that they each start on their own unique frame number.

10 Now that you have a rain sequence nested in a symbol, drag as many instances of this symbol as you need to the stage. Scale them and even tint some darker to suggest more depth to your scene.

Playing with fire

N O FLASH ANIMATION BOOK IS COMPLETE without a topic involving fire. How many times have you ever wanted to animate fire and had no idea how to even approach it?
The first technique that comes to mind for animating flames is Shape tweening. It just seems like the appropriate choice because of the nature of fire and how flames dance and flicker. But in my experience, shape tweening doesn't seem to ever produce realistic results. Often, the shapes "implode" or simply morph in all the wrong ways. The effect of fire is simply not achievable using tweens.

Motion tweens are not an option for the obvious reason that they can only be applied to instances of symbols.

ActionScript might be a solution, but, if you are like me, your scripting skills are not up to the challenge of producing fire from within the Actions panel.

Don't be frightened by what I am about to say, but frame by frame is the best option for animating fire. Don't be fooled; it's not that hard or time-consuming.

1 Start by making several overlapping rectangles (with no stroke outline). Don't concern yourself with color at this stage of the process; any color will do.

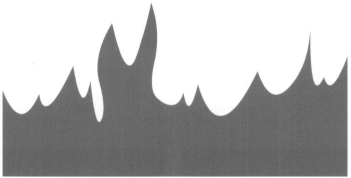

5 Ultimately your flames in frame 1 should look something like this. Try to alternate the direction of each flame. Fire is random and travels in unpredictable ways.

9 Create a Linear gradient using bright red and bright yellow as the two colors.

10 In each keyframe, select all and drag the Bucket tool vertically inside your flames to fill them. The gradient will follow the direction you drag in.

2 Use the Selection tool **V** to pull edges to create peaks.

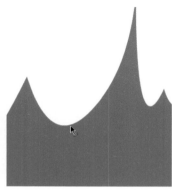

3 Fire is naturally unpredictable. Avoid repetition with your shapes.

4 Try to incorporate some shapes with "S"-shaped curves for some added realism.

HOT TIP

Art imitates life, and there's no substitute for studying the flames of a real fire. Just as Disney's animators went to Africa to study real animals in preparation for production of *The Lion King*, you should also study from life as much as possible. Although your budget may not allow for world travel, something like fire is a bit more accessible.

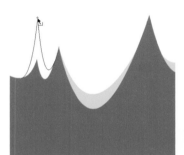

6 Insert a keyframe (F6) on frame 2, turn on Onionskin and begin editing the next frame by pulling each point higher and lower.

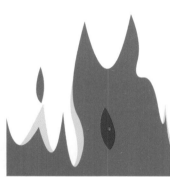

7 "Punch" holes in the flames by drawing different colored shapes and deleting them. Fire is not solid; it will break up as it rises into the air.

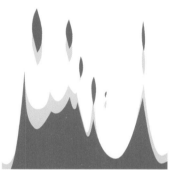

8 Continue to create keyframes and edit the shape of your flames in each one by pulling and pushing with the Selection tool.

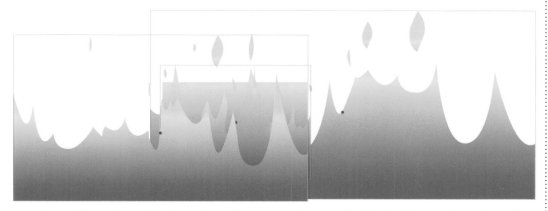

11 Copy all frames of your animation and paste them into a new Graphic symbol. Add three new layers to the main Timeline and drag instances of this symbol to each of them. Delete your original layer. Select one of the instances and flip it horizontally. Scale two of the instances so they are much wider than the stage. Position them off-center from the stage while leaving one of the instances at its original size and position. Create a background shape with the same linear gradient to make it look like the entire scene is ablaze.

Torch

CREATING ANIMATIONS FOR GAMES OFTEN requires creating short looping animations that do not generate large file sizes. These short looping animations work well when they can be reused over and over again throughout the game. This flame example was created for a game where the character carried a torch. The tricky thing about fire as we know from the previous example is that it is unpredictable. Animating elemental effects usually requires a hand-drawn technique because automated tools such as tweening are too consistent in their interpolation to be used for the creation of anything random, such as fire. But don't be intimidated by the thought of hand-drawing each frame because you can use the random nature of fire to your advantage.

1 The first frame is drawn using the brush tool **B** and a graphics tablet with pressure sensitivity. The idea here is to draw a single shape that has long whispy flame-like shapes coming off of it vertically. I try to make each flame different from the next with the tallest flames towards the center and the shorter flames to the sides.

4 Once you have a few frames drawn it is always a good idea to playback the animation in a loop to see how it is shaping up. You can loop the timeline within Flash by choosing Control > Loop Playback.

2 Here I have the original fire drawing on a layer that has been converted to outlines. In a new layer below it is where I draw the next fire drawing. Having the original drawing outline on the layer above helps me use it as a guide. Onionskin would normally be used in this situation but often times the current drawing will hide the edges of the drawing in the previous frame. With an image such as fire it is much easier to draw when you can see the entire outline of the previous drawing.

3 Fire is unpredictable. Keeping this in mind I try to draw the individual flames so that they are animating in different directions. If the flames move in a predictable way then it will not look unrealistic.

5 This flame animation required 7 individual drawings to complete the loop. The flame color was changed to white because the game background was black.

6 All frames were copied into a Movie Clip Symbol so I could apply a Glow filter. Using yellow as my glow color, adjust the amount of Blur and Strength to create a soft glow effect.

7 Test the movie to see the torch flame come to life complete with the glow filter for added effect.

243

Lightning

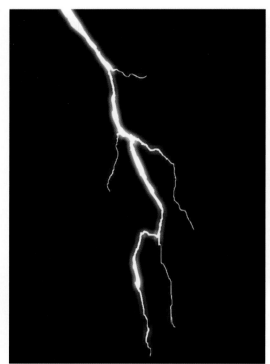

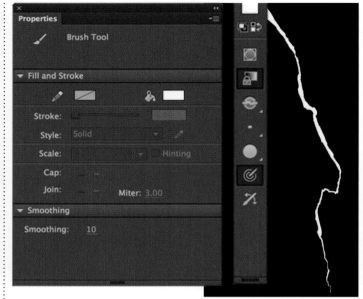

1 The main lightning bolt is drawn using the brush tool **B** and a graphics tablet with pressure sensitivity. Lowering the amount of smoothing helps achieve a realistic looking bolt due to the imperfections caused by the human hand. Nature is not perfect, and therefore your lightning bolt should have imperfections also. Try to vary the weight of the bolt as well as the direction it goes by drawing with a loose carefree hand.

LIGHTNING IS ONE OF THE EASIEST AND most fun elemental effects to animate. Lightning can be used in scenes for atmospheric effect, and it can be very effective to say the least. As an animator, I'm always trying to push my skills as far as they can go, and recently I've been trying to learn how to animate special effects. I've been taking a 2D animation effects course with Adam Phillips, and I highly recommend it. One of the first lessons is learning how to animate lightning and even though I already knew how, Adam's lesson provided me with new tips and tricks. This example is a combination of my own technique as well as what I learned from Adam. Learn more about Adam's course here: bitey.com/2010/08/bca-fx

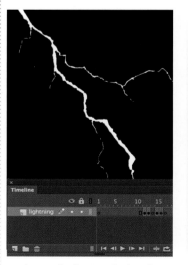

5 Insert a keyframe and select the eraser **E** tool. Carefully remove areas of the lightning bolt from the outside edges to create the illusion that it is breaking apart.

6 As an added effect, convert the first bolt of lightning to a Movie Clip symbol and then apply a Glow filter to it from the Properties panel.

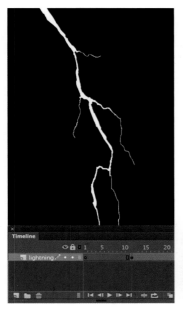

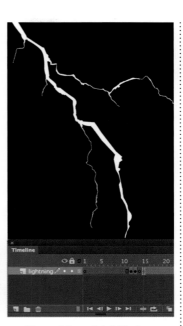

2 You can add thinner branches breaking off from the main lightning bolt itself. These branches are usually very thin so reduce the size of the Brush before drawing them.

3 The frame following the lightning should be completely white. This white frame creates a high contrast effect that leaves a residual image in the viewer's eye. It is a very powerful and easy effect to create.

4 The next frame is left blank, exposing just the black background. The frame after that contains a new lightning bolt drawing.

HOT TIP

Lightning is a very quick and simple animation technique that can easily be over-animated. Don't try and animate the lightning bolt into the frame by building it up over a sequence of keyframes. The entire bolt should "enter" the scene in a single frame, fully drawn. If you've ever had the opportunity to stand and watch a lightning storm on the horizon, then you've noticed that lightning bolts strike within the blink of an eye. Keeping it simple will yield the best results.

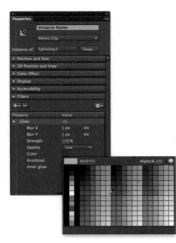

7 The color of the glow is entirely up to you. It can be almost any color depending on the subject matter. Green or blue can suggest a fantasy theme while red may look more real-world.

8 With the color selected, adjust the amount of blur and strength using the hot text sliders. It is easy to abuse the blur effect so remember that being subtle usually works better here.

9 Test the movie to see the lightning bolt in action.

Winter wonderland

L ET IT SNOW, LET IT SNOW, LET IT SNOW. CREATING constantly falling snow is fun. Like the rain example, snow can be animated several different ways. The easiest way is to Motion tween a snowflake symbol along a Motion Guide path. Other methods include using ActionScript-generated snow but don't ask me to show how that is done because I admittedly do not know how to write scripts on that level. Let's stick with my "analog" method of animating in Flash, shall we?

The more snow you create, the more processor intensive your animation becomes. Proceed with caution and test your animation frequently to make sure the constant looping snowfall doesn't cause unexpected playback issues. There's nothing worse than creating a cool animation only to find it skips and chugs during playback.

I highly recommend Chris Jackson's book **Flash + After Effects** (Focal Press) because he teaches you how to create snow in Adobe After Effects that is easily imported into Flash. His book contains a ton of other cool examples that you'll find very useful on a day-to-day basis.

1 Start with a snowflake design using the Line tool. It's hard to make a mistake here since there's no real way to create an incorrect snowflake pattern. Make one "arm" of the snowflake, convert it to a symbol or as an Object Drawing. Copy it using ⌘ C ctrl C and paste it in place using ⌘ Shift V ctrl Shift V, then rotate it 45 degrees. Repeat until you have pasted enough to complete the pattern.

4 Here's what your Movie Clip's Timeline should look like (give or take some frames or layers). Notice the *stop();* action in the last frame of the top layer. This prevents this Movie Clip from looping. Since all instances of the snowflake Movie Clip are present, they will loop by default.

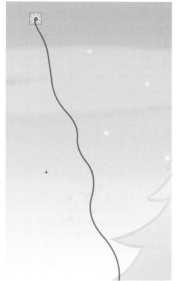

2 Convert your snowflake to a Graphic symbol and then convert the Graphic symbol to a Movie Clip symbol. Double-click the Movie Clip and edit it by inserting a Motion Guide layer. Draw a curvy stroke for the guide and Motion tween your snowflake along the path (traveling downward of course).

3 You now have a Movie Clip containing an animation of a snowflake tweened along a motion guide. Next, in your Library panel, create a new Movie Clip and insert several new layers. Drag an instance of your snowflake Movie Clip into each layer. Position each snowflake Movie Clip randomly throughout your scene. For each layer, select and drag the keyframe in frame 1 to a different frame number so they each start playing at different times. Make sure each snowflake animation begins outside of the viewable area of the stage.

HOT TIP

The length of the Motion tween in your guided snowflake can help make the difference between a soft snowfall or a blizzard. Experiment with the number of frames in your tween to get the best results for your particular animation. To animate a blizzard you would need to shorten the length of the Motion tween and populate the scene with an abundance of snowflake instances. You could even try making the Motion Guide path one big "S" turn to suggest a strong wind that is changing direction.

5 On the main Timeline, place an instance of your Movie Clip containing your snowflake Movie Clips onto the stage in its own layer. You can place multiple instances of this Movie Clip around your stage as many times as you like. But be aware that the more instances of the snowflake animations you have present on the stage, the more processor intensive your movie will be. If maintaining a high frame rate is your priority, you may want to experiment by using a simple oval shape for your snowflake graphic. Remember, fewer vector points means better playback.

3D perspective

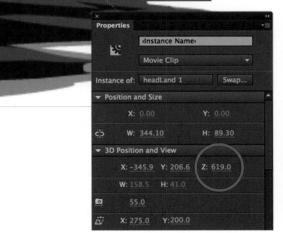

ADAM PHILLIPS IS BEST KNOWN FOR HIS AWARD-WINNING Brackenwood series: http://www.biteycastle.com/content/animation_brk.html. The rest of his animation is equally as brilliant and I highly recommend treating yourself to his entire website: http://www.biteycastle.com/ Adam has generously provided a couple of killer Flash examples that showcase Flash CC's 3D capabilities. Flash CC allows you to create 3D effects by moving and rotating movie clips in 3D space on the stage. Flash represents 3D space by including a *z axis* in the properties of each Movie Clip instance. You can add 3D perspective effects to Movie Clip instances by moving or rotating them along their *z axis* using the 3D Translation and 3D Rotation tools. Moving an object in 3D space is called a *translation* and rotating an object in 3D space is called a *transformation*. You can take advantage of this powerful new 3D feature for scenes like this one where the perspective of a landscape fly-over animation needs to look realistic.

1 Start with a simple background graphic that shows a clear horizon line. Here the sky and ocean are convincingly represented using 2 simple radial gradients. This simple illusion is created due to the alignment of the gradients vertically, thereby making our eye translate the bottom gradient as a reflection.

4 Verify the playhead is in the last frame of your tween span in the Timeline. Open the Properties panel and select the first Movie Clip symbol. Use the Z axis hot text slider in combination with the X and Y axis sliders to position your object off the bottom edge of the stage.

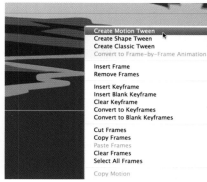

2 Next some background elements are added to provide depth to the scene. A mountain range divides the sky and ocean while some shoreline elements are positioned in the distance. The plan for this scene is to provide the illusion that we are flying towards the horizon along the shoreline. To set this up from the start, begin with your shoreline objects at their starting point, scaled down at their furthest point away from the "camera". Convert them to Movie Clip symbols.

3 Distribute each of these Movie Clip objects to layers, then right click over each of them and select Create Motion Tween. Do not use Classic tweens since they are not supported by the 3D Translation and Transformation tools. I recommend going to View > Pasteboard and making sure you can see beyond the stage area of your document. This will help you when positioning your objects beyond the viewable stage area.

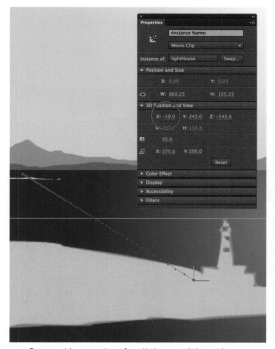

5 Repeat this procedure for all the remaining objects on the stage. You will also want to increase or decrease each tween span to adjust the timing of each object to prevent them from all moving simultaneously.

6 Adding the Gull animation to the foreground adds 2 important elements to the scene: it enforces the illusion of depth as well as something interesting to look at. Even though there's no "camera", upon playback, the human eye will perceive us as literally flying through the scene.

HOT TIP

It's worth noting that these 3D tools will not work with objects on mask layers. You can not convert a layer containing 3D objects to a mask layer either.

Sausage grinder

A POLOGIES IN ADVANCE TO ALL vegetarians. Sausage Kong is a Flash game developed by Thibault Imbert (Product Manager, Adobe Flash Player) and myself to help showcase the more advanced features of the latest Flash Player. This is the type of game that gets created when two guys go completely rogue and put their creative minds together sans a babysitter (and when I say "creative" I really mean "twisted"). The reason I chose the grinder animation for this example is because it takes advantage of several design and animation tools in Adobe Flash CC. From the Pencil tool to Motion and Classic tweens, you don't have to limit yourself to a single tool. It is often the combination of several techniques that make for a better product.

Thibault Imbert: www.bytearray.org

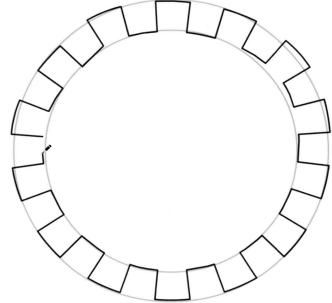

1 The gear was drawn using the Pencil tool **Y**. The light blue circles were used as my guide and drawn using the Oval **O** tool with an outline color only on a different layer below the actual gear layer.

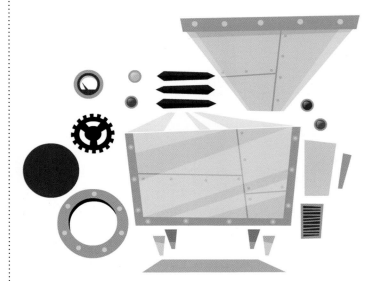

4 The important aspect to this animation is identifying the parts that need to move. Once identified, draw each part separately and convert them to symbols. Here is an exploded view of all the individual parts of the grinder.

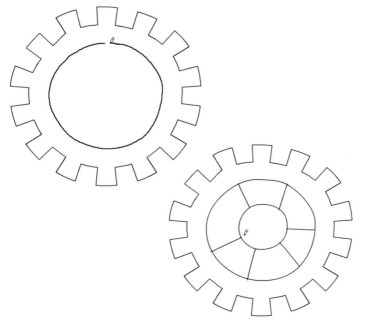

2 Using the pencil tool and the same stroke size, draw 2 inner circles and then attach them by drawing some support sections.

3 Select any overlapping stroke segments and delete them. You can then fill the gear with your color(s) of choice.

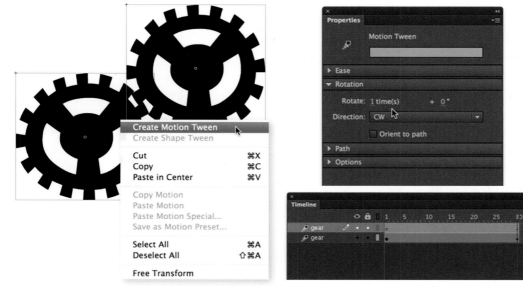

5 Convert the gear to a symbol and then copy and paste it to create a 2nd gear. Distribute each gear to its own layer. Right click over each one and select Create Motion Tween.

6 Select each motion span for each gear and in the Properties panel set each gear to rotate using the Rotation tools. Type in the number of rotations as well as the direction (clockwise or counter-clockwise).

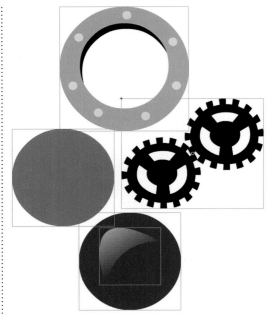

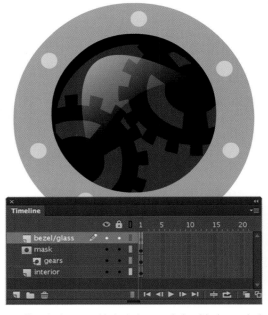

7 Both gear animations were converted to a single symbol. I wanted them to be viewed "inside" the grinder so I designed a porthole style window as separate assets. The red shape is the mask that limits the visibility of the gears to the window area only. The gray circle is the background color, the irregular shape seen on top of the gray shape is the window highlight and the bezel is shown at the very top.

8 Here is the assembled window porthole with the masked gears. You can see the layer ordering of each object in the Timeline. The irregular shape with the alpha gradient is the only artwork inside the bezel. There was no need to provide anything else as this small piece of art was enough to provide the illusion of glass.

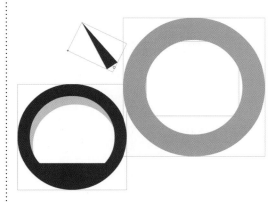

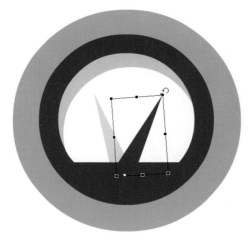

11 Here's the exploded view of the pressure gauge. Once again I have used very simple shapes to build this gauge keeping in mind that it will be scaled down quite small, so keeping it simple was crucial. The needle was kept as a separate object because I intended to animate it.

12 With each object distributed to layers I was able to animate the needle moving back and forth. Notice the center point was positioned at the bottom of the needle to allow it to rotate based on where it would be normally hinged.

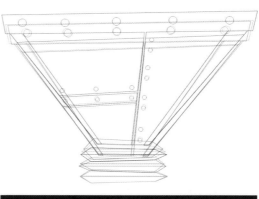

9 The meat catcher is made up of 4 different graphics, each converted to a symbol and is distributed to layers. An 8-frame animation was created of the catcher moving up and down in a slightly erratic nature. Those 8 frames were copied and pasted to lengthen the animation Timeline.

10 With the layers converted to outlines it becomes easier to see the subtle motions of the catcher between the frames. A combination of Motion and Classic tweens was used to create this effect.

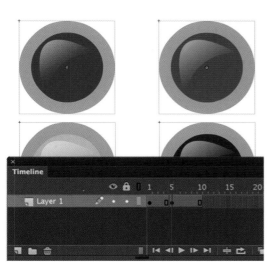

13 The flashing lights couldn't be simpler to create. The glass highlight was reused from the porthole (gears) example and the light flashing effect was simply a 2nd keyframe with a brighter "lens" color.

14 Here's the entire grinder assembled and in fine working order. Check out the source file on the website to see the entire animation.

HOT TIP

Usually several different short looping animations can create a more compelling experience than a single larger motion. I prefer to make everything move small amounts simultaneously, as opposed to animating the entire object as a single asset. It's a lot more work but usually provides a better result.

From the inside out

I AM A DIGITAL ANIMATOR. A "DIGIMATOR" IF YOU WILL. I LEARNED how to animate on a computer, which is inherently different than the traditional animation process. Sure, it shares some similarities when it comes to animation techniques, but ultimately any animation program can have a mechanical feel to it since we work by selecting options from menus much of the time. The trick I have learned is how to make a software program like Flash feel more organic, as if it were a ball of clay, starting with a basic shape and pushing and pulling it into something unique. Just because the Help docs, online resources or even other books tell you how something can or should be done, don't take that as carved in stone. Take it as carved in clay, meaning you can continue to expand upon the ways the tools are used, even beyond what you may have read elsewhere. If 100 people were given their own ball of clay, they would all create something unique.

Many years before Flash even existed, I studied everything from art history to sculpture, color theory to lithography and, above all, how to draw. This combination made the progression to the world of computer graphics and animation tremendously helpful. I feel just as comfortable with a mouse or stylus in my hand as I do with pencil, paintbrush, airbrush or printing press. Each tool is just as powerful as the other. A quick and loosely sketched pencil drawing can have just as much impact visually as a full-blown animated action sequence that took three months to complete. It's the subject matter that counts and this applies to Flash as well.

Several people have asked me why I am so forthcoming with my home-grown tips and techniques and why I'm not afraid that many will use them to emulate my own personal style. As with the ball of clay metaphor, everyone is different, and therefore everyone will express themselves in a unique fashion whether it's through a ball of clay or an animation program like Flash.

I have spent several years adopting and inventing Flash drawing and animation techniques. This book will show you different ways of approaching Flash and how to make it work for you. Whenever possible, I will try and avoid explaining what is readily available in the Help docs and the multitude of online resources. You bought this book for a reason, to learn what isn't found anywhere else. You will get a first-hand look at how I create characters and motion graphics from scratch, and learn how Flash, as a tool, can be pushed and pulled, limited only by your imagination.

My philosophy with tools like Flash is to learn as much as I can, then go back to the first 10% of what I learned and take a left turn.

■ Having the ability to record your own high-quality sound effects, vocals and musical soundtracks opens up a world of artistic possibilities. Many of my daughter's candid recording sessions have inspired popular original animations, one of which was chosen as a Flashforward Film Festival finalist.

8

Working with sound

FOR ME, ANIMATION IS ABOUT TIMING AND RHYTHM. I've always been visually sensitive to the moving image. As a drummer for the past 35 years, I'm very fixed on musical patterns. The combination of animation and the right soundtrack can be a wonderful experience for both senses. When the right sound complements the perfect animation, it can produce a most memorable experience for the viewer.

In this chapter, we'll look at how you can incorporate sounds into your animations, where to find them, and how to record, edit and load them dynamically.

Recording sounds

SOUNDS CAN ENHANCE YOUR ANIMATION in wonderful ways. Recording and designing sounds is an art form all of its own and a job typically left to dedicated sound editors who have an innate ability to edit, mix and craft sounds into works of audible art. But chances are you don't have a dedicated sound designer at your disposal 24 hours a day. Since Flash does not record or create sound files, you need to find or record your own and import them into Flash. So the best way to find, edit and incorporate sounds into your Flash projects is to purchase sound effects from your local music store or online. A quick search on Amazon.com for "sound effects" will return a few dozen audio CDs available for purchase. These are handy to have around but may include some legal restrictions as to how you can use the sounds. Some publishers may retain the royalty rights to the contents of CDs, limiting you to non-commercial usage. These limits may pose some legal issues for you

....

Get yourself a good microphone. I'll be honest – you get what you pay for when it comes to the quality of recording. There are several different microphones designed to record sounds for almost every situation imaginable. The cheapest solution would be something like the Logitech USB microphone that can be found at your local computer supply store for around $20 US. A microphone like that is great for transferring your voice during an Internet phone conversation, but I wouldn't rely on it for high quality recordings.

On the other hand, you don't need to spend your next five paychecks on the most professional studio microphone either. The microphone pictured on the right is an AKG Perception retails for around $249 US. It produces great sound whether you are recording voice, sound effects or musical instruments. It is a condenser microphone, which tends to be more sensitive and responsive, making it well-suited to capturing subtle nuances in sounds. The best feature of all is being able to switch between the three different recording settings depending on the recording situation. You can set it to record only what is directly in front of the microphone, which is great for voice, sound effects and instruments. If you have two voices or instruments next to each other, there's a setting to record bidirectionally.

The third is an omni-directional setting that will record sounds in a 360 degree pattern around the mic. This setting is great for picking up general room or ambient sounds.

and most importantly your client, who would rather avoid paying legal fees for a few *thumps*, *swooshes* and *pops* sound effects. Another potential issue with published sound effect CDs is their sound quality. Depending on the equipment used to record and edit the sounds, there is no guarantee they are of high enough quality to justify using them. It's always a good idea to try to find out the technical information regarding the actual sound files before you purchase the CD. You will want sounds that are high quality, usually 44 kHz, 16-bit stereo. You may also want to edit your sounds by applying effects or editing loops, or you may even want to compose original soundtracks. For editing you'll need to choose decent audio editing software. Some of you may already be using an audio editing application, but for those of you who are unfamiliar in the area, we'll take a look at what's available a bit later in this chapter.

....

Next, you need a way to get your shiny new microphone to connect with your computer. Once again you have a variety of audio interfaces to choose from. Assuming you don't need every bell and whistle available, a good choice is something like M-Audio's FireWire Solo mobile audio interface. It has a standard XLR microphone input and a 1/2" guitar input, allowing you to record guitar and vocals simultaneously. There are also dual line inputs for effects, drum machines and other outboard gear. The biggest decision to make when purchasing an interface like this is whether you want to use USB or FireWire connectivity. FireWire may provide faster data transfer over USB, but double check that your computer's hardware supports FireWire. If not, you can purchase a FireWire card separately.

So now how much can you expect to spend? An audio interface is between $200 and $400 US depending on how many features it offers. The M-Audio FireWire Solo mentioned here will

set you back about $250 US, but I found one on sale for $200 at my local music vendor. Throw in a microphone stand and cable and you could be looking at spending around $600. Keep in mind this information is based on equipment I feel provides the best bang for your buck. There are many less expensive microphones to choose from, some with USB connectivity that avoid the need to purchase a FireWire interface. It's a balance between the level of quality you prefer and the size of your budget.

Samson USB Microphones

CONDENSER MICROPHONE technology is becoming increasingly sophisticated. There are a number of quality microphones that connect to your computer using **USB** only. There's no need to purchase additional hardware and cables and, in most cases the microphones are extremely portable due to their small size.

Any one of the following microphones is an affordable way for the casual or professional animator to capture high quality sounds for their animations. Learn more at **samsontech.com**.

The best bang for your buck may be the **Samson Go Mic**. The **Go Mic** is a portable USB condenser microphone that literally fits in the palm of your hand. The microphone chassis alone is only two and a half inches in height and just over an inch wide. The microphone is attached to a weighted base using a ball joint, allowing it to be angled in almost any direction. The base can sit on any flat surface or be mounted to the top of your laptop screen using the integrated clip. The base has four integrated rubber feet to help limit external vibrations and a hole that lets you mount it to a microphone stand.

The **Go Mic** provides a 1/8-inch output, so you can connect your headphones. The **Mini-B** size **USB** connector is also located on the same side of the microphone.

The **Go Mic** comes bundled with **Cakewalk Music Creator** software, but I opted to stick with **Adobe Audition** because of my familiarity with it. The **Go Mic** is designed to work with a variety of editing software such as **Apple Logic**, **Garage Band**, **Sony Sound Forge**, **Cubase** and more. Out of the box, the Go Mic connected to my **MacBook** Pro was instantly recognized by **OS X** and **Adobe Audition**. No need to download drivers. The **Go Mic** just works. I was recording within seconds, and my initial spoken-word tests were surprisingly crisp and balanced.

What good is portability if it doesn't come with some form of protection when bouncing around the bottom of your laptop bag? **Samson** includes a zipper case with the **Go Mic** to eliminate the fear of the microphone getting dirty or damaged in transit.

You can also tailor the **Go Mic** to your recording environment by switching between **cardoid** and **omni-directional** polar patterns. The cardoid setting records sound in one direction while **omni-directional** captures sound in all directions. Use the cardoid setting for recording vocals in front of the microphone. Sounds from the sides and behind the **Go Mic** will be rejected. **Omni-directional** is great for situations where you are recording the environment - perfect for ambient sounds or live music situations. Good news for those of you on a limited budget; as of this writing, the **Go Mic** can be found on amazon.com for under $40 US. The **Samson Go Mic** is an outstanding product for recording high quality sounds with portability. With a **Go Mic** and a laptop, the world is your stage.

Other quality products from Samson are the **Meteor Mic** and **G-Track** microphones. Both are **USB** condenser microphones with additional features that go beyond the **Go Mic**. The **Meteor Mic** (pictured left) has a large 25mm condensor diaphram (the **Go Mic** diaphram is 10mm). The **G-Track** (picured right) boasts a built-in audio interface and mixer and a 19mm diaphram. The power of the **G-Track** is its ability to record vocals and an instrument at the same time, making it ideal for studio musicians.

Audacity®

Audacity®

AUDACITY IS A FREE DOWNLOADABLE audio editing application that boasts a surprisingly robust feature set. Audacity can record live audio through a microphone or mixer, or digitize recordings from cassette tapes, vinyl records or minidiscs. With some sound cards, it can also capture streaming audio. Audacity supports several popular audio file formats, allowing you to cut, copy, splice and mix various files together as well as change their pitch and speed. If you have a limited budget, look no further – and even if you can afford software that offers more, Audacity still might be enough to satisfy your needs. Go to http://audacity.sourceforge.net/ to learn more and download the installer.

Audacity offers a variety of editing tools consisting of a Selection, Envelope, Time Shift, Zoom and Draw.

These sliders control the mixer settings of the soundcard in your system. The Output slider (left) actually controls the output setting of the soundcard driver while the Input slider (right) controls the recording level setting of the soundcard driver.

Audacity can record live audio through a microphone or mixer, or digitize recordings from cassette tapes, vinyl records or minidiscs. With some sound cards, it can also capture streaming audio.

Audacity's handy Edit Toolbar allows you to cut, copy, paste, trim and silence your audio and more.

Audacity certainly doesn't make its most basic of controls hard to find. Cursor to Start, Play, Record, Pause, Stop and Cursor to End are all oversized and easy to find.

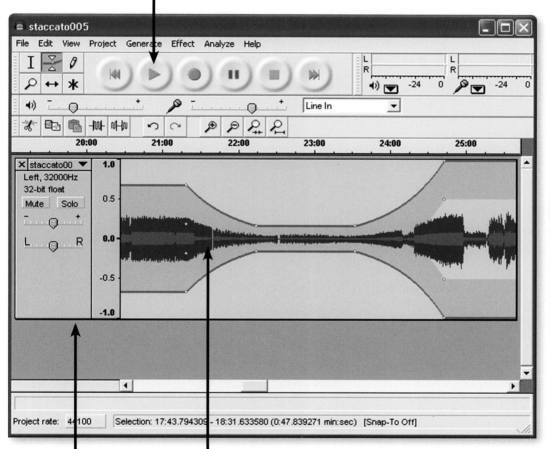

It's free! I can't think of a hotter tip than that. Audacity does a great job of handling a majority of your audio editing needs.

HOT TIP

You can mute and solo (isolate) when working with multiple tracks.

Audio tracks contain digitally sampled sounds. In Audacity, a channel of sound is represented by one mono audio track and a two channel sound by one stereo audio track. You can specify a different sample rate for each track. You can import audio of any sample rate or bit depth, and Audacity will resample and convert it to the project rate and bit depth on the fly.

Adobe® Audition® CC

The workspace in Audition is completely customizable. You can scale and drag panels to new locations and in configurations that suit your working needs. As you rearrange panels, other panels will resize themselves automatically to fit the workspace.

Switch between Edit, Multitrack and CD views easily.

AUDITION IS A VERY robust audio editing program from Adobe that offers a fully integrated set of audio-editing and restoration tools. Audition is a complete audio-editing program, from recording and editing to mixing and exporting.

If you're an experienced sound editor and composer, Audition delivers a full suite of features that rivals the competition. I use it for recording voice overs, sound effects and also sounds from my digital keyboard. I can then switch over to Multitrack View and mix all my sounds together using an unlimited amount of stereo mixing tracks.

Audition offers over 50 real-time audio effects including echo, flange, reverb and more. You can even record and edit MIDI.

Simply put, if you need a complete audio studio out of the box, Audition delivers.

Work with more than 50 real-time audio effects including echo, flange, reverb and more. Manipulate recordings with digital signal processing (DSP) tools, mastering and analysis tools and audio restoration features.

Apply various colors to your tracks for easy identification.

Manage your customizable workspace with the Workspace drop-down menu. You can add or remove workspace layouts similar to how you can in Flash.

HOT TIP

When I'm creating Flash animations for video export, I'll often export a mixdown of the soundtrack from Adobe Audition in MP3 format to animate to in Flash. An MP3 version helps keep the FLA source file smaller. I'll then export a mixdown of the soundtrack in high quality WAV or AIF format for when it comes time to edit the animation to the audio in Premiere Pro.

View and zoom controls provide a helpful way to isolate and focus on specific portions of your audio track(s).

Working with sound

Sound in Flash

THE EDIT ENVELOPE WINDOW offers some limited sound editing features without having to leave the Flash environment. There are enough features here to control the starting and ending points of your sound file, as well as some basic fading effects. But don't expect much more beyond that.

As much as Flash could use a few more bells and whistles in this area, it was never meant to be a sound editing program in the first place. Let's leave that for the dedicated sound editing applications and use Flash for what it is. We can't expect Flash to do everything, can we?

1 Select frame 1 in your Flash document, and then go to File > Import > Import to Stage and select your WAV or AIF file. Your sound will be in frame 1, but you will need to insert enough frames to accommodate its length. By default, the sound will be set to Event. Use the drop-down to change the sound's behavior.
Event: This setting is used to play a sound at a particular point in time but independently of other sounds. An Event sound will play in its entirety even if the movie stops. An Event sound must be fully downloaded before it will play.
Start: This setting is the same as Event except that if the sound is already playing, no new instance of the sound plays.
Stop: This setting stops the selected sound.
Stream: This setting is used to synchronize a sound with the Timeline and, subsequently, the animation. Streaming sounds will start and stop with the playhead.

4 To change the start and end points of a sound, drag the Time In and Time Out controls in the Edit Envelope. The tricky thing about moving these points is, without the ability to scrub the waveform in the envelope window, it's a game of hit or miss (mostly miss). If you need to continue a long sound file across multiple Scenes, you will have to add a new instance of the sound to each scene. Next, determine where the sound ended in the previous Scene and manually adjust the Time In controller for the current Scene so that the sound starts where the previous Scene ended. It's not an exact science and not an ideal solution if your audio file is one continuous sound (such as a musical score).

5 In some situations, having the ability to view the waveform is helpful. For example, having a clear visual indicator of when sounds start and stop can help speed up this tedious process. Right-click over the layer name containing your sound and select Properties from the context menu. In the Layer Properties panel, locate the Layer Height drop-down menu and select 300% to increase the height of the layer to its maximum.

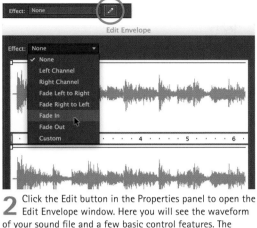

2 Click the Edit button in the Properties panel to open the Edit Envelope window. Here you will see the waveform of your sound file and a few basic control features. The Effect drop-down menu offers some convenient effects to add to your sound.

Left Channel/Right Channel: Plays sound in the left or right channel only.

Fade Left to Right/Fade Right to Left: Shifts the sound from one channel to the other.

Fade In/Fade Out: Gradually increases/decreases the volume of a sound over its duration.

Custom: Lets you create custom in and out points of sound using the Edit Envelope.

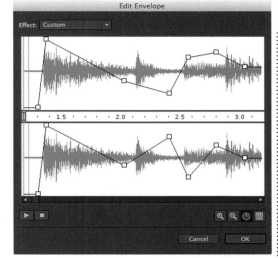

3 You can add up to eight envelope handles by clicking anywhere within the sound window. Each handle can be dragged around to control the volume of the sound at that point in the sound file. The higher the handle is positioned, the louder the sound. To remove a handle, drag it out of the window. To change the sound envelope, drag the envelope handles to change levels at different points in the sound. Envelope lines show the volume of the sound as it plays.

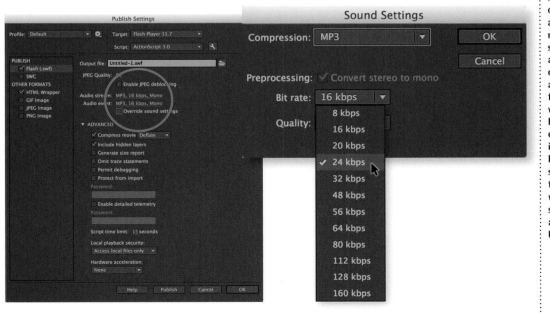

6 Many have experienced an issue with sounds when set to "stream" that manage to fall out of sync with the animation in the Flash Player. The only solution I have found to keep it in sync is to change the default MP3 compression in the document's **Publish Settings** panel. Go to **File >**

Publish Settings and click on the Flash tab. The default MP3 compression is 16 kbps, Mono. Click the "Set..." button next to the "Audio stream..." and change the bit rate to 20 kbps or higher. I personally recommend 24 kbps as the minimum compression setting. Click "OK" and test your movie.

HOT TIP

Once the sound has been set to Stream behavior, you can then drag the play-head across the Timeline to hear your soundtrack. The default Event setting sends the sound to your system's sound card and forgets about it. It is no longer part of the Timeline and will not maintain sync with any animation. The only way to stop an Event sound from playing while in the Flash authoring environment is to hit the Esc key. Event sounds are typically used with shorter sounds and attached to buttons.

Dynamic sounds (AS3)

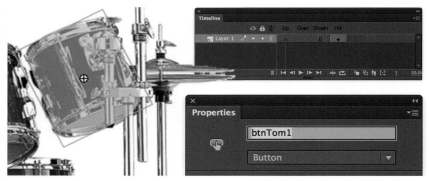

1 The first step is to create an invisible button for the area where you want to assign a mouse command. On a new layer above your image, draw a solid color in the same shape as your image. Convert the shape to a Button symbol and then double-click it to enter Edit Mode. Drag the Up keyframe to the Hit frame. The Hit state dictates the active area of the Button and will not be visible in the compiled movie. Back on the main Timeline the button is semi-transparent for editing purposes. With the instance of the Button selected, type in a descriptive instance name in the Properties panel, so you can assign some commands to it.

I T'S ALWAYS FUN WHEN SOUND and graphics come together to create an engaging and dynamic experience. This example uses ActionScript 3.0 to assign sounds to invisible buttons. The sounds are triggered when you roll over individual drums and cymbals. Each sound file in the Library is exported for ActionScript, allowing you to assign each sound to a different keyboard command as well. As a result, the Flash movie converts your keyboard to a musical instrument.

This example is just one of an infinite number of ways sound and ActionScript can be combined to create a fun, interactive experience.

4 The first line creates a suitably named variable and sets it to an instance of *Tom1*. You'll do this step for each sound clip class, which preps each sound for play. The other lines here show how to trigger the sound with a keystroke. Set the focus to the stage and then add a "key down" event that checks for the event's charCode. In case it's 68 or 100, play the *sndTom1* sound. What are 68 and 100? These happen to be ASCII codes for the letter *D*. See asciitable.com for a chart (you'll want the Dec column).

```
var sndTom1:Tom1 = new Tom1();
stage.focus = this;
addEventListener(
    KeyboardEvent.KEY_DOWN,
    function(evt:KeyboardEvent):void {
        switch(evt.charCode) {
            case 68:
            case 100:
                sndTom1.play();
                break;
        }
    }
);
```

6 Now that you have created a hit area and assigned a mouse and key command to trigger a sound dynamically, repeat steps 1 through 5 for each additional sound you want to add to your project.

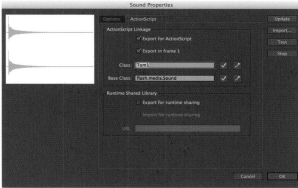

2 Import your sound file into your Flash document. In the Library panel, right-click over the sound and select Linkage from the context menu.

3 In the Linkage Properties panel, click the Export for ActionScript checkbox. That checkbox will automatically check the Export in the first frame for you. Provide a unique Class name. Here, I've named it "*Tom1*". The Base class must be "*flash.media.Sound,*" but Flash is smart enough to fill that in for you. When you click OK, Flash may give you a warning about a missing class in the classpath. That's the *Tom1* class you just named, so let Flash generate its automatic fix. If you like, check "Don't warn me again" to avoid a repeat warning. Click OK.

Choose instance names carefully to help "sort" things in your code. At a glance, it's easy to see that the *Tom1* class relates to the *sndTom1* instance, which is a sound, and to the *btnTom1* instance, which is a button.

5 If you want to trigger the sound with a mouse movement, add the desired mouse event handler to your *btnTom1* button and have the function play the corresponding Sound instance. Check out the sample file to see how easy it is to repeat this small block of code as often as necessary.

```
btnTom1.addEventListener(
    MouseEvent.MOUSE_OVER,
    function(evt:MouseEvent):void {
        sndTom1.play();
    }
);
```

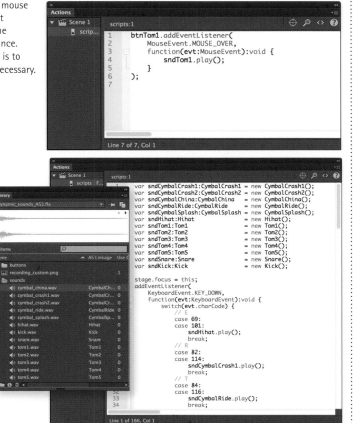

7 Open the Library, and you'll find a total of 13 sounds, each exported to ActionScript and given a unique Class name. Open the Actions panel, and you'll see all the ActionScript has been provided as well.
This example was written by David Stiller (quip.net) in AS3. He has also written a version in AS2 which has also been provided with the example files. We hope that these samples will provide a springboard for your own dynamic sound projects and experiments. Have fun!

269

My wish list for Flash CC

IK

Inverse Kinematics has been deprecated in Flash CC. It is down but not necessarily out. The Bone tool or something very similar could return to Flash someday. If we see an inverse kinematics tool in a future update, I'm hopeful it will boast new and improved pinning and morphing features.

Layer Parenting

This feature is found in other programs (After Effects and Toon Boom Animate) that allows you to drag and link layers to create a hierarchical relationship between them. This hierarchical relationship means that if I have a symbol of a hand on Layer 1 and a symbol of a forearm on Layer 2, I can drag the hand layer to the arm layer, and they will become linked together in a parent/child relationship. On the stage, if I tween the arm, the hand will follow – and most importantly on an arc.

Convert a range of frames and layers to a symbol

Wouldn't it be great to have a button on the Timeline that when pressed, turns on brackets that work the same as the Onionskin and Edit Multiple Frames tools? But this feature would allow us to convert the range of frames across all layers to a Graphic or Movie Clip symbol.

Naming and organizing color swatches

This feature is found in other animation programs that allows you to name and organize color swatches.

After Effects–style timeline

The Motion Editor has been deprecated in Flash CC and may return in a future update after much needed redsigned. The Motion Editor panel demanded a lot of screen real estate and unless you had a second monitor, it was very cumbersome to use. One thought is to integrate the Motion Editor into the existing timeline in a style similar to the After Effects timeline.

A single tween model

As of CS4, the introduction of an additional tween model has been quite confusing for most newcomers to Flash. I get asked frequently what the difference is between the two tween models and when to use one tween type over the other. Fact is, the Motion tween is object-based while the

Classic tween is frame-based. To the seasoned veteran Flash user, both tweens have their distinct purpose. But to the user just launching Flash for the first time, it's not obvious as to what the differences are between the two tween models. A single tween model that combines all the features of both tweens would be an ideal solution.

Filters and Blend Mode support for Graphic symbols

Animators demand frame-accurate sequences, which is why Graphic symbols are favored over Movie Clips. As a result, animators seldom take advantage of the many filters and blend modes offered only for Move Clip objects. I would love to see these features carried over to Graphic symbols someday.

Layer properties

Having the ability to adjust the alpha transparency of an entire layer (and all the contents on that layer) across all frames and keyframes would be very useful. Add to that the ability to apply blend modes to layers and also merge layers together.

Graphic symbol management tools

Flash animators rely on the nesting of assets, especially animations within animations, etc. Managing these Graphic symbols can be blind work because the Flash Properties panel provides limited information as to the symbol's nested content. It would be very valuable to scrub and see a thumbnail preview of the nested frames of a graphic symbol and then have the ability to display the desired frame on the parent timeline using the Properties panel.

There will always be features we'll want to see added or improved in future versions of Flash, which is why Adobe offers us our own wishing well:

adobe.com/cfusion/mmform/index.cfm?name=wishform

Feel free to drop in a coin or two and make your voice heard. The best part is, Adobe is listening.

■ One day your client may request that their online content be re-purposed for video. They may look to you for answers as to how possible this process is. Rest assured, Flash-to-video is widely produced for a variety of broadcast content. The line between online and offline Flash content is officially blurred.

9 Flash to video

FLASH IS EVERYWHERE. NOT ONLY IS FLASH THE development tool for animation, websites, games and applications, but also for DVD and broadcast television. In fact, my first years as a Flash user were spent authoring Flash content for several broadcast animated series. Exporting from Flash to video formats (QuickTime and AVI) to be imported and edited in an Avid workstation was my only authoring requirement of Flash. I had no knowledge of Flash for the Web, including ActionScript, optimizing, preloaders and even buttons of any kind. It was analog Flash at its purest, and that was the Flash world in which I lived. Today, I still use many of the same Flash-to-video techniques for many client projects with the added benefit of an improved QuickTime Exporter from Adobe.

Document setup

SOME OF THE MOST POPULAR FLASH TO video questions I am asked are:

What Flash content can and cannot be exported to video? Why do some animations play in video format while others do not? What frame rate do you use? What is NTSC? What is PAL?

What is the resolution for a 16:9 screen?

What is the correct stage size? Should you be concerned about color correction? What video format should you export to? Do you export the audio from Flash? Are you getting enough sleep? (OK, that last one was from my mother, but you get the idea). This entire chapter is devoted to the topic of getting your Flash project to video format. Sounds simple enough, but there's a lot to know, so let's boogie.

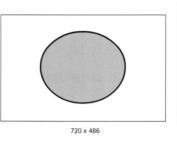

1 Let's start with the basics and open a new Flash document. Open the Document Properties panel using **⌘** **ctrl** **J** or click the "Size" button in the Properties panel. Here you can determine the width and height of the movie and its frame rate. But before we change anything we need to decide what aspect ratio we are authoring to.

720 x 486   720 x 540

3 NTSC doesn't use square pixels; they are rectangular. A problem arises when you develop content for video on your computer because you are creating square pixels to be displayed as rectangular pixels. The problem is your video will look slightly stretched. To compensate for change in pixel shape, adjust the width of the movie so that the aspect ratio is 720 x 540.

720x576

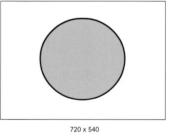

5 PAL (Phase Alternating Line), the predominant video standard outside the Americas, also uses the 4:3 aspect ratio but uses a 720 x 576 pixel aspect ratio. The frame rate is 25 fps. PAL has a greater resolution than NTSC and therefore has a better picture quality. Its higher color gamut level produces higher contrast levels as well. But the lower frame rate, compared to NTSC's frame rate, will not be as smooth.

6 Film uses 24 fps, which is also a popular frame rate among animators. Although you can use 24 fps in your Flash project, when you export it to video, you will need to convert the frame rate as well. This conversion is easily done during the export process by specifying the appropriate frame rate.

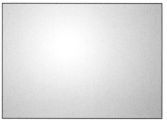

Standard Television
4:3

Widescreen Television
16:9

2 NTSC (National Television Standards Commission), the video standard used in North America and most of South America, uses a 4:3 aspect ratio, which essentially means the width and height of a standard television set. To break it down in even simpler terms, 4:3 means that for

every four units wide, the picture is three units high. Apply this formula to a 16:9 screen, and you'll get 16 units of width for every nine units of height. It's simple arithmetic so far, but it's about to get tricky.

Document Settings

Units:	Pixels
Stage size:	1920 x 1080 px Match contents
Scale:	Scale content
	✓ Locked and hidden layers
Anchor:	
Stage color:	
Frame rate:	29.97

Make Default   Cancel   OK

Save as Template

Name:	My Custom Template
Category:	Media Playback
Description:	Title Safe Area guides for broadcast playback reference.

Preview

Cancel   Save

4 NTSC uses a frame rate of 29.97 fps. You can export Flash movies that have different frame rates such as 12, 15, or 24 fps and convert them to 30 with video editing software, although a movie converted from 12 to 30 fps will not look as smooth as a movie originally authored at 30 fps.

You can save your NTSC Flash document as a Template if you plan to create multiple files (File > Save as Template...). You can also create your own template categories by creating new folders in the "Templates" folder on your local hard drive where Flash CC is installed.

Export PNG

Width:	1920 pixels
Height:	1080 pixels
Resolution:	72 dpi
Include:	Full Document Size
Colors:	32 bit

☑ Smooth

Cancel   Export

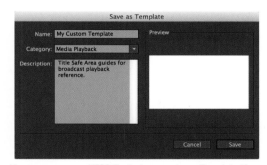

7 Exporting your movie as a PNG image sequence is often the best and most popular method. Go to File > Export Movie and select PNG Sequence as your format. I highly recommend creating a new folder where your image sequence can be saved since the number of images Flash creates is directly related to the number of frames in your

animation (which can easily be hundreds or even thousands). A PNG sequence insures your animation is frame accurate with lossless compression. If you are using After Effects to further refine or add effects to your animation, importing a PNG sequence is not only supported but is also treated as a single object, making it easy to manage.

HOT TIP

Using a video-based aspect ratio for the Web is always a good idea. You never know when the client might ask you to convert the Web-based Flash movie into video format to be burned onto DVD and shown at their next big company summit meeting.

Title and action safety

TELEVISIONS DO NOT GENERALLY display the entire width and height of your movie. In almost all cases, televisons will show a smaller portion of the true display size. Using a visual guide that represents the potential stage area in danger of being cropped will help guarantee that what you create in Flash shows up in its entirety on a variety of television sets.

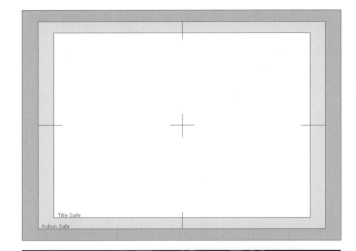

1 There's nothing worse than finding out too late that the title sequence you labored over for ten hours appears on most televisions with several characters cropped, or is even completely invisible. To prevent this cropping, you need to define which area is considered the safe zone within the dimensions of your movie. There are two safe zones to consider: the action-safe zone and the title-safe zone.

2 The title-safe zone is smaller than the action-safe zone because it is much more important to ensure that all titles are clearly legible without any chance of a single letter being cropped. For this reason, the title-safe zone lies 20% in from the absolute edge of the video. When you add titles to your movie, make sure they are positioned entirely within this safer title-safe zone to avoid being cropped.

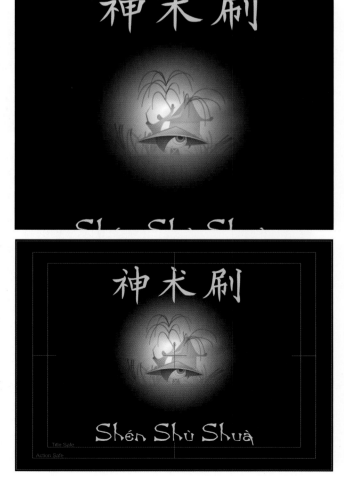

3 The action-safe zone lies 10% inside the absolute edge of the video. You can assume that everything falling within this zone will appear on a television screen. Anything outside this zone can be potentially cropped and not visible. Compose your scenes based on the area within the action-safe zone, assuming this part will be the only area not cropped by the majority of televisions.

4 Place the title-safe zone in your Flash project on its own layer above all other content. When you are ready to export to video, delete this layer to prevent it from being included in the video file. If you don't want to delete it from your document, just convert the layer to a guide layer. Guide layers will not be included in your final export.

Convert the layer containing the title-safe graphic to outline mode to reduce its visual impact and make it less noticeable. You can easily change the color of outline mode by clicking on the color swatch in the layer and selecting a different color in the swatch panel.

5 View > Pasteboard will allow you to see the work area beyond the stage dimensions. This view is useful for working with graphics that extend beyond the width and height of the stage. Having the title safety visible will indicate where the stage is in relation to your artwork. Having the title-safe area visible is particularly useful for simulating camera moves such as panning and zooming.

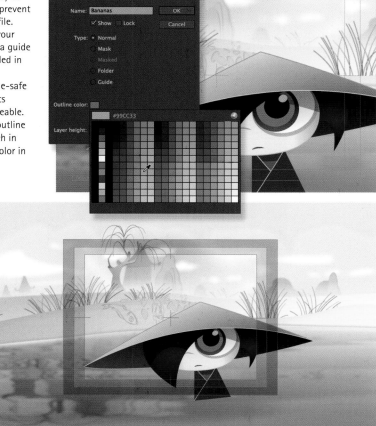

HOT TIP

Flash CC supports the "Include Hidden Layers" option. Go to File > Publish Settings > Flash to locate this feature. When this feature is turned off, all layers with visibility turned off will not be exported. The advantage here is not having to delete the layer from your timeline. You just need to remember to turn off its visibility before exporting.

277

CC video templates

ONE OF THE NICEST features of CC is actually more of a convenience. Adobe has provided us with an easy way to create Flash documents for video output in the form of templates. These template files provide everything you need to get started if you are producing content for video output. In some cases, it's actually a good idea to use these formats for Web content as clients often will need to output their content to both the Web and video formats.

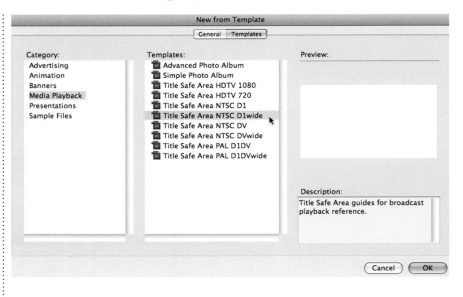

1 Go to File > New... and in the New Document panel click on the Templates button near the top. In the Category section select Media Playback. The Templates section will update with all of the various template files needed to produce content for video output. Select the template that best applies to your needs. The NTSC templates are for video output in America while PAL is used throughout Europe.

3 The title safety provides a clear defining boundary for text-based content as well as action-based content (everything other than text). The title safety region is indicated by guides that represent a 20% margin of the viewable area. The action-safe guides represent a 10% margin of the viewable area. To help discern between these 2 regions, the borders contain a fill color mixed with alpha transparency to allow for the content underneath to still be seen. Keeping within these guides insures your content will not be cropped on older screens.

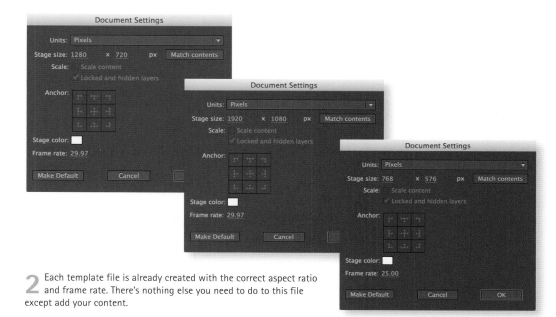

2 Each template file is already created with the correct aspect ratio and frame rate. There's nothing else you need to do to this file except add your content.

4 The timeline consists of two layers; the action-safe layer and an empty layer for content. The action-safe layer is already converted to a guide layer so that it will not be included during export to SWF, to video or as an image sequence. There is only one layer for content, but depending on your needs you may need more. Feel free to add as many layers as you like.

Safe colors

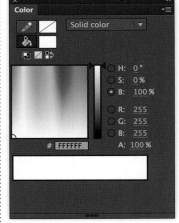

COLOR IS CRITICAL TO THE success of your final file format. Since Flash is technically a Web-based authoring tool, the range of colors far exceeds the color range a television can display. This example will show you how to mix colors while keeping them television-safe and also provide instructions for replacing the default color palette with a color-safe one (included in the downloadable assets from the book website).

1 Your computer monitor is designed to display the full range of RGB color values (0-255). Television can only display a limited range of color values. There's a good chance you may be using colors in your Flash movie that fall outside the television value range, resulting in very noticeable color bleeding.

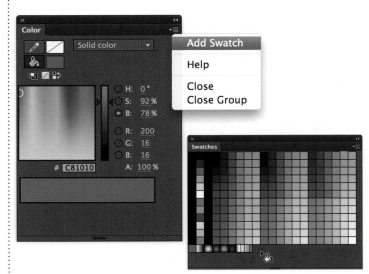

3 To add your new color as a swatch, use the drop-down menu in the upper right corner of the Color Mixer panel. An alternative method for adding colors to your Swatch panel is to hover over the empty area below the existing swatches. Your cursor will automatically become a paint bucket and when you click anywhere in this area, the current color will be added.

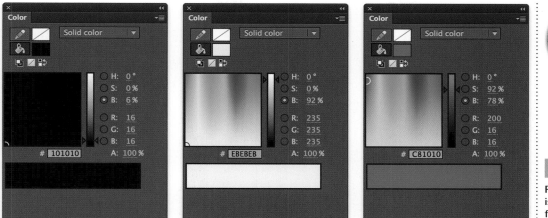

2 You will need to limit this range to between 16 and 235. The RGB color value of the darkest color (black) is 0-0-0. For television this value must be limited to 16-16-16. This setting should be your new black color for any project exported to video. The RGB value of the lightest color (white) is 255-255-255. This television white must be limited to

235-235-235 for export to video format. Since this will be the brightest color in your palette, it will appear to be stark white in comparison to all other colors. The color red has a tendency to bleed more than any other color, so it may be a good idea to compensate more than you need to by lowering the value to around 200-16-16.

HOT TIP

Remember, Flash is resolution-free; as long as you are working in the correct aspect ratio, you can always resize when exporting without a loss in quality. If you have imported bitmaps in your Flash movie, you'll want to use a width and height that is 100% of your final output to avoid having them scaled in Flash.

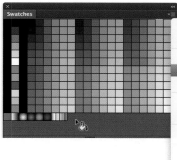

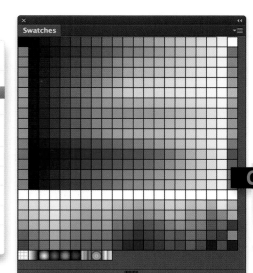

4 Sometimes the default color palette is not needed and simply gets in the way of your workflow. This is a good time to remove or replace the current swatches. You can start over by mixing and adding new colors one at a time or by importing an existing color set, color table

or even a GIF file. From the drop-down menu choose Replace Colors and navigate to the *.clr, *.act or *.gif file containing the colors you want to use. Here I have imported an NTSC safety color palette provided by Warren Fuller (www.animonger.com).

Ape Escape

APE ESCAPE IS BEST KNOWN as a platform game for Sony's PlayStation gaming console, but it's also an animated series for television. Recently I was asked to help animate a few scenes and thought it would make for a great example of how a professional production creates animation with Flash as its primary tool for television broadcast. Many of the animators worked remotely including myself. We shared files via FTP (File Transfer Protocol) and we were initially given storyboards in QuickTime format. The main characters were already set-up for us in Flash and each episode was broken down into several small chunks of time, specifically from 5 to 10 seconds in length. Breaking down the episodes created more files but they were very small in size and easily shared via the Web. All we had to do was upload the Flash source file so that the post-production crew could then export a PNG image sequence or QuickTime movie and edit all the scenes together using a video editing tool.

As you can see here, the duration of this scene is at 2.3 seconds. The entire duration of this shot is only about 5 seconds long. Each episode is a total 2 minutes in duration, made up of several 5 to 10 second shots. Each 2-minute episode could take anywhere from 10 to 20 different scenes.

The Flash stage is set to 1920 x 1080 HDTV widescreen aspect ratio and the frame rate is set to 24 fps.

The safety contains guides for action and text as well as a 4:3 aspect ratio.

All animation is either on the main timeline or nested in graphic symbols, keeping them in sync with the main timeline. The rule used to be: if it plays inside of the Flash authoring tool when you scrub the playhead or play your animation, it will export to video format successfully. This rule is true for all versions of Flash and with the latest Quicktime Exporter, dynamically gener- ated content will also export to video as well.

Keeping it all in sync

1 If your Timeline contains Movie Clips, convert them to Graphic behavior so they sync with the main Timeline. To convert a Movie Clip to a Graphic symbol, select the Movie Clip instance and change its behavior from Movie Clip to Graphic using the Properties panel. Then change its property from Single Frame to Loop or Play Once depending on your needs.

WE HAVE TWO OPTIONS FOR authoring Flash for video output. The old school method requires everything to be on the main timeline. Movie Clip symbols must be avoided altogether since their Timelines are independent of the main Timeline and only render during runtime in the Flash Player.

Flash 8 introduced filters and the ability to add drop shadows, blurring and other cool effects to Movie Clip symbols. But due to the dynamic nature of Movie Clips, they had to be avoided as well. Flash CS3 introduced the QuickTime Exporter which solved this problem. We will take a look at the enhanced QuickTime Exporter in Flash CC later in this chapter.

For now, let's take a look at the old school method of creating Flash animation for export to video. This example is analog Flash in its purest form: straight-ahead timeline animation, streaming sound and nested Graphic symbols.

3 One of the disadvantages of using scenes is confusion during the editing process as it can be difficult to find assets within multiple scenes. Another disadvantage with multiple scenes is having more content in your FLA, which can result in a very large file size. This larger file size increases the chances of corruption and loss of work. It's usually better to work with several smaller files, then edit the individual exported video files together in your video editor.

5 Layer folders are a great way to organize your Timeline, especially if your animation involves a great number of layers, which is often the case with animation. Layer folders combined with nesting animations can go a long way in making efficient Timelines. You can place all your character animations inside a Graphic symbol. One graphic symbol each character makes it much easier to edit and control your entire scene from the main Timeline if you need to position, scale, pan, zoom as if playing the role of a Director. Since the nested animations are inside Graphic symbols, you can still scrub the Timeline with the playhead to see the animations play.

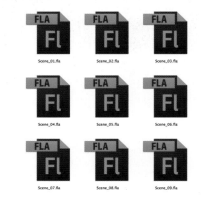

2 Scenes are a great way to manage long Timelines. For example, you could have your title sequence in Scene 1, your story in Scene 2 and ending credits in Scene 3. Using scenes is similar to multiple files chained together since each scene has its own Timeline. The Timeline of each scene combines into a single Timeline in the exported file. The advantage here is having the entire project in one FLA.

HOT TIP

To keep the file size of your FLA as small as possible, it is sometimes good practice to avoid importing high-quality stereo sound files. If you're planning on editing several exported video files together in your video editing program, then import a compressed MP3 audio file into Flash to use as a "scratch track." Place the sound file(s) on its own layer so that it can be easily deleted before export. In Flash CS3, CS4, CS5 and now in Flash CC, you can simply turn off the visibilty of this layer to exclude it from export. Use the high–quality stereo sound file in your video editing program instead.

4 The Flash Timeline has its own limitations. 16,000 is the number that represents the maximum number of layers in a single Flash movie as well as the maximum amount of symbol instances and number of frames. It is rare to see this number reached in any situation, but it is good to understand the limitations in order to avoid them. A Flash document that is 16,000 frames long at 30 fps is nearly nine minutes long. A file that large will cause problems even in the best situations. The file will take longer to open as well as to save. It will exhaust

your system's resources and make it harder to work with multiple Flash documents open at the same time. It will also take a very long time to export to video and will create an enormous file. If you export to AVI, you will very likely exceed the 2 GB limit that is placed on AVI files on most operating systems. Best practice is to break up your project into several smaller FLA files, typically between 30 and 60 seconds each. I often work with FLA files less than 20 seconds in length. It makes the entire process more manageable when animating, exporting and editing.

6 You can quickly expand all layer folders by right-clicking over any one of your folders and selecting "Expand All Folders" from the context menu. Collapsing all folders is done the same way.

7 To sync your animations to a soundtrack, import your sound file and place it on the Timeline in its own layer. You can drag it from the Library to the stage or use the Sound drop-down menu in the Properties panel to select the file. By default, the Sync setting will be Event and must be changed to Stream. The Stream behavior embeds the sound into the Timeline and will be in sync with any Timeline animation. You can adjust the height of a layer by right-clicking over the layer name and selecting Properties. In the Properties panel you can set the layer height to as much as 300%. This height can be useful if you want to see the waveform in as much detail as possible.

285

QuickTime Exporter

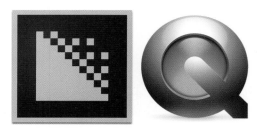

EXPORTING FLASH MOVIES TO VIDEO FORMAT used to require that all animation be on the main timeline. Dynamic content could not be exported to a fixed-frame video format. This content included Movie Clip animations, filters, ActionScript and just about anything dynamically loaded into your SWF file. If it didn't play on the main timeline, then it wasn't included in the exported video.

Welcome the newly enhanced Flash CC QuickTime Exporter. As of Adobe Flash CS5.5, you can export dynamically created Flash content including effects generated with ActionScript as well as effects created with Movie Clips and filters.

The biggest enhancement to the QuickTime Exporter in Flash CC is the integration of the Adobe Media Encoder, providing a number of encoding presets for various devices and platforms. The next biggest enhancement to the exporter is performance. In previous versions of Flash, larger stage sizes, higher frame rates, multiple filters, Blend Modes, animated effects and lack of system resources could contribute to frames being dropped during the export process. As a result, the exported content would suffer from dropped frames or graphic anomalies. In Flash CC, these export issues are now a thing of the past, which is great news for anyone wanting to export their dynamic or timeline-generated Flash content to video format.

1 When you are ready to export your Flash movie to video format, go to **File > Export > Export Video**. In the **Export Video** window, the **Convert video in Adobe Media Encoder** is checked by default – leave it as is. Select **When last frame is reached** for timeline-based animation. If your movie is dynamic, then select **After time elapsed** and then enter the desired duration in **hh:mm:ss.msec** format. Click **Export** when your settings are ready.

3 Preset categories offer several encoding formats to choose. Within the Web Video drop-down you will find a variety of formats within the Vimeo and YouTube sections. These formats will ensure your video will be encoded with the right compression for viewing on these types of web platforms.

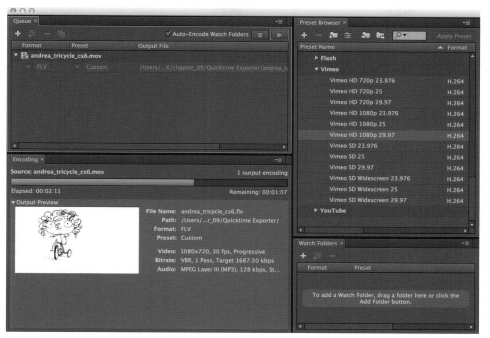

2 Once the export from Flash is complete, the Adobe Media Encoder will launch automatically. The exported MOV file will be automatically added to the queue as seen in the upper left panel. In the lower left corner is the Encoding panel where you can see a preview of the encoded movie along with data specific to the file itself. Along the right side is the Preset panel where you'll find a list of presets for just about any

output you can imagine. From audio and broadcast output, to mobile devices and the web, the Adobe Media Encoder has just about every platform covered. With your preset selected, click the green arrow button in the top right corner of the Queue panel to start the encoding process. The Encoding panel progress bar will indicate the elapsed and remaining time encoding duration.

HOT TIP

Knowing your intended output at the planning stage of your project can help smooth the production process. If you know you want to use a web-based platform such as Vimeo or You-Tube, you can use the Adobe Media Encoder to check out the file format specifications and use that information when setting up your files. Do you want to develop for an Apple iPad 2? The Adobe Media Encoder lists that resolution as 1024x768 with a frame rate of 29.97. Use these settings when you create a new Flash document to ensure compatability with the Apple iPad 2 platform.

4 The encoded movie can be opened and played with the QuickTime Player before uploading to the web. The most notable enhancement besides the integration of the Adobe Media Encoder is the flawless export quality. No more dropped frames and image quality is as expected: excellent.

SWF & FLV Toolbox

BY ELTIMA SOFTWARE

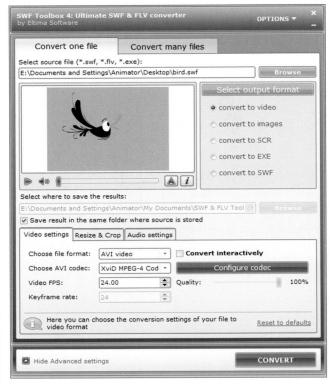

THE SWF & FLV TOOLBOX IS A VERY HANDY 3rd-party program that converts Adobe Flash files (SWF), Flash Video (FLV) and Projector (EXE) files to several different formats (AVI, JPEG, GIF and BMP). You have complete control over the settings for each file format including codec, keyframe rate, movie quality, bitrate, cropping, resizing and more. I've been using this software quite a lot recently, and I really like its ease of use and no-frills interface.

Find out more by visiting www.eltima.com. *SWF & FLV Toolbox is only supported for the Windows platform as of this writing.*

1 The first step is to publish your Flash document to generate a SWF file. Launch SWF & FLV Toolbox, click the Browse button and select the SWF file. Select the output format and click Convert. That's basically all you need to do to convert your SWF files to a different format. Of course you have advanced settings to play with as well.

3 Select an audio codec and configure your desired audio settings to include your sound in the converted video file (if sound was published along with the original SWF file).

2 The advanced settings provide the option to crop your SWF file to any width and height by dragging the edges of the crop marquee or by typing in the numerical values. You can also resize the SWF by providing new values for the width and the height.

4 You can easily convert any SWF, FLV or Projector EXE file to a Windows screensaver file. SWF & FLV Toolbox offers several options that allow you to customize your screensaver by adding a title, website URL and email address.

Wacom tablets

THERE ARE SOME THINGS I JUST CAN'T WORK WITHOUT, AND ONE OF THEM is my Wacom tablet. Graphics tablets are indispensable when it comes to design workflows, and they save valuable production time on a daily basis.

My first graphics tablet was a 12x12 SummaSketch. I distinctly remember the stylus being tethered by a chord, because during the drawing process it would constantly wrap itself around my wrist. Every 20 minutes or so I had to stop, and unravel myself from the stronghold the tablet had on me. Since the only other option was to draw with a mouse, it was a nuisance I easily tolerated. I wasn't aware that a wireless stylus even existed. I didn't know any other way.

After a couple of years of using SummaSketch tablets, I discovered the Intuos series from Wacom. My design life was changed forever. The sleek design of the tablet, its multiple levels of pressure sensitivity and the wireless stylus were all wonders of the modern world for me. Over the years, I've used almost every Intuos and Cintiq model as well as a couple Wacom Bamboo series tablets. Each model has their strengths and weaknesses depending on your design needs.

The Intuos tablets come in three sizes: small, medium and large. The medium size has an overall dimension of 15x9.9" and active drawing area of 8.8x5.5". My personal preference is marketed as the medium size. I don't have to physically move my hand and arm as much as with the larger version, and the small size is a little too small for any serious graphics work. Combine the medium Intuos with the wireless accessory kit, 2048 levels of pressure sensitivity, customizable ExpressKeys, TouchRing and multi-touch gesture support, and you've got a portable tablet that fits alongside your laptop in your backpack.

Lately I have been lucky enough to spend my working days with a Wacom

Cintiq 24HD Touch. Most of my design time is split between Adobe Photoshop CC and Flash CC. The 24HD Cintiq is the Shangri-La of graphics tablets. It's simply huge and incredibly well engineered. I think if our planet exploded, this Cintiq would spend the rest of its life floating around space fully intact. The construction just feels solid.

It's called the 24HD but in terms of its active area, we're really talking about 20.4x12.8" (518.4x324mm). But don't let that sway you. The 24HD's screen size and aspect ratio will surely satisfy your design appetite with no room for dessert. The size of the Cintiq fills the majority of your peripheral field of view, a side effect that tends to draw you into your work (pun intentional). The Cintiq 24HD connects via a DVI output that requires a DVI-to-Thunderbolt adapter. What surprised me, however, was the lack of HDMI-to-HDMI connectivity from the Cintiq to support the newer Retina MacBook Pros. I would think HDMI would be a no-brainer, but for now the DVI-Thunderbolt works fine and supports older, non-Retina display MacBooks. The Cintiq 24HD display can be adjusted by height and incline. The angle of the display itself is adjusted by grasping the levers on both sides and squeezing to release the clutch mechanism. As you squeeze the levers, tilt the display to the desired angle and then release the levers to engage the clutch to lock the display in place. I have fun angling the display due to Wacom's perfectionist build quality in the hinging joints that connect the display to the support arms. It's like opening the hood of a high-end luxury car while still on the showroom floor kind-of-feel. Adjusting the Cintiq almost becomes more about how good it feels than achieving the desired position angle. The support arms lock when in vertical position and unlock by accessing the release latch located at the very back of Cintiq's base. When unlocked, you can lower the entire display to achieve a flatter angle. The Cintiq series offers a 24HD without the touch feature for a little less money.

THE NEXT CINTIQ MODEL IS THE 22HD WITH OR WITHOUT THE MULTI-TOUCH feature. The biggest difference besides the slightly smaller size is the ability to physically rotate the display on a center pivot point. I used the 22HD for an entire day as a demo artist for Wacom and found the rotation feature very useful. Another slight difference in the 22HD is the lack of a TouchRing. To make up for it are 16 customizable ExpressKeys and 2 rear-mounted Touch Strips.

The Cintiq 13HD is the perfect choice if you want a portable Cintiq tablet. The 13" tablet fits easily in most laptop bags, making it extremely handy if you want the Cintiq experience on-the-go. Keep in mind, you'll need a power source wherever your travels take you as the Cintiq 13 is not wireless in any way. In fact, I found the tethered nature of the 13 slightly annoying, but I'll admit I'm splitting hairs with that complaint, so don't take it too seriously. The small

screen also means that everything being displayed is very small. I had a difficult time selecting menu items and tools across Adobe Flash and Photoshop. Over time, the more I worked with the 13" Cintiq, the more used to it I got. The tethering issue all but went away. The screen still felt too small, but it didn't hamper my workflow when drawing. Still the best part: Transporting the Cintiq alongside the MacBook Pro in my backpack between work and home. Portability is this tablet's key strength.

As of this writing, Wacom announced the new Cintiq Companion tablets: Cintiq Companion and the Companion Hybrid. The Cintiq Companion Hybrid is both a Cintiq pen display and an Android™ tablet, giving you the freedom to sketch, draw and paint with Android creative apps. The Cintiq Companion combines the Cintiq pen display with the mobility of a high-performance Windows 8 creative tablet. This combination means you can run applications that support Windows 8 such as the Adobe Creative Cloud. The Cintiq Companion is available with an

Intel® Core™ i7 processor and Intel® HD Graphics 4000, Windows 8, 8 GB DDR memory / 256 GB SSD or Windows 8 Pro, 8 GB DDR memory / 512 SSD.

The Cintiq Companion Hybrid is a quad-core NVIDIA® TEGRA® 4 powered tablet running Android™ 4.2, Jelly Bean, and comes with Wacom Creative Canvas software. You can connect the hybrid to your Mac or PC to transfer your files and use it as a second monitor.

Both the Companion and the Companion Hybrid come with an optional wireless keyboard, 2048 levels of pressure sensitivity and an ergonomic Pro Pen stylus with extra pen nibs and carrying case.

Wacom has defined the graphics tablet industry by offering something for even the most discriminating designer. With the introduction of the Cintiq Companion models, it's clear that portability is the new black in the digital design space.

■ This chapter is divided into 6 stages. Stage 1 will show you how to dynamically create a character that can be controlled to run left, right and jump. In subsequent stages you will then add more characters, interactivity, parallax scrolling, particle effects, sound and even add touch controls for mobile devices

Interactivity

ALL OF THIS DESIGN AND ANIMATION IS FUN, BUT
that's only one side of the Flash authoring experience.
Interactivity is an entirely different, yet complementary
side of Flash that when combined with design, makes for
a compelling experience.

This chapter features a step-by-step process of how to
design and code a game entirely within Flash CC. Thanks
to my talented friend David Crawford we will show you
how to create a character that can be controlled in real
time using keyboard shortcuts and ultimately how to
build a complete interactive game.

David Crawford is the brain child behind PercyPea Ltd., a
company that specializes in advanced online, single and
multiplayer, Facebook and iPhone game development,
with games reaching hundreds of millions of players.

www.percypea.com

Stage 1

S TAGE 1 WILL SHOW
you how to set up a
Movie Clip symbol with your
animated character and how
to include ActionScript to
spawn multiple instances of
this symbol. In addition we
will add ActionScript that
provides the viewer the ability
to control one of the Movie
Clips with keyboard commands.
Press the left arrow key and
the character will run to the
left. Press the right arrow key
and the character will run to
the right. Press the space bar
and the character will jump.
You will create all of this
interactivity using a single FLA
file to keep things as simple as
possible for non-developers. In
later stages we will add more
advanced features, but for now
let's keep it simple.

1 Start with creating new 960x640 FLA. This resolution is the native iPhone4 screen size. It's also a reasonably good size for a web-based game (well maybe a bit too large, but not to worry, the game will scale nicely).

2 Create new Movie Clip for your character. For future coding ease, make the Movie Clip so that the 0,0 center point of the Movie Clip is at ground level and pretty much in the center of the symbol. If the center point is at the bottom and center, the character won't move too much when we flip him horizontally.

If you would prefer you can use 'stage0.fla' from the companion website which contains our pre-animated Ninja. If you use this file rather than creating your own, simply jump to Step 7.

5 The Movie Clip timeline contains 3 animations: still, run and jump. Even though the first animation is **still**, there is some subtle motion of the character moving slightly back and forth. This state is often referred to as an **idle** animation and used for whenever the character is stationary. The subtle motion provides the illusion of breathing or resting which looks more realistic, especially if your character is required to run a lot in what may be a side scrolling game.

6 Create a new layer above all other layers and insert blank keyframes at the beginning and end of each animation cycle. In frame 1 add the label **still** and in the last frame of the still animation add the label **still_end**. Repeat these steps by adding labels to the other 2 animation cycles with descriptive names such as **run**, **run_end**, **jump** and **jump_end**. These labels will be used to control each animation dynamically when ActionScript is added later on.

3 Draw your character with each body part inside it's own movieclip on it's own layer. Before animating, give each body part an instance name (using the properties panel), 'head', 'body', 'rightarm', 'leftarm', 'rightleg', 'leftleg' and 'sword'. Note the cross hairs that represent the center point of the symbol near the character's feet are located as instructed in the previous step.

4 Create three animations: a still, run and jump. You can use tweens, keyframes or a combination of both. Most importantly, make sure the start and end frames are the same for each animation that needs to loop.

Entering a Class name to a Movie Clip requires right–clicking over the Movie Clip in the library, clicking Advanced and subsequently clicking the "Export for ActionScript" checkbox. A quicker way of assigning a Class name for export to ActionScript is to double–click in the empty space in the "AS Linkage" column next to the Movie Clip in the library. You can then immediately type in the Class name you want to use and the appropriate check boxes will have been ticked automatically.

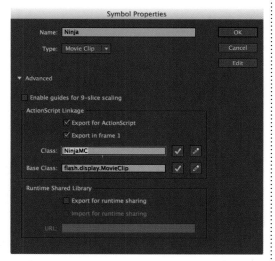

7 In the library is the **Ninja** Movie Clip. Right-click over it and select Properties from the context menu.

8 Open **Advanced** options and click the **Export for ActionScript**. By default the **Class** name will match the name of our Movie Clip, however let's change that to **NinjaMC**. Assigning a Class name for ActionScript linkage automatically sets up the Properties of the Movie Clips so that we can access it via ActionScript and place as many instances of the ninja on screen as desired. Because we are now going to place the character on the screen programmatically, make sure you don't have your ninja already on screen in the main timeline.

9 In your main scene, which should be a nice big empty stage, add the first line of code into frame 1. Open the Actions panel by going to Window > Actions. Click on the empty keyframe in frame 1 in the timeline and type the following code into the Actions panel:

var ground_position:int=500;

This code defines where the character will be placed on the stage when the file is published to the SWF format and played in the Flash Player.

10 Let's add the code that will generate the character from the Movie Clip in the Library:

```
var theNinja:NinjaMC = new NinjaMC();
addChild(theNinja);
theNinja.x = 480;
theNinja.y = ground_position;
```

13 We will create a **newNinja** Function that provides us with the ability to create an instance of our NinjaMC Class and then tell it where on the stage it should be positioned. We will set up the function so that we can add some values to it.

```
function newNinja(x_position:Number, y_
position:Number):void
{
var theNinja:NinjaMC = new NinjaMC();
addChild(theNinja);
theNinja.x = x_position;
theNinja.y = y_position;
}
```

14 To call the function, we just need to write the line **newNinja(480,ground_position);**

For every new ninja, we could then add:
newNinja(580,ground_position);
newNinja(680,ground_position);
newNinja(780,ground_position);

But once again, there's a more efficient way to add multiple instances of this Movie Clip in the next step.

11 Test the Flash movie by going to Control > Test Movie > In Flash Professional. You should now see **theNinja** in the middle of the screen, playing through all of his animations. So far, so good. Let's add more ninjas!

12 As intuitive as it may seem, instead of taking the previous code and duplicating it for each new ninja we want on the screen, let's make the code into a nice simple Function that we only need to write once. The Function will allow us to call upon it as many times as we want. The above image shows how not to write code that duplicates the character. It's not necessarily wrong; there are better and more efficient ways to use ActionScript.

When creating a function we can set up values that get passed to it. In the case of our newNinja function we pass to it x and y position values for our ninjas.

The function itself calls them x_position and y_position and simply assigns them to our new ninja as x and y coordinates.

When we call the function we pass a random number for the x_position but the same ground_position value for the y_position. Changing only the x_position means all our ninjas will have the same y position, but it will be very unlikely that any share the same x position.

15 Add the following code that creates a convenient loop that will add 10 ninjas and place them at a random **x** position on the stage.

```
for(var a:int = 1; a<=10; a++) {
var randomX_Position:Number = Math.random()*960;
newNinja(randomX_Position, ground_position);
}
```

Test the movie to see the code spawn 10 instances of the Movie Clip containing the character playing through each of the animations inside its timeline.

16 But we don't want the animations to loop like this! Let's continue by making the **still** animation simply loop by itself. To loop just the **still** animation, we will need to control the Movie Clips' timeline – more specifically, the frames in between the **still** and **still_end** frame labels.

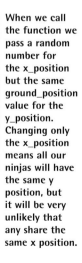

So our **newNinja** function should look like this:

```
function newNinja(x_position:Number, y_position:Number):void
{
var theNinja:NinjaMC = new NinjaMC();
addChild(theNinja);
theNinja.x = x_position;
theNinja.y = y_position;
theNinja.loopStill = function(){theNinja.gotoAndPlay("still")}
theNinja.gotoAndStop("still_end");
theNinja.addFrameScript(theNinja.currentFrame-1,
theNinja.loopStill);
theNinja.gotoAndPlay(1);
}
```

20 We squeeze the above run and jump lines in before the gotoAndPlay(1) line, and at the bottom put in **theNinja.running=false;**

```
theNinja.jumpFinished = function(){
if (theNinja.running)
{theNinja.gotoAndPlay(theNinja,"run")}
else
{theNinja.gotoAndPlay(theNinja,"still")}
} theNinja.gotoAndStop("jump_end");
theNinja.addFrameScript(theNinja.currentFrame-1,
theNinja.jumpFinished);
theNinja.running=false;
```

I N OUR NEWNINJA FUNCTION, WE NEED TO ADD some code to the Ninja itself to automatically loop its animation when it reaches the end of the timeline inside the Ninja symbol. There is an undocumented feature in Flash where we can add function calls at certain frames. When using this method, frame numbers actually start from 0, rather than 1 as in the timeline, so you need to remember to always subtract 1 from the frame number where you want to go to.

Furthermore, we actually want to go to the frame labeled still_end, so we can't very well say *goto "till_end"- 1*, as that will just confuse poor flash.

Thankfully there is a quick fix; we simply tell our NinjaMC to go to the frame **still_end** then grab the real frame number for that frame, subtract 1 from it, and use the addFrameScript command with that number. The command **addFrameScript** unfortunately doesn't allow you to pass values into functions, so we can't directly call the **gotoAndPlay** command passing in **still**, but a simple fix is to give our ninja a new function, which doesnt need any values to be passed but then simply calls **gotoAndPlay("still");**.

Finally, we then add a bit of code to set the ninja back to playing its animation from the first frame.

18 But what about the run and jump parts of our animation? For the run, we simply do something very similar to the still:

```
theNinja.loopRun = function(){theNinja.
gotoAndPlay("run")}
theNinja.gotoAndStop("run_end");
theNinja.addFrameScript(theNinja.currentFrame-1,
theNinja.loopRun);
```

19 For the jump though, this isn't a looping animation, and when it's finished, we need to go back to either still or run animations. We will give our ninja a new property called **running**, which later we will set to be either true or false, and jump will simply check that value.

```
theNinja.jumpFinished = function(){
if (theNinja.running)
{theNinja.gotoAndPlay("run")}
else
{theNinja.gotoAndPlay("still")}
} theNinja.gotoAndStop("jump_end");
theNinja.addFrameScript(theNinja.currentFrame-1,
theNinja.jumpFinished);
```

21 So now we have 10 ninjas on screen all looping their still animations and also set up to loop their run animations and return to either still or run from their jump animation. But what good is it if we don't know which of the 10 ninjas is you, the player? No good at all. Back where we created our newNinja function, you will see the word :void at the end of the first line. This first line tells Flash that when the function is called not to bother returning any information. We can easily change it so that instead we actually return that particular ninja we have just created.

```
function newNinja(x_position:Number, y_position:Number):NinjaMC
{
var theNinja:NinjaMC = new NinjaMC();
addChild(theNinja);
theNinja.x = x_position;
theNinja.y = y_position;
theNinja.loopStill = function(){theNinja.gotoAndPlay("still")}
theNinja.gotoAndStop("still_end");
theNinja.addFrameScript(theNinja.currentFrame-1,
theNinja.loopStill);
theNinja.loopRun = function(){theNinja.gotoAndPlay("run")}
theNinja.gotoAndStop("run_end");
theNinja.addFrameScript(theNinja.currentFrame-1,
theNinja.loopRun);
theNinja.jumpFinished = function(){
if (theNinja.running)
{theNinja.gotoAndPlay("run")}
else
{theNinja.gotoAndPlay("still")}
}
theNinja.gotoAndStop("jump_end");
theNinja.addFrameScript(theNinja.currentFrame-1,
theNinja.jumpFinished);
theNinja.gotoAndPlay(1);
theNinja.running=false;
return theNinja;
}
```

22 Now, after the loop of 10 ninjas, we can have an extra line where we create our 11th ninja, **player**. From this point forward our ninja will always be known as **player** to the rest of the code.

`var player:NinjaMC = newNinja(480,ground_position);`

23 Now let's make our ninja move! Each key on your keyboard has its own unique **keyCode**, for example the **left** cursor key's code is **37**. We don't need to know these codes, as we can look them up in Flash's built in Keyboard Class. The left cursor key is **Keyboard.LEFT**. There are lots of ways to assign key press actions to each key. I like to use a simple Array;

`var keyPressedActions:Array = new Array();`

26 We now need to create our functions that we've already started to assign to key presses. For now, in our move left and move right functions we'll simply subtract 20 pixels from the player's Ninjas x position when moving left, and add 20 when moving right. We'll also remember to set the **running** property to true, so when it comes to jumping we'll know if it's a run, jump or a still jump. You'll see that we also tell our Ninja movieclip to go to (and play) the run animation. We only tell it to run if the ninja previously wasn't running, otherwise the code would always go to the first frame of the run animation and not loop.

```
function moveLeft():void
{
    player.x -= 20;
    if(!player.running)
    {
        player.running=true;
        player.gotoAndPlay("run");
    }
}
function moveRight():void
{
    player.x += 20;
    if(!player.running)
    {
        player.running=true;
        player.gotoAndPlay("run");
    }
}
```

27 Our stopMoving function simply sets our ninja to go back to the **still** animation and also marks that it is no longer running.

```
function stopMoving():void
{
    player.running=false;
    player.gotoAndPlay("still");
}
```

30 Typically, when a user presses a key, they expect to start doing something; while the key is held down, continue doing that something; then when the key is released, stop doing that something. For example, pressing and holding the right arrow key, you would expect your ninja to move right and continue to do so until you release the right arrow. So how can we make the ninja start, continue to stop with just the above **press** and **release** functions, when we don't have a **hold** function too? We can't! We now create possibly the most important piece of code for our game – what we will call the **gameLoop**. We will listen for a special event called ENTER_FRAME which actually gets dispatched every single frame – so many, many times per second (depending on your swf frame rate, of course!).

```
stage.addEventListener(Event.ENTER_FRAME,
gameLoop);
function gameLoop(e:Event):void
{
//check if key is continued being pressed and then do
stuff
}
```

24 We then map function calls to the keys:

```
keyPressedActions[Keyboard.LEFT] = moveLeft;
keyPressedActions[Keyboard.RIGHT] = moveRight;
```

25 We also need an array for when our keys are released

```
var keyReleasedActions:Array = new Array();
keyReleasedActions[Keyboard.LEFT] = stopMoving;
keyReleasedActions[Keyboard.RIGHT]= stopMoving;
```

28 We need to tell Flash to listen for key presses. Then depending on the key that is pressed, get the ninja to do something. We also need Flash to listen for when that key is then released to then stop the ninja from whatever it was doing. So... we add two listeners!

```
stage.addEventListener(KeyboardEvent.KEY_DOWN,
keyPressed);
stage.addEventListener(KeyboardEvent.KEY_UP,
keyReleased);
```

29 We then need to make the keyPressed and keyReleased functions; we will populate them shortly

```
function keyPressed(theKey:KeyboardEvent):void
{
    //Do stuff
}
function keyReleased(theKey:KeyboardEvent):void
{
    //Stop doing that stuff
}
```

31 So we have our 3 listeners that will handle the keyboard: **pressed**, **continued being pressed** (our game loop) and **released**. For simplicity, we are going to actually deal with **pressed** and **released**. We will simply record which key was pressed and then **delete** that recording when we release. To keep track of which key is pressed, we make another new array to **record** or **store** that information. Place this line of code up above your keyPressed function.

```
var keys:Array = new Array();
```

32 We then modify our keyPressed function as follows:

```
function keyPressed(theKey:KeyboardEvent):void
{
keys[theKey.keyCode] = true;
}
```

and keyReleased function to this:
```
function keyReleased(theKey:KeyboardEvent):void
{
delete keys[theKey.keyCode];
if(keyReleasedActions[theKey.keyCode])
keyReleasedActions[theKey.keyCode]();
}
```

33 You will notice the keyReleased function has an extra line which is needed to call our keyReleasedAction immediately. We don't have to call the keyPressedAction when we press the key, as our gameLoop handles that. In our gameLoop code, we examine our key's array to see if any of the values are true (ie, a key has been recorded that it is pressed and still down) and then trigger the corresponding **keyPressedActions**. Because we are storing function references in our keyPressedActions Array, we can trigger these functions by simply putting () at the end.

```
function gameLoop(e:Event):void
{
for(var key:String in keys)
{
if(keyPressedActions[key]) keyPressedActions[key]();
}
}
```

34 You should now be able to test your game and move your ninja! So what's the first problem we see when moving our ninja left and right? That's right, he doesn't face left (assuming we drew him facing right by default). Thankfully the fix is simple. We flip the ninja horizontally via code when moving left and back again when moving right. To flip him, we adjust the Ninja's **scaleX property: -1** means flip it, 1 means default. Our **moveRight** and **moveLeft** functions become:

```
function moveLeft():void
{
    player.x -= 20;
    if(!player.running)
    {
        player.running=true;
        player.gotoAndPlay("run");
    }
    player.scaleX = -1;
}
function moveRight():void
{
    player.x += 20;
    if(!player.running)
    {
        player.running=true;
        player.gotoAndPlay("run");
    }
    player.scaleX = 1;
}
```

37 Now, the trouble is, because we already get our player to start off at our ground_position of 500. If we test the game, we see our player fall off into oblivion. We therefore add another bit of code to make sure that our player ninja never can go lower than the ground. We also will tell our player ninja that it is not jumping (because we know it is on the ground).

```
function gameLoop(e:Event):void
{
    for(var key:String in keys)
    {
    if(keyPressedActions[key]) keyPressedActions[key]();
    }
    player.y += player.gravity;
    if(player.y > ground_position)
    {
    player.y = ground_position;
    player.jumping=false;
    }
}
```

38 Of course now when we test the game, it looks like nothing has happened now as our ninja starts at ground level anyway. Let's add our jump function! First, let's assign a key to perform the jump command. Let's use the A key.

```
keyPressedActions[Keyboard.A] = jump;
```

Now the function

```
function jump():void
{
    if(!player.jumping)
    {
    player.gotoAndPlay("jump");
    player.gravity = -8;
    player.jumping = true;
    }
}
```

To help keep the code organized, we add this block up near the moveleft and moveright functions, and also set the keyPressedAction for **A** with our two left and right settings.

35 Let's add jumping! First we need to understand what a "jump" really is. In the real world, we are constantly pulled down by gravity. By jumping, we are exerting a force from the floor and fighting with the pull of gravity. Once our feet have left the floor, we have no ability to continue to fight gravity, so eventually it wins and pulls as back down. Currently in our game, we have no concept of gravity. Our ninjas all look like they are on the ground simply because we've position them all at the same y value, using our ground_position variable. So the first thing's first, let's actually emulate gravity! Don't worry if physics isn't your favorite subject; we're going to keep things very simple and not accurately simulate real-world gravity. Back in our **newNinja** function, we are going to add a new variable to our ninjas:

```
theNinja.gravity = 10;
```

36 We now go to our gameLoop function and code it so that this gravity value is constantly added to our players y position (eg, the player is always pulled down screen by the gravity, each frame/loop).

```
function gameLoop(e:Event):void
{
    for(var key:String in keys)
    {
    if(keyPressedActions[key]) keyPressedActions[key]();
    }
    player.y += player.gravity;
}
```

a "+=" bit of code is a quick way of writing
player.y = player. y + player.gravity;

HOT TIP

In the jump function in steps 37 and 38 we use a new property of our player, "jumping". This property is so that when we press our key to jump, the jump only happens once, rather than constantly while the key is held down. We just need to set player.jumping back to false when the ninja has landed, as only then do we want him to be able to jump again.

39 Finally, you see that we are setting our ninja's gravity from the default 10, to -8. We come to this value because it's half the number of frames in our jump animation (more on this below). There's one extra thing we now need to do; setting the ninja's gravity to -8 means that in each game loop 8 is subtracted from the player's y position therefore causing the ninja to float upwards. To correct the floating, we simply add an extra line at the end of the game loop:

```
player.gravity += 1;
```

This single line of code means that for each loop, the gravity value gets greater by 1 and eventually becomes a positive number which therefore will start moving the ninja back down to earth. Increasing the gravity value by 1 and starting the gravity setting at -8 when we jump means that gravity will be 8 by the time the ninja is back on the ground. The gravity setting will have changed a total of 16 times which matches our frame count of the jump animation.

40 If we test the game, we will see now the ninja does jump, however, it is a puny and weak jump. To give our ninja more vigor, we just need to play around with the 1 value at the end of player.gravity+=1 and the -8 value that is set when we press jump. The rule is if we double the -8 value, then also double the 1 value. However, you will also find that you may want to change these values independently if you find that your ninja's jump animation is actually over too soon or carries on after he's landed. Alternatively, here is when you can adjust your ninja jump animation so that it fits better. For our ninja with a 16 frame jump animation, let's try

```
player.gravity =- 40;
```

and

```
player.gravity += 5;
```

Perfect! :)

41 The full code for stage 1 looks like this:

```
var ground_position:int = 500;

function newNinja(x_position:Number, y_position:Number):NinjaMC
{
        var theNinja:NinjaMC = new NinjaMC();
        addChild(theNinja);
        theNinja.x = x_position;
        theNinja.y = y_position;
        theNinja.loopStill = function(){theNinja.gotoAndPlay("still")}
        theNinja.gotoAndStop("still_end");
        theNinja.addFrameScript(theNinja.currentFrame - 1, theNinja.loopStill);
        theNinja.loopRun = function(){theNinja.gotoAndPlay("run")}
        theNinja.gotoAndStop("run_end");
        theNinja.addFrameScript(theNinja.currentFrame - 1, theNinja.loopRun);
        theNinja.jumpFinished = function(){
        if (theNinja.running)
        {theNinja.gotoAndPlay("run")}
        else
        {theNinja.gotoAndPlay("still")}
        }
        theNinja.gotoAndStop("jump_end");
        theNinja.addFrameScript(theNinja.currentFrame - 1, theNinja.jumpFinished);
        theNinja.gotoAndPlay(1);
        theNinja.running=false;
        theNinja.gravity = 10;
        return theNinja;
}

for(var a:int = 1; a <= 10; a++)
{
        var randomX_Position:Number = Math.random()*960;
        newNinja(randomX_Position, ground_position);
}

var player:NinjaMC = newNinja(480,ground_position);
var keyPressedActions:Array = new Array();
keyPressedActions[Keyboard.LEFT] = moveLeft;
keyPressedActions[Keyboard.RIGHT] = moveRight;
keyPressedActions[Keyboard.A] = jump;

var keyReleasedActions:Array = new Array();
keyReleasedActions[Keyboard.LEFT] = stopMoving;
keyReleasedActions[Keyboard.RIGHT]= stopMoving;

function moveLeft():void
{
        player.x-=20;
        if(!player.running)
        {
                player.running = true;
                if(!player.jumping) player.gotoAndPlay("run");
        }
        player.scaleX = -1;
}
```

```
function moveRight():void
{
        player.x+=20;
        if(!player.running)
        {
                player.running = true;
                if(!player.jumping) player.gotoAndPlay("run");
        }
        player.scaleX = 1;
}

function jump():void
{
        if(!player.jumping)
        {
                player.gotoAndPlay("jump");
                player.gravity=-40;
                player.jumping=true;
        }
}

function stopMoving():void
{
        player.running=false;
        if(!player.jumping) player.gotoAndPlay("still");
}

stage.addEventListener(KeyboardEvent.KEY_DOWN, keyPressed);
stage.addEventListener(KeyboardEvent.KEY_UP, keyReleased);
var keys:Array = []
function keyPressed(theKey:KeyboardEvent):void
{
        keys[theKey.keyCode]=true;
}

function keyReleased(theKey:KeyboardEvent):void
{
        delete keys[theKey.keyCode];
        if(keyReleasedActions[theKey.keyCode]) keyReleasedActions[theKey.keyCode]();
}
stage.addEventListener(Event.ENTER_FRAME, gameLoop);
function gameLoop(e:Event):void
{
        for(var key:String in keys)
        {
                if(keyPressedActions[key]) keyPressedActions[key]();
        }
        player.y += player.gravity;
        if(player.y>ground_position)
        {
                player.y = ground_position;
                player.jumping=false;
        }
        player.gravity += 5;
}
```

HOT TIP

One final change that we make, as shown in the code on this page, is to modify our moveRight and moveLeft function so that our player ninja only does gotoAndPlay to run our animation if it's not actually jumping.

Stage 1 is now complete!

307

Stage 2

S O! WE'VE COMPLETED STAGE 1. WE KNOW how to take our animated character, attach multiple copies of it to the stage via code, add basic code to control its animations, reference one in particular and make it a playable character.

But we're still a long way off making a full game, and there are some things we'll have to do first to our existing code before continuing in our quest.

Right now, we stand at around 120 lines of code,

give or take a few empty line spaces.

We have a system set up to listen for keystrokes and an easy way to assign different functions and commands to those keys. We also have a nice GameLoop that is set up to manage everything. If we continue down this path, we are going to end up with many more lines of code which will become harder and harder to manage. So, we are going to separate out our code into different files, files which are known as Classes.

1 Our first Class! Go to File > New > ActionScript 3.0 Class, name it Ninja and save it in same directory as the FLA file we created in stage 1.

2 Now for the Ninja Class equivalent of our new Ninja function. It's very similar, however a few places are changed over the function method in stage 1. Put this code into our new class:

```
package
{
        import flash.display.Sprite;
        public class Ninja extends Sprite
        {
                public var theNinja:NinjaMC;
                public var running:Boolean;
                public var jumping:Boolean;
                public var gravity:Number;

                public function Ninja(x_position:Number, y_position:Number)
                {
                        theNinja = new NinjaMC();
                        addChild(theNinja);
                        x = x_position;
                        y = y_position;
                        theNinja.gotoAndStop("still_end");
                        theNinja.addFrameScript(theNinja.currentFrame - 1, loopStill);
                        theNinja.gotoAndStop("run_end");
                        theNinja.addFrameScript(theNinja.currentFrame - 1, loopRun);
                        theNinja.gotoAndStop("jump_end");
                        theNinja.addFrameScript(theNinja.currentFrame - 1, jumpFinished);
                        theNinja.gotoAndPlay(1);
                        running = false;
                        jumping = false;
                        gravity = 10;
                }
                public function loopStill():void
                {
                        theNinja.gotoAndPlay("still");
                }
                public function loopRun():void
                {
                        theNinja.gotoAndPlay("run");
                }
                public function jumpFinished():void
                {
                        if (running)
                        {
                                theNinja.gotoAndPlay("run");
                        }
                        else
                        {
                                theNinja.gotoAndPlay("still");
                        }
                }
        }
}
```

HOT TIP

You will notice that in front of all our variables and functions inside our class, we have a new word "public." This word which means that the variable or function can be reached from any part of our code such as our gameloop for example.

Although we won't be doing it in the course of making this game, it's also possible to use the word "private" instead of "public." Making a variable or function private prevents other parts of code outside of the class from accessing our values and more importantly changing them when perhaps we don't want them changed.

3 In Stage 1, in the main FLA timeline code we have the following line:

var player:NinjaMC = newNinja(480, ground_position);

With our new Class, let's change this line to be these two lines:
var player:Ninja = new Ninja(480, ground_position);
addChild(player);

Let's also change our code that creates the 10 other ninjas to this:
for(var a:int = 1; a <= 10; a++)
{
        var randomX_Position:Number = Math.random()*960;
        var enemy:Ninja = new Ninja(randomX_Position, ground_position);
        addChild(enemy);
}

4 What we will do now, is move our moveLeft, moveRight, stopMoving and jump functions to the new Ninja Class. We can cut them from the timeline as they will be no longer needed there and paste them into our Ninja class beneath the **jumpFinished** function. We need to add **public** before each **function** and remove most of the **player.** references. The ones which are **player.gotoAndPlay** however, we will replace with **theNinja.gotoAndPlay**.

With these functions inside our Ninja Class, we need to make some minor modifications to our keyPressedActions and keyReleasedActions arrays.

Simply stick **player.** in front of all the function names, ie:
keyPressedActions[Keyboard.LEFT] = moveLeft;
becomes:-
keyPressedActions[Keyboard.LEFT] = player.moveLeft;

```
package
{
        import flash.display.Sprite;
        public class Ninja extends Sprite
        {
                public var theNinja:NinjaMC
                public var running:Boolean;
                public var jumping:Boolean;
                public var gravity:Number;
                public function Ninja(x_position:Number, y_position:Number)
                {
                        theNinja = new NinjaMC();
                        addChild(theNinja);
                        x = x_position;
                        y = y_position;
                        theNinja.gotoAndStop("still_end");
                        theNinja.addFrameScript(theNinja.currentFrame - 1, loopStill);
                        theNinja.gotoAndStop("run_end");
                        theNinja.addFrameScript(theNinja.currentFrame - 1, loopRun);
                        theNinja.gotoAndStop("jump_end");
                        theNinja.addFrameScript(theNinja.currentFrame - 1, jumpFinished);
                        theNinja.gotoAndPlay(1);
                        running = false;
                        jumping = false;
                        gravity = 10;
                }

        public function loopStill():void
        {
                theNinja.gotoAndPlay("still");
        }
}
```

```
public function loopRun():void
{
    theNinja.gotoAndPlay("run");
}

public function jumpFinished():void
{
        if (running)
        {
                theNinja.gotoAndPlay("run");
        }
        else
        {
                theNinja.gotoAndPlay("still");
        }
}
public function moveLeft():void
{
        x -= 20;
        if(!running)
        {
                running = true;
                if(!jumping)theNinja.gotoAndPlay("run");
        }
        scaleX=-1;
}

public function moveRight():void
{
        x+=20;
        if(!running)
        {
                running = true;
                if(!jumping)theNinja.gotoAndPlay("run");
        }
        scaleX = 1;
}

public function jump():void
{
        if(!jumping)
        {
                theNinja.gotoAndPlay("jump");
                gravity=-40;
                jumping=true;
        }
}
public function stopMoving():void
{
        running = false;
        if(!jumping) theNinja.gotoAndPlay("still");
}
    }
}
```

HOT TIP

In Stage 1, although we weren't directly using classes, our NinjaMC in the library is actually a Class. Those eagle eyed will have spotted in the Symbol Properties panel that it uses a Base Class of "MovieClip."

The MovieClip Class is known as a Dynamic Class which means you don't have to "declare" the variables and functions that you want to add to it.

With our new Ninja Class, we do have to declare these values. Declaring them actually gives a nice performance boost though, as well as makes our code easier to manage and test, so it's a good thing.

SO, THAT WAS A CLASS EXAMPLE. However, because we want our ninja to exist in a 3D world, the Class is going to be a little bit different. Our Ninja Class isn't actually finished and won't work currently, but we will leave it for now because first of all we're going to set up our pseudo 3D engine. The first thing to create for any self respecting 3D engine is a Camera! For our game and engine, we just need a very simple camera with just 3 properties: an **X**, a **Y**, and a **perspective**. variable. Despite having a 3D engine, we won't need a **Z** property as our Camera will never move into or away from our game (although for those brave enough feel free to add this value and we'll drop some hints along the way as to how you could use it).

5 We create a new Camera Class. Note: we call our x and y properties x3D and y3D for reasons to be explained later.

```
package
{
    public class Camera
    {
        public static var x3D:Number = 480;
        public static var y3D:Number = 300;
        public static var perspective:int = 1000;
        public function Camera()
        {
        }
    }
}
```

As with our new Ninja Class, save this Camera Class into the same folder as our FLA.

Note that there is an important term "static" used when declaring our 3 properties/ variables. In simple terms, what doesn't change about a static property or variable is its memory location which makes it easier for the rest of our code to access these values.

This book isn't about coding ethics, so that explanation is all you need to know for now.

By default, we set our x value to 480 because this is half of our flash game's width. For the y value, we use 300 because our **ground_position** is still 500. If we use 500 for the camera too, it will be as if the camera is actually sitting right on the ground and mean we're actually looking at our ninja's feet which is fine from a distance but not when the ninja comes up close. At 300 we're just above our ninja's head. Perspective is a magical 1000. Why? Because 1000 works well.

In stage 1, we just allowed left and right movement of our ninja, along the **X** axis, and jumping, using the **Y** axis. However, in the full game, we want to move our ninja into and out of the environment along the **Z** axis, using the up and down keys. As our ninja moves into the environment, he gets smaller giving a 3D effect.

It's not just our ninja that will have this 3D effect but pretty much all of the characters and objects in the game. Therefore, we want to code this 3D effect just once and allow all Classes to be able to use it if needed. We create a new Class which will be used as a base for all our other classes: ninjas, blood splats, bunnies, etc.

Because we are now using a 3D world, we need to add the z coordinate. What's more, because our ninja will appear to be moving slower across the screen when he is far off in the distance, we no longer directly move the x and y values of our ninja. So we need some new x and y variables along with our z. We will use **x3D**, **y3D** and **z3D**.

So let's create our new Class that all (or at least most of) our in-game objects will use as their Base. For this reason, we will call the **Class Base3D**.

We extend **Sprite** so that we can incorporate the native features for the Sprite object, ie, its x and y values, the ability to scale it, add it to stage, etc.

6 Because in our 3D world our objects will be scaled (using **scaleX** and **scaleY** properties) when they move in and out of the background, we can no longer set **scaleX** to be **1** or **–1** depending on if we want our ninja to face right or left. Therefore we will create a new variable called **direction**.

In the **convert3D** function of this class, those brave could try and combine their **Camera z3D** with the three **z3D** values if they felt up to the challenge.

```
package
{
        import flash.display.Sprite;
        import flash.display.MovieClip;

        public class Base3D extends Sprite
        {
                public var x3D:Number;
                public var y3D:Number;
                public var z3D:Number;
                public var direction:int;
                public var timeline:MovieClip;

                public function Base3D(x:Number, y:Number, z:Number = 1000)
                {
                        x3D = x;
                        y3D = y;
                        z3D = z;
                        direction = 1;
                }
                public function convert3D():void
                {
                        x = (x3D – Camera.x3D)*(Camera.perspective/z3D)+480;
                        y = (y3D – Camera.y3D)*(Camera.perspective/z3D)+320;
                        scaleX=scaleY = (Camera.perspective/z3D);
                        scaleX*=direction;
                }
        }
}
```

Again we will save this class in the same folder as our FLA.

The **convert3D** function is where the magic happens. This function takes the x, y and z 3D values of our object (in this case the Ninja) and converts them to on screen x and y coordinates, as well as scaling the Ninja to give the illusion of depth. See how our new value **direction** is used right at the end to affect the scaleX value which in turn will "flip" the ninja horizontally if needed.

Finally, there's a **timeline** variable, defined as a MovieClip. We will want our Ninjas (and other Classes that extend Base3D) to be able to easily reference variables we still store in the timeline. This **timeline** variable will become our timeline reference to be able to look up variables such as **ground_position** in our main FLA's timeline.

Now that we have our **Base3D** class, let's go back to our **Ninja Class** and modify it to make use of **Base3D**.

In our **Ninja Class**, change the line towards the top:
public class Ninja extends Sprite
to be:

public class Ninja extends Base3D
Because **Base3D** manages our x and y coordinates, we can delete these lines from the Ninja Class. We also modify the default Ninja function to include **z_position**; we can even set it by default to be the **Camara.perspective** value, **1000**. By setting it to 1000, it means our Ninja will be the exact same size as if we weren't using 3D at all. I know that sounds a bit pointless, but bear with me to find out why.
Finally, because the code in **Base3D** needs to do something too, we add this line at the end of the Ninja function:

super(x_position, y_position, z_position);

HOT TIP

Every Class that we will make must be saved with the same filename that the Class is called. It also must contain a function that matches the Class name too.

You will see our Ninja.as file is our Ninja Class with a Ninja function. Our Base3D.as file is our Base3D Class with a Base3D function.

This Class name function is the first bit of code that will get run when you create a new instance of the class.

As you will see with Camera though, the function doesn't neccesarily have to do anything.

313

7 So the Ninja function of our Ninja Class now looks like this:

```
public function Ninja(x_position:Number, y_position:Number, z_position:Number = 1000)
{
     theNinja = new NinjaMC();
     addChild(theNinja);
     theNinja.gotoAndStop("still_end");
     theNinja.addFrameScript(theNinja.currentFrame 1, loopStill);
     theNinja.gotoAndStop("run_end");
     theNinja.addFrameScript(theNinja.currentFrame 1, loopRun);
     theNinja.gotoAndStop("jump_end");
     theNinja.addFrameScript(theNinja.currentFrame 1, jumpFinished);
     theNinja.gotoAndPlay(1);
     running = false;
     jumping = false;
     gravity = 10;
     super(x_position, y_position, z_position);
}
```

10 Next we need to modify our gravity code to affect y3D of player, instead of .y.

```
player.y3D += player.gravity;
if(player.y3D>ground_position)
{
    player.y3D = ground_position;
    player.jumping=false;
}
player.gravity += 5;
```

11 However, now that we have our Ninja Class extending **Base3D**, which in turn has the **timeline** reference. We no longer need Step 10's bit of code to happen in the main gameLoop. We need to create a new **loop** function inside our Ninja Class, and move the gravity stuff from our main gameLoop to our Ninja's internal loop. So actually, let's replace all that code in step 10 with this single line:

player.loop();

Then inside our Ninja Class, add the code:

```
public function loop():void
{
     y3D += gravity;
     if(y3D >= timeline.ground_position)
     {
          y3D = timeline.ground_position;
          jumping = false;
     }
     gravity += 5;
}
```

8 We also need to swap out our adjustments to **x** in the **moveLeft** and **moveRight** functions to be the new x3D. Remember we also have the new direction variable in **Base3D**, so we will swap the **scaleX = 1** and **scaleX = -1** lines to be **direction = 1** and **direction = -1**. Now we add **moveDown** and **moveUp** functions to our Ninja Class which are very similar to the **moveLeft** and **moveRight**, but instead of adjusting **x3D** we adjust **z3D**. Don't worry about direction as no horizontal flipping needs to happen here.

```
public function moveUp():void
{
        z3D+=20;
        if(!running)
        {
                running = true;
                if(!jumping) theNinja.gotoAndPlay("run");
        }
}
public function moveDown():void
{
        z3D-=20;
        if(!running)
        {
                running = true;
                if(!jumping) theNinja.gotoAndPlay("run");
        }
}
```

9 We've finished changing our Ninja Class for now. Make sure you have saved it, and then let's go back to the main code in our timeline of our FLA and add some keyboard actions to call our new moveUp and moveDown functions.

```
var keyPressedActions:Array = new Array();
keyPressedActions[Keyboard.LEFT] = player.moveLeft;
keyPressedActions[Keyboard.RIGHT] = player.moveRight;
keyPressedActions[Keyboard.UP] = player.moveUp;
keyPressedActions[Keyboard.DOWN] = player.moveDown;
keyPressedActions[Keyboard.A] = player.jump;

var keyReleasedActions:Array = new Array();
keyReleasedActions[Keyboard.LEFT] = player.stopMoving;
keyReleasedActions[Keyboard.RIGHT]= player.stopMoving;
keyReleasedActions[Keyboard.UP] = player.stopMoving;
keyReleasedActions[Keyboard.DOWN]= player.stopMoving;
```

12 The last thing we need to do now, is when we create our player in the timeline, we just add:

player.timeline = this;

Finally, to test our 3D effect we actually need to call our **convert3D** function on our ninja. We also need to call convert3D on our 10 **enemy** ninjas too which is currently very hard, because in our **for loop** where we create the 10 ninjas, we don't actually store any easy reference to them, so that we can later call their **convert3D** function in the same way as we could call **player.convert3D** for our player. So we will come up with a solution. Due to the way our engine works, we know we need to call **convert3D** to all of our on-screen 3D objects (ninjas). Therefore, we will create a new **Array** to store these objects. We will call our array **Objects3D** as unfortunately we can't name an array starting with a number.

Right at the top of our timeline code add:

var objects3D:Array = new Array();

13 Then we modify our for loop for adding our enemies:

```
for(var a:int = 1; a <= 10; a++)
{
    var randomX_Position:Number = Math.random()*960;
    var enemy:Ninja =
    new Ninja(randomX_Position, ground_position);
    addChild(enemy);
    enemy.timeline = this;
    objects3D.push(enemy);
}
```

As with our player, we pass the enemy a reference to our main timeline, so they too can look up variables.

The final addition to our timeline code, after we create player is to add:

objects3D.push(player);

14 At the bottom of the gameLoop function after the **player.loop()** line, add the following 4 lines of code:

```
var a:int;
for(a = 0; a < objects3D.length; a++)
{
        objects3D[a].convert3D();
}
```

Now test your game, and after all this extra code we've done you should see everything looks pretty much exactly like stage1.... um... OK... so what's the point of all this extra code? Don't worry, we've not wasted time. Try using the down arrow key to control your ninja. You will see you can

now move him closer to the camera. Use the up arrow key and he'll move further away. There is of course one problem. As you move your ninja further away from the camera, he doesn't visually move behind the enemy ninjas, rather he just gets smaller.

16 Let's add the ability of the camera to track our Player if he runs off screen. In the Camera Class, underneath the empty **Camera** function, add:

```
public static function track(player:Ninja):void
{
  var scaleValue:Number = perspective/player.z3D;
  var edgeDistance:Number = (280-100*
scaleValue)/scaleValue;
  if(x3D < player.x3D-edgeDistance)
    x3D = player.x3D-edgeDistance
  if(x3D>player.x3D+edgeDistance)
    x3D=player.x3D+edgeDistance
}
```

Then in our **gameLoop** just after the **player.loop()** line and before the **objects3D.sortOn** line put:

Camera.track(player);

17 The second to last thing we need to sort with our ninja is that we need to limit how close to the camera he can come and also how far off into the distance he can run. You may have spotted that if you keep down pressed, your ninja will not only run straight to the camera, but then somehow do a magic trick and start running on an invisible ceiling away from the camera. Not good. Let's fix it! In the Ninja Class, in the **moveUp** function where we have **z3D+=20** we add a little if statement beforehand:

```
if(z3D<5000)
        z3D+=20;
```

and in moveDown:

```
if(z3D>500)
        z3D-=20;
```

15 We need to now add some depth management. The method we will use isn't the most optimized, but it is the most simple and does the job well. In the gameLoop function before our for loop from step 14, where we call

convert3D(), we need to sort all our **3D Objects** by their depth which just happens to be their z value (**z3D**). The **z3D** value is a Numeric value, and we want to sort it from highest to lowest (descending), so we add the single line of code:

objects3D.sortOn("z3D", Array.NUMERIC | Array.DESCENDING);

Now, inside our new for loop from step 14, immediately underneath the objects3D[a].convert3D(); line, we add:

setChildIndex(objects3D[a],a)

This line sets the display ordering of our ninjas to the stage so that the ones in the distance are drawn first and the rest on top. Test the movie now, and you will see you can run in front and behind the ninjas. Yay. But uh oh! You may notice that some of our ninjas flicker. This flickering happens because they all have the same z3D value at the moment, so

when we do our array sort sometimes ninja 1 will be in front of ninja 2, and other times ninja 2 will be in front of ninja 1. Don't worry. We will fix this later by giving our ninjas their own z3D position. In the final game, it's very unlikely two ninjas will share the same z3D position and be close enough to overlap, so it won't be a problem.

18 To complete this stage, we are going to position our enemy ninjas at different depths. In our timeline code, in the **for** loop where we create our 10 ninjas, let's change and add the new **randomZ_Position** line and modify the line that creates the ninjas so that the complete **for** loop looks like this:

```
for(var a:int = 1; a <= 10; a++)
{
        var randomX_Position:Number = Math.random()*960;
        var randomZ_Position:Number = Math.random()*1000+1000;
        var enemy:Ninja = new Ninja(randomX_Position, ground_position, randomZ_Position);
        addChild(enemy);
        enemy.timeline = this;
        objects3D.push(enemy);
}
```

Stage 2 is now complete!

10 Interactivity
Stage 3

1 Let's start stage 3 by making 2 new identical classes, the only difference being their class names. As always, save these in the same folder as your FLA:

Player.as

```
package
{
    public class Player extends Ninja
    {
        public function Player(x_position:Number, y_position:Number, z_position:Number=1000)
        {
            super(x_position, y_position, z_position);
        }
    }
}
```

Enemy.as

```
package
{
    public class Enemy extends Ninja
    {
        public function Enemy(x_position:Number, y_position:Number, z_position:Number=1000)
        {
            super(x_position, y_position, z_position);
        }
    }
}
```

Currently both our enemy and player Ninjas use the same **Ninja.as Class**. Up until this point, using the same class has worked fine. However, we now are going to add some differences to our **Ninjas**, both visually and code-wise. In the same way as our **Ninja Class** extends **Base3D** but adds lots of extra functionality, we can make two new Classes, one **Player** and one **Enemy**, which both extend our **Ninja Class** but then add even more functionality.

4 Next, inside our main Player function in the new Player.as Class, we add the line:

```
setColor(1);
```

In our Enemy Class, in our main Enemy function simply put:

```
setColor(2);
```

5 We need to now make use of our new Player and Ninja **sub-Classes**. Let's go back to the timeline and change our code a little to make new Player and new Enemy Instances instead of just new Ninjas.

Change our line where we create our player to the following:

```
var player:Player = new Player(480, ground_position);
```

2 Let's differentiate the enemies from the hero ninja visually. We will keep our hero ninja in black but make our enemy ninjas red. The easiest way to assign different colors is to use 2 keyframes inside each of our ninja body parts. In the second keyframe we will fill the body parts in with red.

3 Now, when we test the game all our ninjas, including our player, will flash rapidly between colors. So, let's go to our main Ninja Class and add the function below. Because both our new layer and Enemy Classes extend our Ninja Class, they will be able to have access to this function:

```
public function setColor(frame:int):void
{
        theNinja.rightarm.gotoAndStop(frame);
        theNinja.leftarm.gotoAndStop(frame);
        theNinja.leftleg.gotoAndStop(frame);
        theNinja.rightleg.gotoAndStop(frame);
        theNinja.head.gotoAndStop(frame);
        theNinja.body.gotoAndStop(frame);
}
```

HOT TIP

If you have been using the Ninja MovieClip provided in the stage0.fla, you will notice that that there is no leftarm symbol in the library.

Instead the Ninja's left arm is actually the exact same Movie Clip as the rightarm, but mirrored horizontally.

By giving it the instance name of leftarm it means that as far as our code is concerned, it's a completely separate object from the rightarm.

6 We also need to change our for loop that creates our 10 Enemy Ninjas:

```
for(var a:int = 1; a <= 10; a++)
{
    var randomX_Position:Number = Math.random()*960;
    var randomZ_Position:Number = Math.random()*1000+1000;
    var enemy:Enemy = new Enemy(randomX_Position,ground_
    position,randomZ_Position);
    addChild(enemy);
    enemy.timeline = this;
    objects3D.push(enemy);
    enemies.push(enemy);
}
```

Also note, we've added an additional line of code. We now store a reference to our enemy in new array called **enemies** which of course needs creating first. So add the code to create this array just above our for loop. You should know how to create an Array on your own now. The reason we will create this new enemies array is so that when it comes to attacking, we just look in this array, rather than our complete **objects3D** array, to determine which (if any) enemies we will face.

7 Now, we actually have some bits of code still in our **Ninja Class** that our **Enemy Class** doesn't need to worry about, so these should really be moved to just our **Player Class**. These are the movement functions. Cut and Paste these functions and their code from the **Ninja Class** into our **Player Class**:

moveLeft
moveRight
moveUp
moveDown
stopMoving

Having fun yet? In the next step we'll start adding ninjas that will attack our hero ninja!

8 Currently our Ninja MovieClip has 3 animation states. Still, Run and Jump. In each of these states, we want it to be possible to perform an attack. One option could be to make 3 new animations, using the originals as a basis: **StillAttack**, **RunAttack** and **JumpAttack**. However... what if we start an attack while still and then start running while the attack is still happening? Or what if we are running and press attack when the ninja steps onto his right foot, and then the next time, we want to start the attack when he's stepped onto his left foot? To think about and then make animations for all the possible combinations will take a lot of time. What's more, there would be a lot of code to correctly display the animation.

So, we come up with a trick! We give our Ninja a 3rd arm! This arm is complete with sword and contains a 20 frame animation of the arm reaching for the sword, swinging it and then putting the sword away with extra blur for effect.

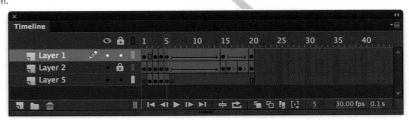

10 When our ninja jumps, we can see that if we keep our **A** key down, our ninja will constantly jump which is perfectly fine.

However, with attacking we want the player to work for that attack and not have the ninja constantly swinging his sword if you just keep the **S** key down. Therefore, we will only trigger the next sword swing if the game has detected that the player has released the attack key after the previous sword swing.

Because this code is only related to our **Player** and not **Enemies** (they won't be controlled via the keyboard), we add a new variable to our **Player** class, **attackKeyReleased**, and then set it to be true. So our Player Class will now look like this:

```
package
{
  public class Player extends Ninja
  {
    public var attackKeyReleased:Boolean;
    public function Player(x_position:Number, y_position:Number, z_position:Number=1000)
    {
      super(x_position, y_position, z_position);
      setColor(1);
      attackKeyReleased=true;
    }

    public function moveLeft():void
    {
      x3D -= 20;
      if (!running)
      {
        running = true;
        if (!jumping) theNinja.gotoAndPlay("run");
      }
      direction = -1;
    }

    public function moveRight():void
    {
      x3D += 20;
      if (!running)
      {
        running = true;
        if (!jumping) theNinja.gotoAndPlay("run");
      }
      direction = 1;
    }
```

9 We place this 3rd **Arm MovieClip** which we will give the instance name **swordarm**, in roughly the same place inside our **Ninja MovieClip** as the **rightarm**. With code, we now make sure that we only show either the **rightarm** or **swordarm** and never both (thus never making our ninja appear to have 3 arms). Also, we need to hide the sword on our ninjas back when the **swordarm** is in swing. In our main Ninja Class inside the Ninja function, let's add the following line of code:

theNinja.swordarm.visible = false;

```
public function moveUp():void
{
    if(z3D<5000)
        z3D += 20;
    if (!running)
    {
        running = true;
        if (!jumping) theNinja.gotoAndPlay("run");
    }
}

public function moveDown():void
{
    if(z3D>500)
        z3D -= 20;
    if (!running)
    {
        running = true;
        if (!jumping) theNinja.gotoAndPlay("run");
    }
}

public function stopMoving():void
{
    running = false;
    if (!jumping) theNinja.gotoAndPlay("still");
    }
  }
}
```

11 In the next two steps we are going to modify our Ninja Class to add support for attacking.

When our Ninja performs an attack, we need to remember to hide the normal **rightarm** and show the new **swordarm**. Likewise, when the attack animation is over we need to hide the **swordarm** and show the **rightarm** again. We also need to hide and show the sword on the Ninja's back appropriately.

So we add **addFrameScript**, a function call to the last keyframe of our **swordarm** animation so that we can change the visibilities. We make a new **attackfinished** function that makes the **swordarm** invisible and the **rightarm** and **sword** visible.

Currently our complete Ninja Class should look like the following:

```
package
{

        public class Ninja extends Base3D
        {
                public var theNinja:NinjaMC
                public var running:Boolean;
                public var jumping:Boolean;
                public var gravity:Number;

                public function Ninja(x_position:Number, y_position:Number, z_position:Number = 1000)
                {
                        theNinja = new NinjaMC();
                        addChild(theNinja);
                        theNinja.gotoAndStop("still_end");
                        theNinja.addFrameScript(theNinja.currentFrame - 1, loopStill);
                        theNinja.gotoAndStop("run_end");
                        theNinja.addFrameScript(theNinja.currentFrame - 1, loopRun);
                        theNinja.gotoAndStop("jump_end");
                        theNinja.addFrameScript(theNinja.currentFrame - 1, jumpFinished);
                        theNinja.swordarm.visible = false;
                        theNinja.swordarm.addFrameScript(theNinja.swordarm.totalFrames-1, attackFinished);
                        theNinja.gotoAndPlay(1);
                        running = false;
                        jumping = false;
                        gravity = 10;
                        theNinja.swordarm.visible = false;
                        super(x_position, y_position, z_position);
                }

                public function setColor(frame:int):void
                {
                        theNinja.rightarm.gotoAndStop(frame);
                        theNinja.leftarm.gotoAndStop(frame);
                        theNinja.swordarm.rightarm.gotoAndStop(frame);
                        theNinja.leftleg.gotoAndStop(frame);
                        theNinja.rightleg.gotoAndStop(frame);
                        theNinja.head.gotoAndStop(frame);
                        theNinja.body.gotoAndStop(frame);
                }

                public function loopStill():void
                {
                        theNinja.gotoAndPlay("still");
                }
```

```
public function loopRun():void
{
        theNinja.gotoAndPlay("run");
}

public function jumpFinished():void
{
        if (running)
        {
                theNinja.gotoAndPlay("run");
        }
        else
        {
                theNinja.gotoAndPlay("still");
        }
}

public function attackFinished():void
{
        theNinja.swordarm.visible=false;
        theNinja.rightarm.visible=true;
        theNinja.sword.visible=true;
}

public function jump():void
{
        if (!jumping)
        {
                theNinja.gotoAndPlay("jump");
                gravity = -40;
                jumping = true;
        }
}

public function loop():void
{
        y3D += gravity;
        if (y3D >= timeline.ground_position)
        {
                y3D = timeline.ground_position;
                jumping = false;
        }
        gravity += 5;
}
    }
}
```

12 Because we will want both our Player and Enemies to be able to attack, we add our attack function to the Ninja Class. In this function, because the first 5 frames of the **swordarm** animation are the actual attack part and the remaining frames are a much slower animation of the ninja putting the sword away, we actually want our ninja to be able to reattack after frame 5. So we check to see if the

swordarm animation is currently either on the first frame or on a frame after frame 5, before animating the sword attack. In the same way that our **attackFinished** function hides our **swordarm** and shows our normal **rightarm** and **sword**, the attack function hides the **rightarm** and **sword** and shows the **swordarm**. We also tell the **swordarm** to play the animation from frame 1.

```
public function attack():void
{
        if(theNinja.swordarm.currentFrame == 1 || theNinja.swordarm.currentFrame > 5)
        {
                theNinja.swordarm.gotoAndPlay(1);
                theNinja.swordarm.visible=true;
                theNinja.rightarm.visible=false;
                theNinja.sword.visible=false;
        }
}
```

15 Now let's start working with the enemy! Currently we are only calling **loop** on our ninja player. We now want to get all the enemy ninjas doing new things too, so we need to start calling **loop** for them. We already have a bit of code that loops through all of our Objects and runs a command on them **convert3D**, we can delete our **player.loop** line and add **objects3D[a].loop();** in our for loop, like so:

```
for(a = 0; a < objects3D.length; a++)
{
        objects3D[a].loop();
        objects3D[a].convert3D();
        setChildIndex(objects3D[a],a)
}
```

16 Give the enemy a brain! We know that Enemy extends Ninja and that Ninja has a function in it called **loop** which gets called every frame. Currently this function just handles gravity. However, we can add extra features to this function, features just for our Enemies, just like we did with our Player attack function in Step 13. So in our Enemy Class, add this:

```
override public function loop():void
{
        super.loop();
}
```

19 But what about movement!? We need our enemy to **decide** on where he wants to run to and then make **steps** towards getting there. First of all, we need to add 3 new variables to the top of our Enemy Class:

```
public var steps:int;
public var xStep:Number;
public var zStep:Number;
```

20 Let's make a new **runTo** function inside our Enemy Class.

```
public function runTo(x:Number, z:Number):void
{

}
```

Note that we pass **x** and **z** (not **y**, as **y** is for jumping) to our **runTo** function.

13 So both our enemies and player now can attack, but we actually need some extra code for our **Player** to check if they are allowed to attack (have they let go of the attack key). Instead of rewriting a complete **attack** function in our Player Class, we can use the special keyword **override** which means we can then add some extra code to the function that already exists in our Ninja Class. The other special keyword used is **super** which means that we then perform all the code that exists in the Ninja Class attack function. Add this code to your Player Class:

```
override public function attack():void
{
        if(attackKeyReleased)
        {
            super.attack();
        }
        attackKeyReleased=false;
}
```

14 Finally we need to add to our Player Class a **stopAttacking** function. This function sets our **attackKeyReleased** Boolean to true which means that our code will allow us to attack again.

```
public function stopAttacking():void
{
        attackKeyReleased = true;
}
```

Of course, what good are **attack** and **stopAttacking** functions if we have no keyboard command to trigger them? In our main timeline code, we add **keyPressedAction** and **keyReleasedAction**. You should know where to place these:

```
keyPressedActions[Keyboard.S] = player.attack;
```

```
keyReleasedActions[Keyboard.S]= player.stopAttacking;
```

HOT TIP

In the code in Step 12, you will notice || in the line. This symbol is not the number eleven, instead it represents the word "or." In our attack function we are telling Flash to perform the commands if the swordarm is on frame 1, "or" the "swordarm" is on a frame greater than 5.

Sometimes you will see && instead of ||, which means "and."

17 The **super.loop** means that we keep running our loop function with gravity-related code in our Ninja Class, rather than getting rid of it all together. But let's add some new code that will be unique to our enemies.

```
override public function loop():void
{
        if(int(Math.random() * 100) == 1) jump();
        super.loop();
}
```

18 The code in the previous step is basically saying that there is a 1 in 100 chance the enemy will **decide** to jump. Let's add this line in too:

```
if(int(Math.random() * 100) == 1) attack();
```

If we test our game we'll see that we have red, random sword-swinging, jumping enemy ninjas. Yay.

21 Let's say our enemy ninja is currently standing at 100, 100 in x, z coordinates. And we want to tell him to **runTo(500, 200)**, possibly because that's where our player is. First of all we have to work out the distance from where our enemy currently is to where he wants to go. We need a bit of Pythagorean Theorem. Inside our new **runTo** function, we add:

```
var distanceX:Number = x-x3D;
var distanceZ:Number = z-z3D;
var totalDistance:Number = Math.sqrt(distanceX * distanceX + distanceZ * distanceZ);
```

22 Now that we know the **totalDistance** our enemy has to run, we can work out how many steps it will take him to get there. For now we are going to use a speed value of **20** (literally, moving 20 pixels per **gameLoop**) which is the same as our player Ninja. Continue putting this code inside our **runTo** function:

steps = totalDistance / 20;

We know how many steps our ninja will need to take to get from 100,100 to 500,200, so we then use that to work out each step (or distance) in x and z he will need to make per **gameLoop**:

xStep = distanceX / steps;
zStep = distanceZ / steps;

23 Finally, we need to work out which direction our enemy should be facing when moving:

direction = 1;
if(distanceX < 0) direction = -1;

and then set his animation to running

running=true;
if(!jumping)theNinja.gotoAndPlay("run");

25 Since our enemy can **runTo** somewhere, let's actually tell him where to run. Make a function called **runToRandomPosition**. We always want our ninjas to be close to the player, so we make sure the random position the enemy runs includes our players **x3D** and **z3D** coordinates. We then make sure our Enemy won't run too close or far from the camera. Finally we call the **runTo** function.

```
public function runToRandomPosition():void
{
    var x:Number = Math.random()*600-300 + timeline.player.x3D;
    var z:Number = Math.random()*400-200 + timeline.player.z3D;
    if(z > 5000) z = 5000;
    if(z < 300 ) z = 300;
    runTo(x,z);
}
```

26 Just like the jump and attack, we add the line to our loop function. Note this time we just use **50**, instead of 100 giving a 1 in 50 chance our Enemy will choose to run somewhere. We also want to only choose a new position to run too, if our Ninja isn't mid-jump.

if(int(Math.random() * 50) == 1 && !jumping) runToRandomPosition();

24 So our complete runTo function:

```
public function runTo(x:Number, z:Number):void
{
        var distanceX:Number = x−x3D;
        var distanceZ:Number = z−z3D;
        var totalDistance:Number = Math.sqrt(distanceX * distanceX + distanceZ * distanceZ);
        steps = totalDistance / 20;
        xStep = distanceX / steps;
        zStep = distanceZ / steps;
        direction = 1;
        if(distanceX < 0) direction = −1;
        running=true;
        if(!jumping)theNinja.gotoAndPlay("run");
}
```

27 We need to continue modifying our loop function to get our Enemy to take these new steps we have. We also need to tell our enemy ninja to go back to its **still** animation if it's taken all its steps and arrived at its goal. We only go to **still** if the enemy isn't also jumping. Our loop function is now:

```
override public function loop():void
{
     if(int(Math.random() * 100) == 1) jump();
     if(int(Math.random() * 100) == 1) attack();
     if(int(Math.random() * 50) == 1) runToRandomPosition();
     if(steps > 0)
     {
          steps−−;
          x3D += xStep;
          z3D += zStep;
     }
     else
     {
          if(running)
          {
          running=false;
          if(!jumping)theNinja.gotoAndPlay("still");
          }
     }
     super.loop();
}
```

28 Currently all our attack function does is handle the sword swinging. We don't yet see if the swing will hit an enemy (or if the enemy's swing will hit the player). Before we can check for a hit, we are going to add some extra variables to our Ninja Class to simulate some very basic physics, namely, when a Ninja is attacked, we want it to be pushed away by the force of the sword swing. At the top of our Ninja Class, add these two lines:

```
public var forceX:Number = 0;
public var forceZ:Number = 0;
```

Then at the bottom of our **loop** function, we put:

```
x3D += forceX;
z3D += forceZ;
forceX *= .8;
forceZ *= .8;
```

HOT TIP

Creating a force variable and then using the multiplication assignment operator means that whatever the force was, is now reduced to 80%.

327

29 Let's apply these forces to our enemies if our player successfully hits them. We loop through our enemies array in the timeline and test for all ninjas within a certain distance from the player. The ones that are close enough, we then affect their force. Place this code in our Player Class.

```
public function checkEnemies():void
{
    var attackReachX:int = 280;
    var attackReachZ:int = 150;
    var attackForce:int = 80;
    for each(var enemy:Enemy in timeline.enemies)
    {
        var distanceX:Number = enemy.x3D- x3D;
        var distanceZ:Number = enemy.z3D - z3D;
        if(distanceX * direction > 0 && Math.abs(distanceZ) < attackReachZ && Math.abs(distanceX) <attackReachX)
        {
            var angle:Number = Math.atan2(distanceZ,distanceX);
            enemy.forceX = attackForce * Math.cos(angle);
            enemy.forceZ = attackForce * Math.sin(angle);
        }
    }
}
```

The distanceX * direction > 0 check in our if statement means we only look for ninjas our player is facing (not those close behind).

31 We now modify the attack function in the Player Class again:

```
override public function attack():Boolean
{
        if(attackKeyReleased)
        {
                if(super.attack())
                    checkEnemies();
        }
        attackKeyReleased = false;
        return true;
}
```

32 Remember where we limited the Ninjas z3D value so that it couldn't go less than 300 or more than 500? Since we are now using forceZ it's possible that the ninjas could exceed these values. We need to add some more code to our **loop** function of the Ninja class so that the Ninjas appear to bounce off of this boundary. Note we shall also only reduce our force variables if our ninja is on the ground.

```
public function loop():void
{
        y3D += gravity;
        if(y3D >= timeline.ground_position)
        {
            y3D = timeline.ground_position;
            jumping = false;
        }
        gravity += 5;
        x3D += forceX;
        z3D += forceZ;
        if(z3D < 300 || z3D > 5000)
        {
            forceZ =-forceZ;
            z3D += forceZ;
        }
        if(y3D == timeline.ground_position)
        {
            forceX *= .8;
            forceZ *= .8;
        }
}
```

30 We need to **checkEnemies** when we know an attack has been performed. In our Ninja Class, we need to modify our attack function slightly so that it will return a **true** or **false** value depending on if the attack (sword swing) was made successfully.

```
public function attack():Boolean
{
        if(theNinja.swordarm.currentFrame == 1 || theNinja.swordarm.currentFrame > 5)
        {
                theNinja.swordarm.gotoAndPlay(1);
                theNinja.swordarm.visible=true;
                theNinja.rightarm.visible=false;
                theNinja.sword.visible=false;
                return true;
        }
        return false;
}
```

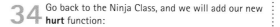

33 We can physically hit the enemy ninjas, but they never die. To be able to die you first need to live. Let's give the Ninja Class "life." We will also stun our Ninjas for a short time when we hit them so that ultimately they can't immediately hit us back as that would be mean! Make a second new variable **stunned**:

```
public var life:int;
public var stunned:int;
```

While we are in the Ninja Class in our loop function add:

```
stunned--;
```

Now in Enemy class in the main Enemy function add:

```
life = 3;
```

We'll give our Player life too. A higher value makes him tougher, so in the Player Class in the main function add:
```
life = 20;
```

In the **checkEnemies** function of the player, let's add a function call just below our **enemy.force** lines:

```
enemy.hurt();
```

34 Go back to the Ninja Class, and we will add our new **hurt** function:

```
public function hurt():void
{
        stunned = 15;
        life--;
        if(life ==0)
        {
                dead();
        }
}
```

Now add the "dead" function. In case our ninja was attacking when it died, we hide the swordarm and make the right arm and separate sword visible.

```
public function dead():void
{
        theNinja.swordarm.visible=false;
        theNinja.rightarm.visible=true;
        theNinja.sword.visible=true;
        theNinja.gotoAndPlay("die");
}
```

35 We don't have a death animation, so we'll need to make one. Just a simple animation of our ninja falling over will suffice. If you make the animation fade out at the end, your ninja will disappear nicely. This fade can be handled via code, but a Motion Tween works just as well. The death animation was created using keyframes poses and Classic Tweens. No new assets for the ninja were necessary as the death animation uses the same body parts. Just animate the ninja collapsing to his knees first before keeling over and eventually lying flat against the ground. You may find the use of keyframes works better than Motion Tweens or a combination of both. There's no right or wrong way to create this animation. Use your imagination and come up with something unique if you'd prefer.

36 As with the other animations, we need the frame labels **die** at the beginning of the death animation and then **die_end** in the final frame of the animation. As shown below, a new layer was created just for Frame Labels to reside. Having a dedicated layer for labels is just for file management purposes.

HOT TIP

If you make the animation fade out at the end where the ninja is in his last frame of dying, your ninja will disappear nicely. This fade can be handled via code, but we aren't going to do that as it's just as easy to apply a Motion tween and some alpha to make him disapear.

37 Because we have a new animation sequence in our ninja, we need to add the following 2 lines of code to our Ninja Class, place them just below the other **addFrameScript** lines in our main function:

```
theNinja.gotoAndStop("die_end");
theNinja.addFrameScript(theNinja.currentFrame-1, dieFinished);
```

Then the following function:

```
public function dieFinished():void
{
       removeChild(theNinja);
       markForRemoval = true;
}
```

The function **removeChild** removes the MovieClip from wherever it is sitting. We remove both **theNinja** MovieClip but not the actual Ninja Class just yet. Instead we mark it for removal. The **markForRemoval** is a new variable we haven't used before and want to define in our Base3D Class:

```
public var markForRemoval:Boolean;
```

38 Rather than removing Class instances straight away when we no long need them, it's often good practice to do a "tidy up" of your instances right at the end of the main game loop. There should be no other code running associated with those class instances, and therefore you are less likely to get any bugs when removing them. To remove everything that has **markForRemoval** set to "true," we add a new **for** loop right at the bottom of our **gameLoop** in the timeline:

```
for(a = 0; a < objects3D.length; a++)
{
       if(objects3D[a].markForRemoval)
       {
              removeChild(objects3D[a]);
              objects3D.splice(a, 1);
              a--;
       }
}
```

When the ninja dies, not only does he visually disappear from the stage, but he gets removed from the **objects3D** array which means there is no longer any **loop** or **convert3D** code running for this Ninja. Because we have now removed all references to this Ninja, Flash will free up some of the memory used and your game will continue to perform well.

331

39 When our Enemy has no life or when he is stunned, we don't want him to still randomly decide if he wants to jump, run, attack etc. In the Enemy Class we add 2 **if** statements around this code in the **loop** function:

```
if(life > 0)
{
        if(stunned <= 0)
        {
                if(int(Math.random() * 100) == 1) jump();
                if(int(Math.random() * 100) == 1) attack();
                if(int(Math.random() * 50) == 1)runToRandomPosition();
                if(steps > 0)
                {
                        steps--;
                        x3D+= xStep;
                        z3D += zStep;
                }
                else
                {
                        if(running)
                        {
                                running=false;
                                if(!jumping)theNinja.gotoAndPlay("still");
                        }
                }
        }
}
```

40 When our Enemy has died, we need to remove it from the **enemies** array so that our player can no longer hit/attack it. To remove it, in the Enemy Class we add a new variable:

public var removedFromEnemies:Boolean;

In our **loop** function where we already have the **if(life>0)** statement add the following after it:

```
else
{
        if(!removedFromEnemies)
        {
                removedFromEnemies = true;
                for (var a:int = 0; a < timeline.enemies.
                length; a++)
                {
                        if(timeline.enemies[a] == this)
                        {
                                timeline.enemies.splice(a,1);
                                break;
                        }
                }
        }
}
```

43 We also need to put an **if** statment in the Players **stopMoving** function too:

public function stopMoving():void
```
{
    if(life>0)
    {
        running = false;
        if(!jumping)theNinja.gotoAndPlay("still");
    }
}
```

44 To be fair to our enemies, let's allow our player to get hurt. Similar to how our Player hits an Enemy, we can get our Enemy to hit our Player. In our Enemy Class, we override the attack function just like in the Player Class but call a **checkPlayer** function instead. We only call this function if we know our player still has life left:

override public function attack():Boolean
```
{
        if(super.attack() && timeline.player.life > 0)checkPlayer();
        return true;
}
```

41 If you kill an enemy when he is jumping, we don't want the run or still animation to be played when he falls to the ground. So we put the if statement in our Ninja Class too:

```
public function jumpFinished():void
{
    if(life > 0)
    {
        if (running)
        {
            theNinja.gotoAndPlay("run");
        }
        else
        {
            theNinja.gotoAndPlay("still");
        }
    }
}
```

42 Although our Player can't get hurt yet, let's make sure that if he has no life or if he is stunned, he no longer can be controlled. It's best if we actually go to where the keys are pressed in our main timeline's **gameLoop**:

```
if(player.life > 0 && player.stunned <=0)
{
    for(var key:String in keys)
    {
        if(keyPressedActions[key]) keyPressedActions[key]();
    }
}
```

45 Our **checkPlayer** function will be very similar to check Enemies. The only difference is that we don't do the **for** loop as there's only one player to check:

```
public function checkPlayer():void
{
    var attackReachX:int = 280;
    var attackReachZ:int = 150;
    var attackForce:int = 80;
    var distanceX:Number = timeline.player.x3D - x3D;
    var distanceZ:Number = timeline.player.z3D - z3D;
    if(distanceX * direction > 0 && Math.abs(distanceZ) < attackReachZ && Math.abs(distanceX) <attackReachX)
    {
        var angle:Number = Math.atan2(distanceZ,distanceX);
        timeline.player.forceX = attackForce * Math.cos(angle);
        timeline.player.forceZ = attackForce * Math.sin(angle);
        timeline.player.hurt();
    }
}
```

Interactivity

46 Having 10 enemies all running around at the start of a game is a bit exessive. Let's ease the Player into the game by starting with just one enemy. Back in our main timeline we are going to delete all our code for adding the 10 enemies (the entire **for** loop). Then, after we create our player, put in this code:

```
function addEnemy()
{
        var randomX_Position:Number = Math.random()*2000 + player.x3D - 1000;
        var randomZ_Position:Number = 2000+Math.random()*1000;
        var enemy:Enemy = new Enemy(randomX_Position, -500, randomZ_Position);
        enemy.jumping = true;
        addChild(enemy);
        enemy.timeline = this;
        objects3D.push(enemy);
        enemies.push(enemy)
}
addEnemy();
var totalEnemies:int = 10;
```

48 Not to be insulting but the enemy Ninjas are a bit dumb. They currently attack randomly regardless of their location on screen, and they don't make any extra effort to aim their attacks at your player. Currently they operate on a 1 in 100 chance of *deciding* to attack. We'll leave the decision making up to them but code it so that when they get closer to the player the chance of attack increases. In the

loop function in the Enemy Class we work out the distance the enemy is from the player. If that distance is less than 1000, we will divide that distance by 10 (that way we never get above our 1 in 100 chance). Then we'll use that value **attackChance**, when determining if the enemy should attack. We'll do a quick check to make sure that chance is never less than 1 in 3:

```
override public function loop():void
{
        if(life > 0)
        {
                if(int(Math.random() * 100) == 1) jump();
                var attackChance:int = 100;
                var distanceX:Number = timeline.player.x3D x3D;
                var distanceZ:Number = timeline.player.z3D z3D
                var totalDistance:Number = Math.sqrt(distanceX * distanceX + distanceZ * distanceZ);
                if(totalDistance<1000) attackChance = totalDistance/10;
                if(attackChance < 3) attackChance = 3;
                if(int(Math.random() * attackChance) == 1) attack();
                ....................
```

47 Notice how we've changed the code a little? Enemies will now start far away in the background as well as in the air which is why we set jumping to be "true." Creating enemies this way gives them the nice effect of "dropping in" to give the player a little warning. We also now have a **totalEnemies** variable. In our main **gameLoop** we can check if we have less enemies on screen than the total allowed (**totalEnemies**). If the number of enemies starts to drop off we can randomly add new enemies as needed. Add this code right at the top of the **gameLoop**:

```
if(int(Math.random()*50) == 1 && enemies.length < totalEnemies)
{
      addEnemy();
}
```

49 It would be a good idea to make sure the enemy is facing our player when they attack:

```
override public function attack():Boolean
{
      if(super.attack() && timeline.player.life > 0)
      {
            checkPlayer();
            direction = 1;
            if(timeline.player.x3D < x3D) direction = -1;
      }
      return true;
}
```

Stage 3 is now complete!

Stage 4

S O WE HAVE THE BASICS OF A GAME! You can attack and die as can your enemies attack and die. Let's keep going and add some UI elements!

But we have a slight problem. In our code we do some depth sorting on our ninjas so that when they are in the foreground they are above the ninjas in the background. This depth sorting uses the **setChildIndex** command to put each ninja in the correct order, typically putting them on top of everything else in the game.

If we start to put our UI elements on the stage, when we run the game our ninjas will be placed on top of them. What we really want is for the UI elements to always be on top of the ninjas. We could run some code in our **gameLoop** to always call **setChildIndex** on each of our UI elements after the depth sorting for the ninjas. However this method is a little messy and there is an easy trick for better separation of the game from the UI. We can make 2 MovieClips, one called "game" and one called "ui." From this point forward we make sure that all of our game objects (our ninjas) are initially added to our game MovieClip via **addChild** and all our UI objects are inside "ui." We then place "game" on our stage first and then "ui" on top. No more worrying about having to change the **childIndex** of our UI elements.

1 Because we will visually want to edit our UI, let's create the instance of the Movie Clip the normal Flash way by using the Library panel's drop-down menu. Create a new empty MovieClip called **ui** and place it in a new Layer on the stage at **0,0** in **x** and **y** coordinates. Give it the instance name **ui**.

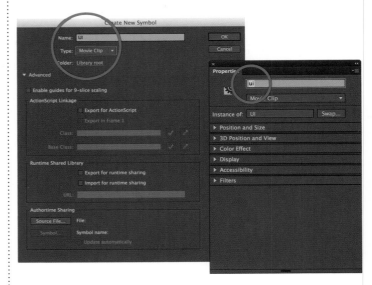

4 Let's now add the UI. The first thing we need to do is add a text field to our **ui** Movie Clip to show the score. "Edit in Place" the **ui** MovieClip and create a new dynamic textfield in the top left of screen. Select a large font and add the instance name **scoreTF** (which stands for score TextField). If you type **0123456789** into the text field, we can be sure the font will be embedded easily.

2 In the timeline code above everything else, add these 3 lines of code:

```
var game:MovieClip = new MovieClip();
addChild(game);
addChild(ui);
```

Because our ui is already created and on stage we call the **addChild** command to make sure it's on top of our game MovieClip.

3 There are four places where we need to reference our new **game** MovieClip. In our two **addChild** lines for the player and the enemy, then where we call setChildIndex(objects3D[a],a); and finally where we call **removeChild**.

Find those 4 lines in our main timeline code and change them to the following:

```
game.addChild(player);
```

```
game.addChild(enemy);
```

```
game.setChildIndex(objects3D[a],a);
```

```
game.removeChild(objects3D[a]);
```

HOT TIP

Entering a Class name to a MovieClip requires right-clicking over the MovieClip in the library, clicking Advanced and subsequently clicking the "Export for ActionScript" checkbox. A quicker way of adding a class is to double-click in the empty space in the 'AS Linkage' column next to the Movie Clip in the library. You can then immediately type in the Class name you want to use and the appropriate check boxes will have been ticked automatically.

5 In your timeline code add the following:

```
var score:int = 0;
ui.scoreTF.text="00000";
```

And then we add a new **updateScore** function:

```
function updateScore():void
{
    score++;
    var fullScore:String = String(score);
    while(fullScore.length<5)
    fullScore="0"+fullScore;
    ui.scoreTF.text = fullScore;
}
```

6 In our **Player.as Class** let's call **updateScore** after our **enemy.hurt** line in the **checkEnemies** function. Remember we need "timeline" first:

```
timeline.updateScore();
```

Whenever we hit an enemy, our score increases by 1. But let's make it more fun. Let's add a basic combo scoring system where if we hit enemies in quick succession, we get more points for each new hit. Back in the main timeline, we add 3 new variables:

```
var comboCounter:int = 0;
var lastHitTime:int = 0;
var maxCombo:int = 0;
```

7 Let's now modify our **updateScore** function:

```
function updateScore():void
{
  if(getTimer() - lastHitTime < 500)
  {
    comboCounter++;
  }
  else
  {
    comboCounter = 1;
  }
  lastHitTime = getTimer();
  score+= comboCounter
  var fullScore:String = String(score);
  while(fullScore.length<5)
    fullScore="0"+fullScore;
  ui.scoreTF.text = fullScore;
}
```

8 Let's add 2 more text fields to our **ui** MovieClip using the same font as the score: 1 textfield to show our last combo and a 2nd to show our maximum combo. Give these 2 text fields instance names of **lastComboTF** and **maxComboTF** and type into them "Max Combo: 0" and "Last Combo: 0." We don't need to include numerals 1 through 9 as they are already embedded in the score text field. Let's modify the **updateScore** function again. This time where we have **comboCounter = 1** we add these lines before it:

```
else
{
    if(comboCounter > 1)
    {
        if(maxCombo < comboCounter) maxCombo = comboCounter;
        ui.maxComboTF.text = "Max Combo: " + maxCombo;
        ui.lastComboTF.text = "Last Combo: "+comboCounter;

    }
    comboCounter = 1;
}
```

11 In **gameLoop** we'll add an extra line of code:

```
ui.healthBar.scaleX = 1/20*player.life;
```

We use **20** because that is our player's maximum life.

12 Finally we're going to add a timer countdown. In the top right of the **ui** MovieClip, add a final text field and name it **countdownTF**

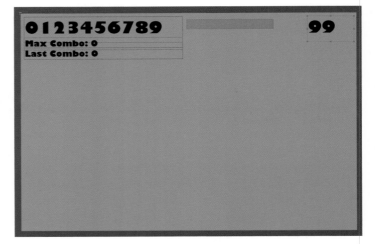

9 Let's add a health bar for our player. Inside our **UI** MovieClip make a new MovieClip with a red rectangle and place it along the top of the screen. Name the MovieClip **healthBar** and make sure the anchor point is on the left somewhere (either top, bottom or center).

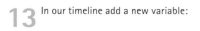

10 Select the **healthBar** MovieClip and give it the instance name **healthBar**.

13 In our timeline add a new variable:

```
var timer:Number=99;
```

and in our game loop add:

```
timer -= 1/30;
ui.countdownTF.text = String(Math.ceil(timer));
```

Our game will run at 30fps. For each frame we subtract a 30th of the time. So what happens when time runs out or we run out of health? Yes, game over!

14 Make a new MovieClip inside our **ui** called **"gameover."** Give it an instance name **gameoverMC** and place three text fields inside it. The 1st and 3rd can be static text fields while the 2nd will be dynamic for showing the score. Give this dynamic text field an instance name of **scoreTF**.

339

15 The first textfield can say something like "Game Over, You scored" and be placed above or next to your dynamic text field.

16 Then underneath the score, the 3rd text field can say "click anywhere to play again" or something similar. Note, I've put a large blue rectangle containing 80% alpha behind my text so that you can read the black font easily (otherwise it will clash with our player ninja).

18 Let's create our **gameover** function which we can add to the bottom of our main timeline code:

```
function gameover():void
{
    if(!gameIsOver)
    {
        ui.gameoverMC.visible=true;
        ui.gameoverMC.scoreTF.text=ui.scoreTF.text;
        gameIsOver = true;
        player.stopMoving();
        addEventListener(MouseEvent.CLICK, resetGame)
    }
}
```

19 We need to call that function when our player dies and when the time runs out. For a timer in our game loop after we have the line **timer-= 1/30**, we add these lines:

```
if(timer < 0)
{
    gameover();
    timer = 0;
}
```

For a **gameover** when our player dies, we're going to be a little clever. In our Player Class, we're going to override our **dieFinished** function from Ninja but not **super()** it, meaning all the code will be ignored. We will just call **timeline.gameover()**. This cheat means that our **Player** instance is never actually removed from the game. Instead, we will be reusing it when the user clicks to start a new game. If we don't remove the **Player** instance, then we don't have to reassign all the **keyboardActions**.

In the Player class let's add the following code:

```
override public function dieFinished():void
{
    theNinja.stop();
    timeline.gameover();
}
```

17 Back in our timeline code, we want to make sure this **gameover** MovieClip isn't visible when the game starts.

```
ui.gameoverMC.visible = false;
```

We also want a new variable to tell the code whether or not the game is over. For example, we don't want the player to be able to continue to attack once **gameover()** has been called.

```
var gameIsOver:Boolean = false;
```

All we then need to do is adjust our **if** statement in the game loop to also check to see if **gameIsOver** is not true:

```
if(player.life > 0 && player.stunned<=0 && !gameIsOver)
```

20 Back to the timeline you'll notice our **gameover** function calls **resetGame** when you click the mouse, but we don't have a **resetGame** function! Basically this function needs to reset everything back to the first time you start the game: 20 health, 99 seconds, 0 points, 0 enemies etc. It's kind of a cleanup function. The only thing we don't clean up is **Player** as we reposition him and revive him:

```
function resetGame(e:MouseEvent):void
{
    removeEventListener(MouseEvent.CLICK, resetGame);
    gameIsOver = false;
    ui.gameoverMC.visible=false;
    timer=99;
    score=0;
    ui.scoreTF.text="00000";
    comboCounter=0;
    lastHitTime=0;
    maxCombo = 0;
    ui.maxComboTF.text = "Max Combo: "+maxCombo;
    ui.lastComboTF.text = "Last Combo: "+comboCounter;
    player.stopMoving();
    for(var a:int=0; a<objects3D.length; a++)
    {
        if(objects3D[a]!=player)
        {
        game.removeChild(objects3D[a])
        }
    }
    objects3D = [player];
    enemies = [];
    player.theNinja.gotoAndPlay("still");
    player.life = 20;
    player.x3D = Camera.x3D;
    player.z3D = 1000;
}
```

THERE ARE SEVERAL WAYS TO handle the preloading of Flash files, and countless tutorials exist on the web as to how to create them. Given that preloading plays a relatively small part of our game, let's not get too complicated with animated bars and percentages. For this example we'll just show a little bit of text to inform the player that their game is indeed loading. You can always come back to this preloader and add a looping animation if you prefer, but it's not necessary.

1 In our main Timeline, currently we have placed everything in frame 1. Our code, our UI and even our Classes in the library are set up to be exported on frame 1. To make room on our Timeline for a preloader, select the 2 keyframes on our layers, and drag them to frame 2. Frame 1 should now be empty.

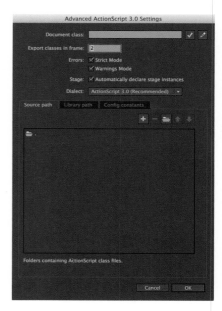

4 Finally, go to File > ActionScript Settings, and change the 1 in "Export classes" input field to the value of 2. Now when a user starts the game, frame 1 will load quickly, showing the user that the rest of the game is loading. When the load is complete, frame 2, and therefore the game, will start automatically.

2 Add a text field to the stage in frame 1 and type the text "loading..." into it

There's nothing preventing you from creating a looping animation in a MovieClip instead of or alongside the text field above. Often we see preloaders with various spinning graphics to indicate something is being loaded. Whatever you decide to create should be as small as possible as not to bloat the file size and defeat the purpose of the preloader.

3 In our code layer, which is in frame 2, just add at the top a **stop();** command:

```
1    stop();
2
3    import flash.display.MovieClip;
4    import flash.geom.Point;
5    import flash.events.TouchEvent;
6
7    Multitouch.inputMode = MultitouchInputMode.TOUCH_POINT
8
9    var game:MovieClip = new MovieClip();
10   addChild(game);
11   addChild(ui);
12   ui.gameoverMC.visible=false;
13
14   var gameIsOver:Boolean = false;
15
16   var ground_position:int = 500;
17
18   var objects3D:Array = new Array();
19   var enemies:Array = new Array();
20
21   var score:int=0;
22   ui.scoreTF.text="00000";
23   var comboCounter:int=0;
24   var lastHitTime:int=0;
25   var maxCombo:int = 0;
26   var timer:Number=99;
27   var controller:Controller = new Controller();
28   ui.addChild(controller)
29   controller.visible=false;
30   controller.gotoAndStop(1);
31
32   var player:Player = new Player(480, ground_position);
33   player.global = this;
34   game.addChild(player)
35   objects3D.push(player)
36
37   function addEnemy()
38   {
39       var randomX_Position:Number = Math.random()*2000 + playe
40       var randomZ_Position:Number = 2000+Math.random()*1000;
41       var enemy:Enemy = new Enemy(randomX_Position, -500, rand
```

Line 1 of 302, Col 8

5 Stage 4 is complete. At this point you have a pretty cool game built entirely in Adobe Flash. In Stage 5 we will add support for touch controls, so the game will work on mobile devices (Android and iOS). Finally, in Stage 6 we will add sounds, a background and a cool Particle System.

Stage 4 is now complete!

343

Interactivity

Stage 5

A NDROID AND IOS! THE INITIAL CHUNK OF code we need to add when dealing with both iOS and Android apps is support for when the app is in the background. By default AIR apps slow down to 4fps when minimized which means that slowly but surely the player will get beaten up if you suddenly have to answer a phone call mid-play. We need to get the game to *listen* out for when it's been minimized and maxmized, in other words deactivated and activated. We then pause it or unpause it appropriately.

1 First, let's add the ability to pause the game. In our main Timeline code create a new variable:

```
var paused:Boolean = false;
```

4 We're going to cover three different types of touch controls here. A simple "tap" for attacking, a "drag" for moving and a "swipe" for jumping. We are going to add three new listeners to handle each of these, but first we need to enable **MultiTouch** control. Add this line into the Timeline code:

```
Multitouch.inputMode = MultitouchInputMode.TOUCH_POINT;
```

6 We are going to use two new Arrays to store data on each touch that is made. The first Array will store the time that the touch was made. The second Array will record the **Y** coordinate of the touch. Both of these arrays will be used when working out whether an upward swipe has been made, in which case we'll make our ninja jump.

```
var timeTouched:Array = new Array();
var touchPointsY:Array = new Array();
```

2 Because we know that everything that happens is executed or triggered from within the main **gameLoop**, we add an **if** statement around everything:

```
function gameLoop(e:Event):void
{
        if(!paused)
        {
        .......
        all game loop code
        .......
        }
}
```

3 We add our listeners (a good place would be to put them with the other listeners)

```
stage.addEventListener(Event.DEACTIVATE, deactivate)
stage.addEventListener(Event.ACTIVATE, activate)
```

and their functions:

```
function deactivate(e:Event):void
{
        paused = true;
}
function activate(e:Event):void
{
        paused = false;
}
```

5 Next let's add your listeners. For code neatness and organization, add these near to our existing **keyPressed/keyReleased** listeners:

```
stage.addEventListener(TouchEvent.TOUCH_BEGIN, touchDown);
stage.addEventListener(TouchEvent.TOUCH_MOVE, touchMoving);
stage.addEventListener(TouchEvent.TOUCH_END, touchUp);
```

7 For movement we will need three things: two "point" objects that store x and y coordinates of our initial touch and where we move that to. Because we can make multiple touches at once, we add a new variable that keeps track of which touch is our movement touch.

```
var touchPoint:Point = new Point();
var movePoint:Point = new Point();
var movingTouch:int = -1;
```

8 For jumping we first add our **touchDown**, which records the time and y value (**stageY**) of our touch:

```
function touchDown(e:TouchEvent):void
{
    timeTouched[e.touchPointID] = getTimer();
    touchPointsY[e.touchPointID] = e.stageY;
}
```

9 Then we create our **touchUp** function. We check to see if the touch has been released within 500ms (half of a second) of it first being made and if it's released at a y position of more than 40 pixels higher than it was started. A quick vertical swipe would achieve this and when triggered, we make our **Player** jump. We need to reuse our **if** statement found in the **gameLoop** to make sure we only allow this jump to happen if our Player is still alive, isn't stunned or if the time hasn't run out.

```
function touchUp(e:TouchEvent):void
{
        if(player.life > 0 && player.stunned<=0 && !gameIsOver)
        {
                if(getTimer()-500< timeTouched[e.touchPointID])
                {
                        if(e.stageY < touchPointsY[e.touchPointID] -40)
                        {
                                player.jump();
                        }
                }
        }
}
```

11 On to moving. In this game we do something unusual. Rather than having set controls on the screen, we allow movement control to happen from any touch point on the screen. If our gamer places their finger or thumb anywhere on the touchscreen and then starts to move it around, our on-screen game pad appears and our gamer can make the player move up, down, left or right. Of course while we play the game, we will make multiple touches to the screen for attacking, jumping and moving. So we only want one of these touches to create the Directional pad (dpad) that allows thumb-operated control of player movement. We therefore find the first touch that seems to be treated as a movement and assign the **id** value for this touch to our **movingTouch** variable. To work out if a touch appears to be a movement-type touch, we measure the distance from where the touch was started to where it is now. If it's more than 10 pixels, it's likely the player wants to use this touch as the controller. We add our **touchMoving** function:

```
function touchMoving(e:TouchEvent):void
{
    if(movingTouch == -1 || movingTouch == e.touchPointID)
    {
        movePoint.x = e.stageX;
        movePoint.y = e.stageY;
        var dx:Number = e.stageX-touchPoint.x;
        var dy:Number = e.stageY-touchPoint.y;
        var dz:Number = Math.sqrt(dx*dx+dy*dy);
        if(dz>10)
            {
            if(movingTouch == -1)
            {
                touchPoint.x = e.stageX;
                touchPoint.y = e.stageY;
            }
            movingTouch = e.touchPointID;
            }
    }
}
```

10 We also want to handle our attack in the **touchUp** event too. If we handle it in **touchDown**, then we wouldn't actually know if the touch was the start of a swipe for jumping or an attack. In the **touchUp** function, we add a temporary variable to record if the touch was for jumping or not. We set this to true at the same point of telling our Player to jump. We only then call **player. attack()** if **touchIsJump** is not true. Note: we also call **player.stopAttacking()**, if you remember, **stopAttacking** is normally called to make sure that the gamer has released the attack key when playing on a computer. As a **touchUp** is the same as releasing a key, we call it here as well.

```
function touchUp(e:TouchEvent):void
{
        if(player.life > 0 && player.stunned<=0 && !gameIsOver)
        {
                var touchIsJump:Boolean;
                if(getTimer()-500< timeTouched[e.touchPointID])
                {
                        if(e.stageY < touchPointsY[e.touchPointID]-40)
                        {
                                touchIsJump = true;
                                player.jump();
                        }
                }
                player.stopAttacking();
                if(!touchIsJump) player.attack();
        }
}
```

12 We need to update out **touchUp** function so that movement is stopped. Note that if the movement is being stopped, we don't do the attack:

```
function touchUp(e:TouchEvent):void
{
        if(player.life > 0 && player.stunned<=0 && !gameIsOver)
        {
                var touchIsJump:Boolean;
                if(getTimer()-500< timeTouched[e.touchPointID])
                {
                        if(e.stageY < touchPointsY[e.touchPointID]-40)
                        {
                                touchIsJump = true;
                                player.jump();
                        }
                }
                player.stopAttacking();
                if(!touchIsJump && movingTouch != e.touchPointID) player.attack();
        }
        if(movingTouch==e.touchPointID)
        {
                player.stopMoving();
                movingTouch = -1;
        }
}
```

13 Finally, inside our **gameloop** we need to handle the player movement, so just before our for loop for checking the **keyPressedActions** add these new lines:

```
if(player.life > 0 && player.stunned<=0 && !gameIsOver)
{
        if(movingTouch != -1)
        {
                var dx:Number = movePoint.x-touchPoint.x;
                var dy:Number = movePoint.y-touchPoint.y;
                if(dx > 20) {player.moveRight();}
                if(dx < -20){player.moveLeft();}
                if(dy > 20) {player.moveDown();}
                if(dy < -20){player.moveUp();}
                if(Math.abs(dx) < 20 && Math.abs(dy) < 20) {player.stopMoving();}
        }
        for(var key:String in keys)
        {
                if(keyPressedActions[key]) keyPressedActions[key]();
        }
    }
```

16 In our **touchMoving** function where we set our **touchPoint** x and y values, we add 3 lines:

```
if(movingTouch == -1)
{
        touchPoint.x = e.stageX;
        touchPoint.y = e.stageY;
        controller.x = touchPoint.x;
        controller.y = touchPoint.y;
        controller.visible = true;
}
```

17 Then to make the controller invisible again, we modify the **touchUp** function:

```
if(movingTouch==e.touchPointID)
{
        player.stopMoving();
        movingTouch = -1;
        controller.visible = false;
}
else .........
```

14 We currently have movement, attacking and jumping all handled by the touch screen. The last thing to do is to add our visual control pad. Make a new MovieClip and draw a classic Nintendo Entertainment System-style cross control pad in it. Make sure the center of the cross is the center of the MovieClip. Give it an AS Linkage name "Controller." Give the MovieClip 9 different frames. The first frame will be still (no direction pressed), then the subsequent frames need to be as follows:

Frame 2 = down
Frame 3 = up
Frame 4 = down right
Frame 5 = up right
Frame 6 = right
Frame 7 = down left
Frame 8 = up left
Frame 9 = left

15 The frame numbers have a slightly random ordering as opposed to creating frames of the dpad being pressed in a clockwise type motion. Assigning directions to different frames means we can more easily choose which frame to show with code, which we shall come to in a bit.

First though, we need to add our controller MovieClip to our UI. We add it at the start of our timeline code, but we make the MovieClip invisible as we only want to show it when the gamer is touching the screen.

```
var controller:Controller = new Controller();
ui.addChild(controller)
controller.visible = false;
controller.gotoAndStop(1);
```

18 Finally, to set the correct frame (direction) for the controller, we modify **gameLoop** again:

```
if(movingTouch!=-1)
{
        var dx:Number = movePoint.xtouchPoint.x;
        var dy:Number = movePoint.ytouchPoint.y;
        var controllerFrame:int = 4;
        if(dx > 20) {player.moveRight();controllerFrame += 2;}
        if(dx < -20){player.moveLeft();controllerFrame += 5;}
        if(dy > 20) {player.moveDown();controllerFrame -=2;}
        if(dy < -20){player.moveUp();controllerFrame - =1;}
        if(Math.abs(dx) < 20 && Math.abs(dy) < 20) {player.stopMoving();controllerFrame = 1;}
        controller.gotoAndStop(controllerFrame);
}
```

19 Let's test our game on a touch device! This section doesn't go into creating your icons or submitting the compiled game to an app store. We're going to keep it simple and test locally, meaning on your own computer. You can choose between testing on an iOS or Android device. Android testing is the easier option because Flash CC compiles much quicker for Android than it does for iOS, and it's free and easier to set up. Apple iOS development has a $99 annual charge from Apple whereas Google Play requires only a $25 registration fee. But it's still free to test your app with the Android OS by simply connecting your Android device to your computer.

Up until now when we've been testing our game for the default Flash Player. Let's change the default testing platform by going to **File > Publish Settings** and change the target drop down to **AIR 3.6 for Android**.

21 You can choose between **Portrait**, **Landscape** or **Auto** from the **Aspect ratio** drop-down menu. You can select **Full screen** as well as **Auto orientation** using the tick boxes. We've selected **Auto** in the drop-down menu and ticked **Auto orientation** for our game. This setting means the user can choose to play in landscape or portrait, and due to the nature of our game, either works well. The most important thing here is to set **Render mode** to **GPU**. Because we use vectors in our game and no fancy filter effects or features not supported by **GPU** mode, this render mode gets us the best performance/frame rate out of our **Android** device. This render mode is also the case with **iOS**. If you were to use Starling or another **Stage3D** engine, you would use **direct** instead here. CPU mode would be used if you found some of your visuals don't look correct in **GPU**. Thankfully, all of ours do.

20 Click the little settings button next to the Target drop-down menu represented by the little wrench icon. In the General tab you can leave the default Output file and App name as it is. In the App ID field enter:
com.mydomainname.ninja
(I used *com.percypea.ninja*).

22 The **Deployment** tab is the most important tab for testing. Click the **Create** button, fill out the fields and add a password in the Password field. Specify a location where you want to save your file to and then click OK. Whatever password you used when creating the certificate, just type it into the password box back in the Deployment tab. Leaving deployment type as **Device release** is fine as we aren't going to be doing any real debugging.

23 Embedding the **AIR runtime** with the application adds 9.4MB to the file size of the app. Our app would only be around 60KB without the AIR runtime, so this file size is comparatively huge and makes it very tempting not to Embed it. If it's not embedded and the user doesn't have AIR already, they should automatically be taken to the Google Play store and given the option to download AIR. We are going to embed it in our game so that the end user won't have to worry about this step. Also, not all Android devices have access to the Google Play store.

24 Back to our **Deployment** panel, if you have your Android device connected to your computer, you can select to install and launch it directly after it's compiled. Select **Publish** and you should have your game running on your Android device with touch controls fully integrated!

Testing devices on iOS works exactly the same way, but you'll need a P12 Certificate for iOS distribution which is harder to get. You'll need to be registered with Apple as a developer, get the UDID for your iDevice and add it to your Apple developer account. We won't provide details as to how to become an iOS developer as that information can be found by going to apple.com. We also don't want you to spend $99 just to test your game on an iOS device since you can test for free on an Android device. If you want to learn more about becoming an iOS developer you can visit these links below.

https://developer.apple.com

https://developer.apple.com/support/technical/certificates

http://www.adobe.com/devnet/air/articles/packaging-air-apps-ios.html

AIR for Android Settings

General Deployment Icons Permissions Languages

Certificate: [▼] [ ] [Create...]
Password: [   ]
☐ Remember password for this session

Android deployment type
⦿ Device release
○ Emulator release
○ Debug
   Network interface for remote debugging
   [Default   ▼]

AIR runtime
⦿ Embed AIR runtime with application
○ Get AIR runtime from: [Google Play   ▼]

After publishing
☑ Install application on selected Android devices
   ☑ Launch application on selected Android devices

   Select   Device Serial No.

                                    [Refresh]

(?)   [Publish] [Cancel] [OK]

Stage 5 is now complete!

Stage 6

M USIC, SOUND AND visual effects! Currently our player can attack enemies and our enemies can attack the player, but other than that there's no visual effect to enhance the attack. This section will show you how to add some blood splatters as well as sound effects and music. A huge special thanks goes out to Tom McCaren of **www.tommccaren.co.uk** for graciously designing the awesome sound effects and music for this game. Tom is a talented UK-based sound designer and composer working primarily in the gaming industry.

1 Let's add some blood! Rather than have code in our timeline to set up and add our blood particles, in the same way that we add our enemy ninjas we are going to create a manager class. Make a new ActionScript 3.0 Class file and call it **ParticleManager**. This class is our first one that will need to have a **Timeline** reference, but it also doesn't extend our **Base3D** class. So we need to create a new timeline variable and pass it the timeline when we initiate it. The code to put into this class is in Step 2, but first, back in our main timeline code, add this single line of code:

```
var particleManager:ParticleManager = new ParticleManager(this);
```

3 Let's create our Blood Class (Blood.as). This Class will extend Base3D as we want our particle to be in our 3D world:

```
package
{
    public class Blood extends Base3D
    {
        public var blood:BloodMC;
        public function Blood(x_position=0, y_position=0, z_position=0)
        {
            blood = new BloodMC();
            blood.stop();
            addChild(blood);
            super(x_position, y_position, z_position);
        }
    }
}
```

2 In our new ParticleManager Class file add the following
code:

```
package
{
    import flash.display.MovieClip;
    public class ParticleManager
    {
        public var timeline:MovieClip;
        public function ParticleManager(timeline)
        {
            this.timeline = timeline;
        }
    }
}
```

4 Finally we need to create our Blood MovieClip
(BloodMC) in our library. In the FLA make a new
MovieClip and inside it create an animated blob of blood.
This blob should be just a looping animation that doesn't
move except for some kind of oscillating effect. In the
Stage6.fla included with the downloaded example files,
you can find this symbol in the file's Library panel. Open
the blood symbol and play the timeline animation to see the
animated effect. The overall movement of the blood during
game-play will be handled via code. Make sure it has the AS
Linkage name BloodMC by right-clicking over the symbol in
the Library panel and selecting Properties. In the Advanced
section type BloodMC in the Class input field.

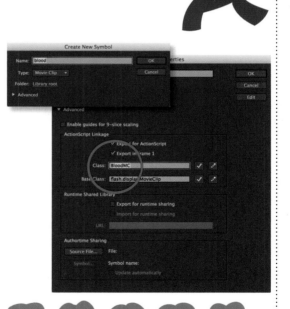

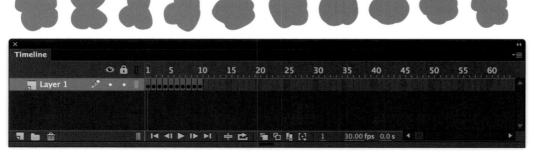

5 Why are we using a **ParticleManager** rather than adding our blood to the game area in the same way as we add our Ninjas? With our blood we want to be able to add several blood drops at a time and possibly end up having close to 50 particles on screen at once. At the same time we want to manage the number of particles on screen for performance reasons. Finally, initiating a Class and an **addChild** function to the stage can cause performance issues if we do it a lot at once So this **ParticleManager** will work around these performance issues. First of all, we do what is termed as **Object Pooling**. Let's decide that the maximum blood particles we want on the screen at any time is 50. We can now create all 50 blood instances right at the start of the game and then store them in our "pool" to easily grab and show them via code when needed. In our **ParticleManager** add this code:

```
package
{
        import flash.display.MovieClip;
        public class ParticleManager
        {
                public var timeline:MovieClip;
                public var bloodPool:Array;
                public function ParticleManager(timeline)
                {
                        this.timeline = timeline;
                        bloodPool = new Array();
                        for(var a:int=0;a<50;a++)
                        {
                                var blood:Blood = new Blood();
                                blood.timeline = timeline;
                                bloodPool.push(blood);
                        }
                }
        }
}
```

7 The **removeParticle** function is a little simpler. It marks our blood particle for removal so that our main code loop knows to remove it from screen and then pushes it back into the pool. Although in this tutorial we won't add any more particles to the game, the **ParticleManager** is actually coded to handle more than just our blood particles, so we look up which **particlePool** is the one where we push our particle back into.

```
public function removeParticle(particle)
{
        particle.markForRemoval = true;
        this[particle.particlePool].push(particle);
}
```

8 Let's update our **Blood** class now. First add some new variables to the class. The three velocity variables are going to be our speed in each direction for the blood particle. The **y_velocity** is actually the same as our "gravity" value for the ninjas. The **particlePool** is the reference our **particleManager** uses to know which pool is where the particle is in. The **fadeOut** boolean is used to determine if the blood particle should be fading out or not, and the **waitForFade** is a value we use as a little timer before the fade out happens.

```
public var x_velocity:Number;
public var y_velocity:Number;
public var z_velocity:Number;
public var particlePool:String = "bloodPool";
public var fadeOut:Boolean;
public var waitForFade:int;
```

6 We now want to add two functions: one to take the blood particles from our **bloodPool** and display them on screen and the other to remove them again and put them back into our **bloodPool** to be able to be reused. The first function **addBlood** will be created so that we can tell the **particleManager** how many blood particles to add along with where to add them in our 3D world. The **shift()** command means we "shift" the first item (in this case a Blood drop) out of the **bloodPool**. We then call a function called **init** which we have yet to create in our **Blood Class**. Finally, we check to see if we are already using that blood particle, and if not, we push that blood particle into our main **objects3D** array so that its loop function (also not yet created) can be called and so that it will be positioned in our world:

```
public function addBlood(totalBlood:int, x_position:Number, y_position:Number, z_position:Number)
{
        for(var a:int=0; a<totalBlood;a++)
        {
                if(bloodPool.length>0)
                {
                        var blood:Blood = bloodPool.shift();
                        blood.init(x_position, y_position, z_position);
                        var alreadyInObjects3D:Boolean = false;
                        for(var b:int=0;b<timeline.objects3D.length;b++)
                        {
                                if(timeline.objects3D[b]==blood) alreadyInObjects3D = true;
                        }
                        if(!alreadyInObjects3D)
                        {
                                timeline.objects3D.push(blood);
                                timeline.game.addChild(blood);
                        }
                }
        }
}
```

9 We then add our **init** function to the **Blood Class**. The **init** function is also like a reset function. Because this blood instance gets reused from our **bloodPool**, properties like its alpha and animation need to be reset:

```
public function init(x_position, y_position, z_position)
{
        x3D = x_position;
        y3D = y_position;
        z3D = z_position;
        x_velocity = Math.random()*40-20;
        z_velocity = Math.random()*40-20;
        y_velocity = -Math.random()*40-30;
        fadeOut=false;
        this.alpha = 1;
        waitForFade = 30;
        blood.play();
        markForRemoval=false;
}
```

10 Finally, our main loop code gets added to the **Blood Class**. While the blood particle is still in the air, we adjust its x, y and z position by the velocities (we also adjust the **y_velocity** in the exact same way as we adjust the gravity value in our Ninja Class). Then if the blood particle hits the floor, we make its animation stop and tell it to **fadeOut**. The **fadeOut** part of the code first of all reduces our **waitForFade** timer. When it is less than 0 it reduces the alpha of our blood until it is less than .1 (10%). Then we call the **removeParticle** function from the **particleManager**.

```
public function loop()
{
        if(!fadeOut)
        {
                y_velocity += 5;
                x3D += x_velocity;
                y3D += y_velocity;
                z3D += z_velocity;
                if(y3D >= timeline.ground_position)
                {
                        y3D = timeline.ground_position;
                        fadeOut=true;
                        blood.stop();
                }
        }
        else
        {
                waitForFade--;
                if(waitForFade<0)
                {
                        this.alpha-=.1;
                        if(this.alpha<.1)
                        {
                            timeline.particleManager.removeParticle(this);
                        }
                }
        }
}
```

12 In our game we'll just have one background which will repeat as you move left to right (and right to left). Make a Graphic symbol (not a MovieClip) called **backgroundImage** in your main fla and create a lovely background. Make sure this background is wider than your screen area (ideally by at least 30%). Making it wider is necessary because not all mobile handsets/tablets are created equal, and some will have wider screens than others. Remember we're currently working on a screen that matches the iPhone 4 which certainly isn't even the widest iPhone screen, let alone handset screen.

11 We have our **particleManger** and blood particle complete, so let's create some blood! In our **Ninja Class** you will remember that we have a **hurt** function. Let's add these two lines inside that function:

```
var totalBlood:int=Math.random()*3+3;
timeline.particleManager.addBlood(totalBlood, x3D, y3D-100, z3D);
```

So we determine that we want between three and five Blood particles (Math.random()*3 will be 0, 1 or 2 when made into an int). And we position them at our ninjas x3d, y3d and z3D values. Note we actually subtract 100 from the y3D value because y3D is at the ninja's feet. Blood Complete! Feel free to increase the **totalBlood** value for more gore.

If you increase it too much though, you will notice that some attacks give no (or very little) blood. This result is because you've got all the particles from your **Blood Pool** on screen already and have to wait until they've gone back in for reuse. A solution is to start with more than 50 particles but beware of the performance impact!

13 Make a new empty MovieClip called "background" and place two copies of your **backgroundImage** in it side by side. Make sure that these two copies are aligned to the left edge and bottom edge of the MovieClip. The reason we place two copies next to each other is because if we only had one **backgroundImage**, eventually we would get to the end of it when we keep scrolling it to the left (or right). By having two copies, the second **backgroundImage** looks like it's the start (or repeat) of the the first **backgroundImage**. We then use some clever code to make sure we never go past this second copy. Rather we jump back enough pixels so the camera shows the first background again and our player never notices. Magic!

14 We have our two **backgroundImage** Graphic symbols inside our **background** MovieClip. Manually place our background into the game by dragging an instance of it from the Library panel to the stage. Make a new layer for it below the **UI** and put it in the second keyframe. Give it the instance name **background**.

16 let's make a function in our main timeline code. Feel free to place it anywhere, though I have it directly beneath the **gameLoop** function:

```
function moveBackground()
{
}
```

17 Inside our **gameLoop** itself just after we call the **Camera.track(player)** command and before **objects3D.sortOn** is where to call our new function:

```
Camera.track(player);
moveBackground();
objects3D.sortOn(["z3D","uniqueID"], Array.NUMERIC | Array.DESCENDING);
```

20 If you actually test your game now, you should see your background move at the correct speed and fit nicely in our 3D world. However, it won't loop/repeat. The fix is to keep moving the background by half its width (remember you have 2 background images next to each other, so half the width is 1 complete image) in the correct direction. So we add these 2 lines:

```
function moveBackground()
{
    background.x =-Camera.x3D*(Camera.perspective/6000);
    while(background.x<-background.width/2) background.x+=background.width/2
    while(background.x>0) background.x-=background.width/2;
}
```

15 Set the "x" value of the MovieClip to 0, although this isn't really that important. What is important is the y value which we need to set to 353.3. Why this strange value, I hear you ask? Well our background won't be controlled by our 3D code that controls all other movement; however, it does need to look like part of our 3D scene. So to get the 353.3 value, we pretend that our background has a z3D value of 6000 (remember our Ninjas can't go beyond 5000). We also know that it sits on the **ground_position** of 500. Finally, we know that all our other 3D objects have their y coordinate worked out with this line:

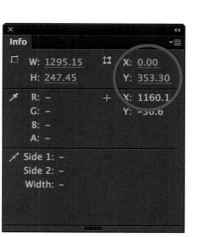

y = (y3D Camera. y3D)*(Camera.perspective/z3D)+320;

If we plug in our background values to that equation, we'll get:

y = (500 Camera. y3D)*(Camera.perspective/6000)+320

Which after reminding ourselves what our Camera.y3D and Camera. perspective values are gives 353.3. Now in fairness, we could quite easily get away with just 353 or even 354, but there's no harm in using 353.3. So y is worked out. In our game we don't ever adjust Camera.y3D (ie pan the camera up and down), so we won't have to worry about moving the background up and down either. However, "x" we do want to move.

18 Let's have a quick reminder of our equation for all our other 3D objects starting with x:

x = (x3D–Camera.x3D)*(Camera.perspective/z3D)+480;

19 We've put our background at 0 currently, so we can remove **x3D** from the equation. We also don't need to worry about that +480 at the end really, as we know we want our background to loop as we move and are not really that worried about where it starts in relation to the game. So we simplify it a little and create this:

```
function moveBackground()
{
background.x = –Camera.x3D*(Camera.perspective/6000);
}
```

21 If you test now, your background should loop seamlessly. And to the untrained eye, it all looks perfect. Sadly, it's not quite as simple as that. On your computer, on an iPhone 4 which has the resolution of 960x640 or on any device which has the same screen ratio the background will look correct. However, on an iPhone 5 where we have a wider screen we will actually see a gap occasionally on the left hand side where the background hasn't correctly wrapped itself. This gap is because our Flash game scales itself so that it fits onto any size screen. Scaling is a very handy feature as it means our UI and enemies will always show, no matter the screen size or orientation. On wider screens the user gets to see more of the game, so they have the benefit of possibly seeing more attacking ninjas that would perhaps be off screen on an iPhone 4. It

is because they can see more of the sides that they then see the missing piece of the background because the coordinate 0,0 is no longer right on the left hand side of the screen; rather extra space has been added there, so the coordinates go into negative numbers. For example, on an iPhone 4 with a screen size of 960x640 the coordinate 0,0 will be the top left. This is because our game is also 960x640 in Flash and therefore no scaling has to be done. The iPhone 5's screen is 1136x640. Our game automatically gets centered on the screen which means there is an extra 88 pixels to both the left and the right. We'll call these our **leftMargin** and our **rightMargin** although we won't mention the right again. However, because of the 88 pixel **leftMargin**, the coordinate -88,0 is actually the top left of the screen on an iPhone 5 in landscape mode.

22 We need to modify our **moveBackground** function to account for whether the screen is more widescreen than an iPhone 4. We work out what our **leftMargin** is. There are many, many different screen ratios, so it's no good just knowing what each screen is. We need a way to work it out. First of all we work out the screen ratio of our phone/handset.

```
var screenRatio = stage.fullScreenWidth/stage.fullScreenHeight;
```

23 We know our default screen ratio is 1.5 (960/640). We only need to worry about whether the **leftMargin** ratio is bigger than 1.5:

```
var leftMargin:int = 0;
if(screenRatio>1.5) leftMargin = 640*(1.5-screenRatio)/2;
```

25 Almost there! There is one other slight issue. We want the web version of our game to be able to be distributed to gaming portals, but not all of them will embed it in their site at the correct ratio. However, because the web game won't be fullscreen, we can't use the **fullScreenWidth** and **fullScreenHeight** properties to work out our **screenRatio**. Instead we have to use the **stageWidth** and **stageHeight** properties. We look at our stage **displayState** property to see if the game is running in fullscreen (on a device) or not (web). The bad news is because our game is created using scaling (so that it will scale to fit any device nicely and the UI stays centered etc.), **stageWidth** and **stageHeight** always return 960 and 640, our default width and height, no matter what size the portal has made the game on their website. However, there is an easy solution. We sneakily tell Flash that we don't want to have scaling any more, which then cheats Flash into working correctly and being able to accurately get **stageWidth** and **stageHeight**. We then quickly work out the **screenRatio** and then tell Flash, "Sorry, we actually do want scaling after all." So finally, our **moveBackground** function becomes this:

```
function moveBackground()
{
        var screenRatio:Number;
        if(stage.displayState == StageDisplayState.NORMAL)
        {
                stage.scaleMode = StageScaleMode.NO_SCALE;
                screenRatio = stage.stageWidth/stage.stageHeight;
                stage.scaleMode = StageScaleMode.SHOW_ALL;
        }
        else
        {
                screenRatio = stage.fullScreenWidth/stage.fullScreenHeight;
        }
        var leftMargin:int = 0;
        if(screenRatio>1.5) leftMargin = 640*(1.5-screenRatio)/2;
        background.x = -Camera.x3D*(Camera.perspective/6000);
        while(background.x<-background.width/2+leftMargin) background.x+=background.width/2;
        while(background.x>leftMargin) background.x-=background.width/2;
}
```

24 We can use the **leftMargin** in our while loops:

```
while(background.x<-background.width/2+leftMargin) background.x += background.width/2;
while(background.x>leftMargin) background.x =background.width/2;
```

Music & Sound Effects

26 Go to **www.howtocheatinflash.com** and download the ZIP file containing all of the example files for this book. In the Chapter 10 folder you will find all of the sound effects and music for this game courtesy of talented sound designer Tom McCaren of **www.tommccaren.co.uk.**

Import all of the sound effects and music into the library and give them AS Linkage names. We will use Linkage names that start with SFX (even for the music) so that it's easy to remember they are Sound Classes.

File Menu	
New...	⌘N
Open	⌘O
Browse in Bridge	⌥⌘O
Open Recent	▶
Close	⌘W
Close All	⌥⌘W
Save	⌘S
Save As...	⇧⌘S
Save as Template...	
Save All	
Revert	
Import	▶
Export	▶
Publish Settings...	⇧⌘F12
Publish	⌥⇧F12
AIR Settings...	
ActionScript Settings...	

Import submenu:
- Import to Stage...   ⌘R
- Import to Library...
- Open External Library...   ⇧⌘O
- Import Video...

Library — stage6.fla — 54 items

Name	Linkage	Use Count	Date Modi...	Type
▼ 📁 Audio				Folder
Music_Intro_Countdown.wav	SFXIntro	0	12/19/13...	Sound
Music_Level_Loop.wav	SFXMusic	0	12/19/13...	Sound
Ninja_Attack_01.wav	SFXAttack1	0	12/19/13...	Sound
Ninja_Attack_02.wav	SFXAttack2	0	12/19/13...	Sound
Ninja_Attack_03.wav	SFXAttack3	0	12/19/13...	Sound
Ninja_Attack_04.wav	SFXAttack4	0	12/19/13...	Sound
Ninja_Death_01.wav	SFXDeath1	0	12/19/13...	Sound
Ninja_Death_02.wav	SFXDeath2	0	12/19/13...	Sound
Ninja_Death_03.wav	SFXDeath3	0	12/19/13...	Sound
Ninja_Death_04.wav	SFXDeath4	0	12/19/13...	Sound
Ninja_Death_05.wav	SFXDeath5	0	12/19/13...	Sound
	SFXHurt1	0	12/19/13...	Sound
	SFXHurt2	0	12/19/13...	Sound
	SFXHurt3	0	12/19/13...	Sound
Ninja_Hurt_04.wav	SFXHurt4	0	12/19/13...	Sound
Ninja_Jump_01.wav	SFXJump1	0	12/19/13...	Sound
Ninja_Jump_02.wav	SFXJump2	0	12/19/13...	Sound
Ninja_Jump_03.wav	SFXJump3	0	12/19/13...	Sound
Ninja_Jump_04.wav	SFXJump4	0	12/19/13...	Sound
Ninja_Jump_Whoosh_01.wav	SFXJumpWhoosh1	0	12/19/13...	Sound
Ninja_Jump_Whoosh_02.wav	SFXJumpWhoosh2	0	12/19/13...	Sound
Ninja_Jump_Whoosh_03.wav	SFXJumpWhoosh3	0	12/19/13...	Sound
Sword_Imp_01.wav	SFXStab1	0	12/19/13...	Sound
Sword_Imp_02.wav	SFXStab2	0	12/19/13...	Sound
Sword_Imp_03.wav	SFXStab3	0	12/19/13...	Sound
Sword_Imp_04.wav	SFXStab4	0	12/19/13...	Sound
Sword_Imp_05.wav	SFXStab5	0	12/19/13...	Sound
Sword_Swish_01.wav	SFXSwing1	0	12/19/13...	Sound
Sword_Swish_02.wav	SFXSwing2	0	12/19/13...	Sound
Sword_Swish_03.wav	SFXSwing3	0	12/19/13...	Sound
Sword_Swish_04.wav	SFXSwing4	0	12/19/13...	Sound
Sword_Swish_05.wav	SFXSwing5	0	12/19/13...	Sound
Tick_01.wav	SFXTick1	0	12/19/13...	Sound
Tick_02.wav	SFXTick3	0	12/19/13...	Sound
Tock_01.wav	SFXTick2	0	12/19/13...	Sound
Tock_02.wav	SFXTick4	0	12/19/13...	Sound
Vox_Fight.wav	SFXFight	0	12/19/13...	Sound
Vox_Game_Over_Gong.wav	SFXGameover	0	12/19/13...	Sound

HOT TIP

For organization purposes, create a new folder within your Library (using the upper right corner drop-down menu) for all imported audio files. As seen in Step 26, all imported sound files are in a folder named "Audio." Organizing files using folders helps keep your Library clean and organized.

27 By default, when we publish a swf file, Flash will use relatively poor audio quality settings. You can change these in **File > Publish Settings**. For web games I find that **MP3, 64 kbps, Mono** gives a good balance between quality and file size.

If publishing for mobile though, particularly on older devices, it's actually best to select **Disable** from the **Compression** option in **Sound Settings**. Disabling this option will drastically increase your app file size but will give the best performance in terms of playing audio.

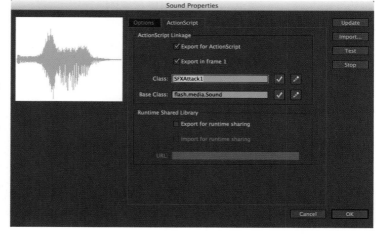

30 In AS3 whenever a sound is played, a new sound channel is created. Once **soundchannel** is created, we have more control over the sound. We can monitor it, stop it, check it to see if the sound has finished or adjust the volume of the sound as it is playing. As soon as the **introSFX** has finished and also on Android devices if the game is minimized, we need to make sure the music stops. So let's start the audio!

```
function startAudio():void
{
        if(!musicChannel)
        {
                musicChannel = intro.play();
                musicChannel.addEventListener(Event.SOUND_COMPLETE, playMusic)
        }
}

startAudio();
```

28 Give or take a few empty lines, we're getting close to 300 lines of code in our Timeline now. This amount of code is over double to what we had at the start of Stage 2 when we decided to use Classes. What we're going to do now will be very frowned upon by most developers. In fact they will already be gnashing their teeth at our use of the Timeline to house code. But for simplicity's sake we're going to add a new layer in our Timeline, name it **Audio Code** and add more code into it.

29 You may have noticed that for a lot of the sounds, there are multiple versions, 4–5 of each sound. We use multiple versions to give a slight variation on each sound effect so that the audio doesn't become too repetitive to the player. Let's start with the simple sounds though, the ones with only one version. In the new **Audio Code** layer, add the code:

```
var intro:SFXIntro = new SFXIntro();
var fight:SFXFight = new SFXFight();
var gameoverSFX:SFXGameover = new SFXGameover();
var music:SFXMusic = new SFXMusic();
var musicChannel:SoundChannel;
```

This initial block of code has initiated but won't start playing 4 sounds, three sound effects and one music track. The last line sets up a **SoundChannel**.

31 We create a **startAudio** function that starts playing our 3, 2, 1 countdown intro sound effect, but then also adds a listener to that sound channel to see when it is complete. When that happens it will call the **playMusic** function which we need to write:

```
function playMusic(e:Event):void
{
        musicChannel.removeEventListener(Event.SOUND_COMPLETE,playMusic)
        musicChannel = music.play(0,9999);
        playSound(fight);
}
```

This function tells the **musicChannel** we don't need to worry about listening for when the sound has completed playing. Notice the 9999, in the **music.play()** command. This number tells the sound to repeat 9999 times before stopping. This setting is potentially a bug as it will eventually mean our music will stop playing if someone plays the game long enough, but as our music track is almost a minute long that's over 150 hours of looping music – pretty much a week. So it's not something we need to worry about, especially as we'll restart the music after our 99 second **gameplay** time anyway.

32 Note the last line of our **playMusic** function is a call to a new function **playSound**. Let's add to that:

```
function playSound(sound):void
{
        sound.play();
}
```

We should be able to test our game, hear the intro countdown with music start and have the intro followed seamlessly by the full music track and also the fight sound effect.

33 Let's get more complicated. Underneath our line **var musicChannel:SoundChannel;** add:

```
var swordSounds:Array = new Array();
swordSounds.push(new SFXSwing1());
swordSounds.push(new SFXSwing2());
swordSounds.push(new SFXSwing3());
swordSounds.push(new SFXSwing4());
swordSounds.push(new SFXSwing5());
```

What we have done is made a small Array containing 5 Sword Swinging sound effects. Let's add a function that will play one of them:

```
function swordSFX():void
{
        playSound(swordSounds);
}
```

35 Finally, we need to call our **swordSFX** function from somewhere. Let's open up our **Player.as** Class. In our **checkEnemies** function at the bottom before the closing } add:

timeline.swordSFX();

A sword sound should be played whenever you swing your sword.

36 But why do we call the **swordSFX** from **Player.as** and not from **Ninja.as** in our **attack** function? Surely that would then mean that both the player and the enemy ninjas make use of our lovely sword swing sound effect. Well, we want our **swordSFX** to only play if the sword does not hit an enemy. If it hits an enemy we want a different set of sound effects to play.

There are 3 different types of sounds we will want to play depending on what happens when we swing our sword: the normal swish which we'll call type 0, an impact when we hit an enemy which we'll call type 1 and a death sound if that hit is the final blow which we'll call type 2. In our **Player Class**, at the top of our **checkEnemies** function before the "for each" line add:

var swordSFXType:int = 0;

34 Our **playSound** function is expecting a normal sound to **play()** but we are passing it an Array of 5 sounds. So let's modify our **playSound** function:

```
function playSound(sound):void
{
        if(sound is Array) sound = sound[int(Math.random()*sound.length)];
        sound.play();
}
```

What we have done is checked to see if what is being passed is an Array, and if it is, then it selects one of the sounds at random from within the Array to play.

37 Then after our **enemy.hurt()** line inside the **for** loop and before the **timeline.updateScore()**, insert the following code:

```
enemy.hurt();
if(enemy.life>0) swordSFXType = 1;
else swordSFXType = 2;
timeline.updateScore();
```

38 We then modify our timeline.swordSFX() line to become:

timeline.swordSFX(swordSFXType,this);

Not only do we pass our swordSFX function the type of effect to play, but we also pass it "this" which is our **Player** character. Why? Find out in Step 40!

39 Back to our Audio Loop layer in the main timeline. First let's add our stab, hurt and death sounds:

```
var stabSounds:Array = new Array();
stabSounds.push(new SFXStab1());
stabSounds.push(new SFXStab2());
stabSounds.push(new SFXStab3());
stabSounds.push(new SFXStab4());
stabSounds.push(new SFXStab5());

var hurtSounds:Array = new Array();
hurtSounds.push(new SFXHurt1());
hurtSounds.push(new SFXHurt2());
hurtSounds.push(new SFXHurt3());
hurtSounds.push(new SFXHurt4());

var deathSounds:Array = new Array();
deathSounds.push(new SFXDeath1());
deathSounds.push(new SFXDeath2());
deathSounds.push(new SFXDeath3());
deathSounds.push(new SFXDeath4());
deathSounds.push(new SFXDeath5());
```

40 Then let's modify our swordSFX function:

```
function swordSFX(type:int, from:Base3D):void
{
        if(type == 0)
        {
                playSound(swordSounds, from);
        }
        else if(type == 1)
        {
                playSound(stabSounds, from);
                playSound(hurtSounds, from);
        }
        else if(type == 2)
        {
                playSound(deathSounds, from);
        }
}
```

Notice that if the sound effect type is 1, meaning that your sword has connected to an enemy but not killed them, we play two different sounds: the sword stab sound as well as a hurt ouch sound.

42 If you test it now, one thing you will notice is that the death sounds aren't quite so loud compared to the other sounds. We could take these audio files into some audio editing software to increase their volume and then reimport into flash, but let's give them a volume boost from within Flash itself. Modify the **playSound** function yet again, to be this:

```
function playSound(sound:*, from:Base3D = null, volumeMultiplier:Number = 1):void
{
        if(sound is Array) sound = sound[int(Math.random()*sound.length)];
        if(!from) volumeController.volume=1; else volumeController.volume=.125+400/from.z3D;
        volumeController.volume*=volumeMultiplier;
        sound.play(0,0,volumeController);
}
```

Then go up to our **swordSFX** function and change the **deathSounds** line to be:

```
playSound(deathSounds,from,3);
```

This code will make **deathSounds** play three times their volume which should certainly be loud enough to be heard above any other sounds.

41 We need to modify our **playSound** function again to handle this new **from** object which if you remember is our Player But first, why do we actually want to know where the sound is being triggered? Because, as our player moves away from the **camera** we want the sound effect to be quieter. So the **playSound** function needs to know how

far an object is from the camera and adjust the volume of the sound accordingly. First we need to create a volume controller from a **SoundTransform** Object as we use it to transform sound. At the top of your Audio Code, place

```
var volumeController:SoundTransform = new SoundTransform();
```

Let's modify **playSound** to make use of it:

```
function playSound(sound, from:Base3D = null):void
{
        if(sound is Array) sound = sound[int(Math.random()*sound.length)];
        if(!from) volumeController.volume=1; else volumeController.volume=.125+400/from.z3D;
        sound.play(0,0,volumeController);
}
```

Because **playSound** is also called with our **Fight** SFX which isn't associated with a Ninja, we need to allow for our **from** variable to be nonexistant (or null). Our new line checks how

whether the sound comes from **from**. If so, it sets the volume to be default which is 1. If the sound has come from a Ninja, we use the z3D value of that Ninja to work out the volume.

43 We have sound effects associated with our player, but what about the enemies? Open **Enemy.as** and find the **checkPlayer** function, and we mirror what we have done to **Player.as**:

```
public function checkPlayer():void
{
        var attackReachX:int = 280;
        var attackReachZ:int = 150;
        var attackForce:int = 80;
        var swordSFXType:int = 0;

        var distanceX:Number = timeline.player.x3D - x3D;
        var distanceZ:Number = timeline.player.z3D - z3D;
        if(distanceX * direction > 0  && Math.abs(distanceZ) < attackReachZ && Math.abs(distanceX) < attackReachX)
        {
                var angle:Number = Math.atan2(distanceZ,distanceX);
                timeline.player.forceX = attackForce * Math.cos(angle);
                timeline.player.forceZ = attackForce * Math.sin(angle);
                timeline.player.hurt();
                if(timeline.player.life>0) swordSFXType = 1; else swordSFXType = 2;
        }
        timeline.swordSFX(swordSFXType, this);
}
```

44 There are two final things we need to do for the **swordSFX**. You may notice that if you run away from the enemies, you still hear them loud and clear. So we make a new function to determine if the sound effects for the enemies are allowed. Add this code to the bottom of the Audio Code layer:

```
function allowSFX(from):Boolean
{
        if(from.x<-100 || from.x>1060) return false;
        return true;
}
```

47 Now we need one more type of sound for both our player and enemy ninjas: a jump sound. As with the sword sound, we have a 1 in 3 chance for a jump type grunt sound to play too. Unlike sword though, we don't need to have a type. Because our whoosh sounds are quite loud, we actually use a value of .4 for the **volumeMultiplier to** reduce the sound. This reduces the sound volume to 40% for the jump whoosh sounds.

```
var jumpSounds:Array = new Array()
jumpSounds.push(new SFXJump1());
jumpSounds.push(new SFXJump2());
jumpSounds.push(new SFXJump3());
jumpSounds.push(new SFXJump4());

var jumpWhooshSounds:Array = new Array();
jumpWhooshSounds.push(new SFXJumpWhoosh1());
jumpWhooshSounds.push(new SFXJumpWhoosh2());
jumpWhooshSounds.push(new SFXJumpWhoosh3());


function jumpSFX(from:Base3D):void
{
        if(allowSFX(from))
        {
                if(int(Math.random()*3)==1)playSound(jumpSounds,from);
                playSound(jumpWhooshSounds,from,.4);

        }
}
```

45 And finally, let's add a bit of extra random sound to the attack, a nice occasional grunt from a Ninja as he swings his sword. The below code shows both the check to see if a SFX is allowed and the new line which gives a 1 in 3 chance to add a grunt (attack sound):

```
function swordSFX(type:int, from:Base3D):void
{
    if(allowSFX(from))
    {
        if(int(Math.random()*3)==1) playSound(attackSounds, from);
        if(type == 0)
        {
            playSound(swordSounds,from);
        }
        else if(type ==1)
        {
            playSound(stabSounds,from);
            playSound(hurtSounds,from);
        }
        else if(type == 2)
        {
            playSound(deathSounds,from,3);
        }
    }
}
```

46 For **attackSounds**, we have a new array:

```
var attackSounds:Array = new Array()
attackSounds.push(new SFXAttack1());
attackSounds.push(new SFXAttack2());
attackSounds.push(new SFXAttack3());
attackSounds.push(new SFXAttack4());
```

48 Because we don't need to work out the type of jump sound as we did the sword sound, we can put the trigger for the **jumpSFX** in our main **Ninja.as** Class so both the Player and Enemy can trigger it. Open up Ninja.as, and in the **jump()** function above the **Ninja.gotoAndPlay("jump");** line add:

timeline.jumpSFX(this);

49 There are two more types of sounds we want to include, a game over and ticking clock noises for the last 10 seconds remaining. We already have our **gameoverSFX** sound initiated, and we already have a function in our main code layer that gets called when **gameover** happens, so we modify this function to include two lines:

```
function gameover():void
{
    if(!gameIsOver)
    {
        ui.gameoverMC.visible=true;
        ui.gameoverMC.scoreTF.text=ui.scoreTF.text;
        gameIsOver = true;
        player.stopMoving();
        stage.addEventListener(MouseEvent.CLICK, resetGame)
        musicChannel.stop();
        playSound(gameoverSFX);
    }
}
```

Note that the first line will stop our music from playing as we don't want that to continue. The second line plays our **gameoverSFX**.

50 We then need to make sure we start the music again when the user hits "try again." At the end of our **resetGame** function, add these two lines:

```
musicChannel=null
startAudio();
```

51 The Tick sounds are a little more complicated. Back in our Audio Code layer, add the following to initiate the 4 tick sound effects and a little counter that we will use to determine which of the 4 ticks to play for each of the remaining 10 seconds:

```
var tick1:SFXTick1 = new SFXTick1();
var tick2:SFXTick2 = new SFXTick2();
var tick3:SFXTick3 = new SFXTick3();
var tick4:SFXTick4 = new SFXTick4();
var tickCounter:int = 1;
```

Then add a **tickSound** function:

```
function tickSound()
{
        playSound(this["tick"+tickCounter])
        tickCounter++
        if(tickCounter>4) tickCounter=1
}
```

54 In our Main Code Layer, add to the existing **deactivate** function:

```
function deactivate(e:Event):void
{
        paused = true;
        stopAudio()
}
```

55 And then add to our **activate** function:

```
function activate(e:Event):void
{
        paused = false;
        startAudio();
}
```

372

52 To trigger the **tickSound** on each second, in the Main Code Layer we go down to the line
timer-=1/30; and sandwich it between these lines:

```
var oldTimer:int=timer;
timer-=1/30;
if(Math.ceil(timer)<10 && int(timer)!=oldTimer)
    tickSound();
```

If we didn't use **oldTimer** then we would get a tick sound happening on every single frame which would be 30 times for every one second.

53 There's one last tweak for sounds. As previously mentioned on Android devices when the game is minimized, the music still plays which we don't want. So add this function to our Audio Code Layer:

```
function stopAudio():void
{
        if(musicChannel) musicChannel.stop();
        musicChannel = null;

}
```

Congratulations! If all went well, you were able to build an interactive game complete with animation, particle effects, sound effects and music using Adobe Flash CC! Feel free to use this game example as a template and get creative! By changing the graphics and code, you could easily expand upon what we've already started.

This chapter would not have been possible if not for the amazing work and dedication from David Crawford himself. Not only did he write the code and set up the Flash files, he painstakingly documented each step for this book. Without his talent and efforts, this example may not have been possible.

Special thanks goes out to Tom McCaren as well for his awesome sound effects and music. Tom brought this fun little game to a whole new level with his sound design, and I can't thank him enough.

As for the ninja, we have our own plans to continue working on this game by adding exploding bunnies, more animations, effects and maybe even levels.

Thank you

BEING THE AUTHOR OF THIS BOOK HAS BEEN THE MOST HUMBLING experience of my design and animation career. Focal Press asked me to write *How to Cheat in Adobe Flash CS3* back in 2006. Five editions and seven years later, nobody is more surprised than I am at the longevity of this series and the number of readers who have embraced it. Tens of thousands of copies are in the hands of Flash hobbyists and professionals worldwide, and several schools and educators have even adopted How to Cheat in Adobe Flash as part of their animation curriculum.

When I was asked to write this series, I considered my options and sought advice from several author friends. What was I getting myself into? Was it a good move financially? How much of my time would it take? Their advice was honest:

> "Don't write the book for money. Instructional, how-to books don't typically generate much income because they don't sell enough and have a very short shelf life."

> "Write the book because you love to write."

> "Be prepared to write for long hours. Then be prepared to write some more."

> "Write the book if you love to teach."

For me, writing this book wasn't about the time or money. It was about sharing all of my techniques and experiences that have made me a better designer and animator. I'm lucky for the opportunity to have a career as an artist and, this book represents all that I am thankful for.

Between writing every chapter, creating each example, designing every cover and laying out each page, I easily regard *How to Cheat in Adobe Flash* as the biggest accomplishment of my career. More meaningfully, this book is also my biggest artistic success based on how well received it has been from all of you.

Thank you all for your emails, tweets, Facebook messages and in some very special cases, actual handwritten letters. They are all reminders that every minute spent, every sacrifice made and every hour of sleep lost have all been worth it.

Thank you for reading.

Index

Index